6140124872

D1759694

Contemporary Scottis

Contemporary Scottish Plays

Caledonia
Alistair Beaton

Bullet Catch
Rob Drummond

The Artist Man and the Mother Woman
Morna Pearson

Narrative
Anthony Neilson

Rantin
Kieran Hurley

B L O O M S B U R Y
LONDON • NEW DELHI • NEW YORK • SYDNEY

Bloomsbury Methuen Drama

An imprint of Bloomsbury Publishing Plc

50 Bedford Square	1385 Broadway
London	New York
WC1B 3DP	NY 10018
UK	USA

www.bloomsbury.com

Bloomsbury is a registered trade mark of Bloomsbury Publishing Plc

First published in 2014

Introduction copyright © Bloomsbury Methuen Drama 2014.
Caledonia first published in Great Britain in 2010 by Methuen Drama. Copyright © 2010 by
Alistair Beaton.
Bullet Catch first published in Great Britain in 2013 by Bloomsbury Methuen Drama. Copyright
© 2013 by Rob Drummond.
The Artist Man and the Mother Woman first published in Great Britain in 2012 by Methuen
Drama. Copyright © 2012 by Morna Pearson.
Narrative copyright © 2014 by Anthony Neilson.
Rantin first published in Great Britain in 2014 by Oberon Books. Copyright © 2014 by Kieran
Hurley. Used by permission.

British Library Cataloguing-in-Publication Data
A catalogue record for this book is available from the British Library.

ISBN: PB: 978-1-4725-7443-5
EPUB: 978-1-4725-7446-6
EPDF: 978-1-4725-7444-2

Library of Congress Cataloging-in-Publication Data
A catalog record for this book is available from the Library of Congress.

Typeset by Fakenham Prepress Solutions, Fakenham, Norfolk NR21 8NN
Printed and bound in India

Contents

Chronology

1997 11 September: A pre-legislative referendum, which had been promised in the Labour manifesto for the UK general election in May 1997, results in overwhelming support for the establishment of a Scottish Parliament with tax-varying powers. Of those who vote 74.3 per cent support the establishment of a devolved parliament and 63.5 per cent agree that the parliament should have tax-varying powers.

1998 17 November: The Scotland Act is passed by the UK Parliament at Westminster. The Act assigns powers to a devolved Scottish parliament although rather than listing areas over which the Scottish Parliament has control the Act specifies matters over which it does not, including, for instance, obligations under the *European Convention on Human Rights.*

1999 6 May: Elections are held for the new parliament. A Labour and Liberal Democrat coalition is formed with Labour leader Donald Dewar as First Minister. On 1 July, the Scottish Parliament, adjourned on 25 March 1707, reconvenes in the General Assembly Hall of the Church of Scotland in Edinburgh.

2000: The Federation for Scottish Theatre (FST) under the chairmanship of Hamish Glen, then artistic director of Dundee Rep, publishes a report outlining a buildingless model for a new national theatre company. The recently elected Scottish Executive agrees in principal to the idea of funding such a company but does not specify what form the proposed company should take.

2001: A working group set up by the Scottish Arts Council to explore available options recommends the FST model. The new theatre company will be buildingless, co-producing and essentially nomadic. 11 September: Aeroplanes hijacked by Al-Qaeda affiliates are flown into the Pentagon in Washington DC and the Twin Towers in New York City, signalling a radical shift in international relations.

2003 1 May: Elections are held for the Scottish Parliament. A Labour and Liberal Democrat coalition is returned with Labour leader Jack McConnell as First Minister.

2004 July: Vicky Featherstone, formerly of Paines Plough, takes up the post of the first artistic director of the National Theatre of Scotland. 9 October: The new Scottish Parliament Building, adjacent to Holyroodhouse in Edinburgh, is officially opened by Queen Elizabeth II.

2005 January: The NTS announces that David Greig will be its first dramaturg.

2006 c. 25 February: The NTS launches with not one but ten productions: *Home Aberdeen, Home Caithness, Home Dumfries, Home Dundee, Home East Lothian, Home Edinburgh, Home Glasgow, Home Inverness, Home Shetland, Home Stornoway. Home* is a free event, attended by an estimated 10,000 people. In August, Gregory Burke's *Black Watch* opens at the Edinburgh Fringe and Anthony Neilson's *Realism* is premiered in a co-production between the NTS and the Edinburgh International Festival.

2007 3 May: For the third time since devolution elections are held for the Scottish Parliament. The Scottish National Party wins the most seats and forms a minority government. Alex Salmond becomes Scotland's First Minister.

2009 25 January: Homecoming Scotland, a series of events designed to attract people of Scottish ancestry to visit Scotland, is launched on the 250th anniversary of the birth of Robert Burns. The series of events runs across the country until St Andrew's Day, 30 November.

2010 6 May: The UK General Election results in a Conservative and Liberal Democrat coalition being established at Westminster. David Cameron becomes the UK's Prime Minister. Scotland returns one Conservative MP.

2011 5 May: The Scottish National Party becomes the first to win an overall majority in Scottish parliamentary elections. An overall majority for any party was not an outcome envisaged by the UK government when the parliament was established in Edinburgh. Alex Salmond remains First Minister.

2012 25 January: the Scottish government launches the consultation, *Your Scotland, Your Referendum.* 15 October: The Edinburgh

Agreement, which will allow for a referendum on Scottish independence, is signed by Alex Salmond and David Cameron.

2013 March: Laurie Sansom succeeds Vicky Featherstone as Artistic Director of the National Theatre of Scotland. 7 July: Andy Murray becomes the first Briton to win the Wimbledon Gentlemen's Singles since 1936 and the first Scot in the modern era, following Harold Mahony's victory in 1896.

2014 23 July: The twentieth Commonwealth Games open in Glasgow. 18 September: a referendum is held on Scottish independence.

Introduction

New Scottish Plays

This anthology of recent Scottish plays lays no claim to be a 'best of' selection. Instead, it seeks to offer a timely snapshot of the richness and diversity of contemporary Scottish writing for the stage. Scottish theatre is currently in extremely rude health. Indeed, it has developed at a pace and in directions that would hardly have seemed possible twenty years ago. There are a number of reasons for this flowering. While there were signs of a renaissance in the 1980s and 1990s the opening of the devolved Scottish parliament in 1999 definitely energized Scottish theatre, not least because questions about how post-devolutionary Scotland should perform itself became additionally live and pertinent. In 2000 the recently elected Scottish Executive agreed in principle to the idea of funding a national theatre company. Subsequently, the establishment of the National Theatre of Scotland (NTS) in 2006 put Scottish theatre on the map, nationally and internationally and signalled a very welcome injection of cash. Scotland now boasts a number of playwrights of international reputation and several award-winning shows, most famously John Tiffany's internationally acclaimed production of Gregory Burke's *Black Watch* (NTS 2006). All of this is surely a cause for celebration. In 2011, the critic and commentator Joyce McMillan spoke for many when she described the present as a 'golden age for theatre production in Scotland'.[1] The plays in this collection can be considered part of this golden age and taken together they provide an overview of some of the more interesting developments in new Scottish theatre-writing. They are Alistair Beaton's *Caledonia* (2010); Rob Drummond's *Bullet Catch* (2012); Morna Pearson's *The Artist Man and the Mother Woman* (2012); Anthony Neilson's *Narrative* (2013), and Kieran Hurley, Gav Prentice, Julia Taudevin and Drew Wright's *Rantin* (2013).

Alistair Beaton's *Caledonia* premiered at the King's Theatre in Edinburgh in a co-production between the Edinburgh International Festival (EIF) and the NTS. Born in Glasgow, Beaton has an established reputation as one of the UK's leading political satirists. He earned his stripes in the late 1970s and early 1980s as a writer on the BBC's *Not the Nine O'Clock News* and ITV's *Spitting Image*, for which he was a regular contributor between 1984 and 1996. More recently he emerged as a leading critic of New Labour via two full-length television dramas, *A Very Social Secretary* (2005) and *The Trial of Tony Blair* (2007). The first of these lampooned the sexual affair between Labour Home Secretary David Blunkett and *Spectator* journalist Kimberley Quinn, the lurid complications of which led to Blunkett's resignation in 2004. The second, *The Trial of Tony Blair,* was rather more serious in tone and intent. Set in 2010 it posited an all too plausible future in which a legacy-obsessed Blair finally resigned to make way for Gordon Brown. Haunted by the consequences of earlier decisions Beaton's Blair begins to crack under the strain. British soldiers continue to die daily in Baghdad, civilians continue to be blown up, and a second wave of bomb attacks hits London in response to a military strike against Iran. These events 'are in no way connected', insists Blair in his final political broadcast as PM.

Although best known as a television satirist, Beaton had in fact written quite extensively for the stage before being commissioned by the NTS to produce their summer show for 2010. Several adaptations and translations, including Gogol's *The Government Inspector* (2005) and Max Frisch's *The Arsonists* (2007), had showcased his not inconsiderable skills as a linguist, for instance. Perhaps more pertinently, his political satire *Feelgood* (2001) – an early attack on the spin culture of New Labour – won the Evening Standard Award for Best Comedy and was nominated for an Olivier. Set in a posh seaside hotel on the eve of the Prime Minister's annual conference speech, *Feelgood* focuses on the machinations of a manically aggressive press secretary and a guileless young speechwriter. At the time, the *New Statesman* praised it for revealing a 'ruthless world of political spin in all its double-dealing glory' and it might easily be seen as a forerunner to Armando Iannucci's celebrated *The Thick of It*.[2] It was his skills as a satirist rather than a translator that Beaton brought to bear on the historical events that were to be the subject matter for *Caledonia*.

The Darien Expedition of 1698 was Scotland's only attempt to establish a colony and overseas trading post of its own. It ended disastrously, not only in death and disease, but also with the loss of around half of the nation's capital. The economic and cultural consequences of this failure were enormous and cannot really be overstated. Not only did the financial implications of Darien signal the death knell of Scotland as an independent nation – the Treaty of Union with England was signed in 1707 – it left scars and insecurities that haunt the Scottish psyche to this day. Clearly this is fertile subject matter for contemporary satire, not least because the financial crisis of 2008 had recently laid bare the dangers of combining crazed devotion to venture capitalism with overblown aspirations. It is also a tale of personal hubris and loss. William Paterson, the visionary Scottish financier behind Darien, had been one of the founders of the Bank of England. He accompanied the expedition himself only to suffer financial ruin and the death of his wife and child. When *Caledonia* opened in Edinburgh in August 2010 questions of Scotland's fitness in managing its own affairs were also on the agenda, as the Scottish National Party gained in the polls, partly by promising a referendum on Scottish independence.

In the event, *Caledonia*, in a production by the playwright and director Anthony Neilson, dealt with the chronology of the disaster relatively straightforwardly, while applying a kind of caricatured comic-book aesthetic to the telling of the tale. More interestingly, both Neilson's production, which received mixed reviews, and the play itself, revealed a timely ambivalence about its own subject matter. Allan Hunter's description of it as 'a breezy satire, a broad, gallus comedy, a quasi-musical, a pseudo pantomime and a morality tale', gives some indication of its competing discourses.[3] But perhaps this unevenness is entirely appropriate. After all, the independence debate, whether in the past or the present, is about more than economics. It is about emotions – which currently range from optimism and fear, to rage, resentment, confusion and even incomprehension. *Caledonia* takes this emotional conflict seriously, resisting the temptation merely to satirise seventeenth-century Scotland as a European backwater with ridiculous delusions of grandeur. Nor does Beaton give way to a victim mentality by giving too much weight to the suggestion that Scotland's attempt to participate in a global trading boom was sabotaged by the machinations of the English. *Caledonia* is as much a play about courage and optimism as it is about hubris and stupidity. Alongside David Greig's *Dunsinane* (2010) and Rona Munro's new trilogy *The James Plays* (2014) it can also be thought of as signalling a resurgence of the history play in Scotland, as increasing numbers of playwrights 'attempt to find episodes and stories from the past that resonate in the present'.[4]

Caledonia can be usefully understood in relation to a long tradition of Scottish history plays that includes John McGrath's *The Cheviot, the Stag and the Black, Black Oil* (1973). Rob Drummond's *Bullet Catch* (2012), while ostensibly dealing with an event in the past, owes much of its theatrical power to its mobilising of more contemporary developments in participatory performance. *Bullet Catch* re-enacts the notorious 'bullet catch' trick – an illusion in which the magician appears to catch a bullet directly fired at him or her – as performed in 1912 by William Henderson, a gifted young illusionist and protégé of Houdini. Henderson, the audience learns, handed a loaded gun to a labourer who has been randomly selected from his audience. The gun misfired, Henderson was killed, and Garth, for that was the unfortunate labourer's name, subsequently became the subject of a murder enquiry. In *Bullet Catch* Drummond both narrates Henderson's story and plays him, while at each performance a different co-star, or 'Garth', is selected from the audience. The piece is thus a solo show for two performers that relies for its effects and affects on audience participation.

As Jen Harvie has noted, the last twenty years have witnessed a 'proliferation of performance and art practices that engage audiences *socially* – by inviting those audiences to participate'.[5] This trend is worth noting because traditionally audience participation has been the preserve of popular forms such as the pantomime, or certain types of political or applied performance including children's theatre. Its increasingly widespread use on contemporary main stages raises interesting questions about how theatre-makers are engaging with developing ideas about social relations. In *Bullet Catch* the investigation into Henderson's death – which may or may not have been suicide – becomes Drummond's means of exploring not only the trick, but also other pertinent and profound questions about the nature of the theatre itself, which regularly deals in transformation, illusion, pretence and physical and emotional risk. Oddly, although Drummond performs a number of impressive illusions in the course of the piece, the most striking way in which the audience glimpses the power of theatrical transformation is in bearing witness to the journey undertaken by the second member of the cast. This co-star is different at every performance, of course, but his or her relationship with Drummond remains of central importance because the climax of both Henderson's story, and also Drummond's show depends on Drummond convincing a volunteer to shoot a loaded gun into his face. 'Is it possible', Drummond asks his audience near the beginning of the evening 'to make someone do something they don't want to do?' The answer seems to be yes, or almost always yes. Occasionally a volunteer refuses. Each performance of *Bullet Catch* therefore carries a potential risk of failure, or rather, foregrounds the risk of failure that accompanies all live performance. The show won both a Herald Angel and a Total Theatre Award at the Fringe in 2012.

Drummond is a young Glaswegian theatre maker with a growing reputation both as an innovator and as someone who immerses himself in each of his projects in a manner that might be considered extreme. For his 2011 show *Wrestling* he spent five months in training as a professional wrestler, for instance. His other theatre credits include *Mr Write* (2010), an improvised NTS show for teenagers, and *Top Table* (2011) a dark comedy set at a wedding party. *Top Table* was produced at Glasgow's Òran Mór, the venue for the lunchtime theatre club, A Play, a Pie and a Pint, which has become a major player in the development of new writing in Scotland. Founded in 2004 by David McLennan, a veteran of 7:84 and Wildcat, A Play, a Pie and a Pint has become Scotland's largest de facto commissioner of new plays, providing a welcome and accessible training ground for emerging writers and directors and a platform for more established dramatists. In 2013 alone Òran Mór hosted thirty-eight premieres and over the last few years has co-produced work with the NTS, the Traverse, Paines Plough, Live Theatre Newcastle, Bewley's Dublin, Bristol Tobacco Factory and Dundee Rep.

Like many theatre artists of his generation, Drummond has been well placed to benefit from McLennan's groundbreaking initiative, but he has also received support from elsewhere. In 2011, along with

Claire Cunningham, Nic Green, Kieran Hurley and Gary McNair, Drummond was selected for the National Theatre of Scotland's inaugural Auteurs project. Conceived in collaboration with the Arches in Glasgow, this project was designed specifically to support the artistic and professional development of emerging Scottish theatre artists and was consequently tailored to meet individual needs. Drummond's 2013 show *The Riot of Spring*, inspired by the centenary of Stravinsky's controversial ballet was a product of the Auteurs project. Created and performed with dancer Robbie Synge and musician Peter Nicholson, *The Riot of Spring* sought to reflect on the themes of the ballet, including the sacrifice of the young and the frenzy of the tribe. In the same year Drummond's *Quiz Show*, a clever and disturbing take on the dark underbelly of light entertainment in the 1970s, written presumably at least partly in response to the Jimmy Savile scandal, was produced at Scotland's premier new writing theatre, the Traverse in Edinburgh.

The Traverse celebrated its fiftieth birthday in 2013. Since its early years as a theatre club in an abandoned brothel in Edinburgh's Lawnmarket, the theatre has proved a fertile breeding ground for new Scottish talent. Contemporary Scottish dramatists whose early careers developed there include Henry Adam, David Harrower, Gregory Burke, Zinnie Harris and Rona Munro. Morna Pearson, whose first full-length play, *The Artist Man and the Mother Woman* (2012), is included in this collection, burst onto the scene at the Traverse in 2006 with her short play *Distracted*, her earliest play, *Untogether*, having been developed while she was part of the Traverse Theatre's Young Writers Group in 2002/3. *Distracted* won the Meyer-Whitworth Award for new writing in 2007, and established Pearson as an acute if idiosyncratic observer of life in her native North East – she was born in Elgin in Morayshire. Its portrayal of a boy scarred by the death of his junkie mother, living in a caravan park with his domineering grandmother and a lascivious neighbour, was as vivid as it was tender. *The Artist Man and the Mother Woman* revisits the territory of tortured intergenerational relationships. Like its predecessor, it also evidences Pearson's flair for a kind of dark, skewed poetry rooted in the Doric dialect of Scots spoken in her native North East. The esteem in which Pearson is currently held is evidenced by the fact that *The*

Artist Man and the Mother Woman was the first show directed for the Traverse by Orla O'Loughlin, who took over as Artistic Director of the theatre in January 2012.

In Pearson's play, Edie, the mother woman of the title, is a disturbing mixture of late middle-aged sensuality and smugness, outwardly serene, but vicious when thwarted. Although in his thirties, her unfortunate son Geoffrey is an innocent, a stranger to his own passions until he runs into an attractive former pupil in the local Sainsbury's. As Mark Fisher noted in his *Guardian* review of the piece, Pearson has a definite knack for rooting 'Doric poetry in a disturbingly credible world'.[6] Geoffrey and Edie battle over their increasingly fraught domestic arrangements, in a play that includes moments of grotesque comedy, hyper-realism and finally absolute horror. Pearson's use of comedy is both hilarious and disconcerting because it is counterbalanced at the play's climax with a savage reminder that we have been laughing at the wilful stunting of human potential. As a playwright, Pearson appears relatively uninterested in social realism but her heightened and skewed domestic comedies nevertheless hold a welcome mirror up to the dark underside of contemporary Scottish culture.

Since the establishment of the devolved Scottish Parliament in 1999, Scotland's theatre artists have benefited from both a general increase in cultural confidence and also funding arrangements that are largely favourable, at least in comparison with those south of the border. Successive administrations in Edinburgh have been willing to invest in arts and culture in the belief that the sector could act as an attractive shop window for Scotland both within the UK and on the international stage. Since its acclaimed inaugural season in 2006 the NTS has achieved sustained cultural prominence, attracting praise for its extensive work in Scotland and also for the ways in which it has brought the work of Scottish theatre-makers to national and international attention. One such theatre-maker is Anthony Neilson who was commissioned to create one of the company's inaugural projects, *Home Edinburgh* (2006) and whose play *Realism* (2006) was also commissioned by the NTS for its first summer season. By 2006 Neilson was already an established and award-winning playwright having been identified alongside Sarah Kane and Mark Ravenhill as a leading member and progenitor of the 'in-yer-face' school of British playwriting with its trademark focus on sexual violence and intense explorations of 'the darker side of the human psyche'.[7] During the early part of his career Neilson produced a number of remarkably intense and disturbing relationship plays, including *Penetrator* (1993), *The Censor* (1997) and *Stitching* (2002). However, the new century saw him begin a period of formal experimentation in works as diverse as *Edward Gant's Amazing Feats of Loneliness* (2002), *Realism* (2006), *God in Ruins* (2007) and most famously *The Wonderful World of Dissocia* (2004), which went on to be recognised as a contemporary classic. In 2004 Simon Stokes and David Prescott at the Theatre Royal Plymouth, who produced *Edward Gant* in 2002, agreed to co-produce *The Wonderful World of Dissocia*, with the Tron theatre in Glasgow and the EIF. The production, which opened at the Tron, went on to win five of the ten awards at the Critics' Awards for Theatre in Scotland, including Best Direction and Best New Play for Anthony Neilson, and Best Theatre Production for the company. In 2007 the NTS funded a revival and extensive tour. Among other things, Neilson's association with the NTS has led to his being repositioned as a distinctively Scottish artist; very little mention of his nationality had been made in criticism of his earlier work. Nevertheless Neilson has continued to live and work in London and the play included in this anthology, *Narrative* (2013) was commissioned for the Royal Court with whom Neilson has had a long association.

In common with *Realism* and *The Wonderful World of Dissocia*, *Narrative* is deliberately organised in such a way as to make it difficult for the audience to distinguish between fiction and reality, or even to develop a clear sense of the basis on which its characters are drawn. In fact, as its title implies, *Narrative* is to some extent a play 'about' the distinction between fiction and reality. What does a sequence of events need, in dramatic terms, to qualify as a narrative? What do characters need to do, and how do they need to explain what they do in order to qualify as 'dramatic'? These themes are perhaps most effectively explored in the story of Imogen, a young woman who kills her friend in an action that seems entirely unmotivated. She is subsequently banished from the world of the play, a strange echo effect added to her voice, until she can offer an explanation for her behaviour that makes sense in 'dramatic' terms. This banishment also precipitates a rather beautiful and haunting breakdown in Imogen's language. 'Sophie please – I'm soppy! You had to forget me, please! I'm scarce!' she sobs. ' . . . My weirds are word.' In *Narrative*, as in much of his recent work, Neilson rejects the more comfortable certainties of dramatic theatre, particularly the laws of cause and effect that typically structure realist narrative, in favour of a theatre of indeterminacy, poignancy and atmosphere.

The final play included in this anthology is *Rantin* (2013), a show produced as part of the Auteurs Project by the young theatre-maker Kieran Hurley and his collaborators Gav Prentice, Julia Taudevin and Drew Wright. Along with *Caledonia*, *Rantin* is the piece collected here that deals most directly and explicitly with issues of Scottish national identity. It has been remarkably successful. After debuting in Glasgow in 2013 as part of the Arches Theatre's Behaviour Festival, *Rantin* embarked on an NTS-sponsored nationwide tour of small community venues across Scotland in early 2014. Drawing on Scottish folk traditions in music and storytelling and on current events, *Rantin* is performed in a relaxed and welcoming ceilidh atmosphere, and in form, although perhaps not in content, it echoes the radical traditions of Scottish theatre in the 1970s, particularly the work of John McGrath with 7:84 Scotland and its seminal production, *The Cheviot, the Stag, and the Black, Black Oil* (1973). *Rantin* does not touch directly on the independence referendum but it offers a timely examination of contemporary Scottish identity. At its heart the show consists in a series of monologues in which characters offer contrasting interpretations of what it means to be Scottish. Howard, a sixty-seven-year-old from the United States, arrives on a pilgrimage, hoping to reconnect with his ancestral Scottishness. A young man leaves his native Stornoway on the Isle of Lewis for Glasgow University, uncertain if he will ever return. In Port Glasgow, on the Clyde, Shona muses on the philosophy of Adam Smith and finally determines to apply Luddite tactics to the installation of self-service checkpoints in her local supermarket. Meanwhile, Miriam, a Palestinian refugee long exiled from her native Ramallah, journeys to her cleaning job. The monologues that form the core of *Rantin* are punctuated by music and chat. Sometimes this involves the reworking of popular Scottish songs.

A cheeky rewrite of *Donald, Where's Yer Troosers (Donald, You're A Loser)* brings light relief, for instance, while a new setting of Hamish Henderson's classic *Freedom Come All Ye* (1960) brings added weight to the show's close. Sometimes thought of as an alternative national anthem, *Freedom Come All Ye* is a song much beloved of the Scottish Left for its defiant optimism but also for its unromantic and clear-sighted view of the role of the Scots in Britain's imperial project. This use of music as a tool for engaging audiences is an established pattern in Scottish theatre and evidences the strong and continuing influence of popular traditions. Neilson's *Realism* and *The Wonderful World of Dissocia* include a number of songs, for example, as do David Greig's *Midsummer* (2008) and more recently his play *The Strange Undoing of Prudencia Hart* (2010). Music also featured prominently in Hurley's earlier work.

Hurley, who was the National Theatre of Scotland's Pearson Playwright in Residence in 2013, made a significant impact at the Edinburgh Fringe in 2012 with his monologue *Beats*, a coming-of-age tale about mid-1990s rave culture and the efforts of the establishment to suppress it, which toured the UK in 2013. An earlier Fringe show *Hitch* (2010) used live music to accompany an autobiographical monologue about Hurley travelling, with no money and little sense of direction, to the G8 conference in L'Aquila in 2009, pausing to attend a Patti Smith concert in Rome on the way. Like Hurley's later work, *Hitch* is relatively simple in structure although it deals, with intelligence and subtlety, with a number of themes that are of striking relevance, particularly for young people. Like *Rantin*, it is about, among other things, the challenges of becoming politically engaged in an increasingly confused world; the remarkable kindness of strangers; the hesitancy one inevitably feels in a world that seems overwhelmingly large; and how one might connect with others and consequently make a meaningful contribution. Alongside Drummond, Hurley is one of the most exciting Scottish theatre-makers to appear in the last five years.

As I said at the beginning of this introduction, Scottish theatre continues to thrive. The innovative and flexible co-producing model on which the NTS was constituted – it has no permanent theatre building – meant its success was predicated from the outset on collaboration with existing theatre artists, companies, and venues. The new company was consequently, by virtue of its structure, plugged in. Subsequently, it has provided a genuinely inclusive framework, both geographically and conceptually, through which twenty-first century conceptions of Scotland and its people can be articulated. The continued success of the Traverse in identifying, developing and producing new Scottish playwrights in combination with the mighty efforts of David McLennan at Òran Mór would also seem to suggest a bright future for Scottish playwriting. Furthermore, that theatre, and the arts in general, have a significant role to play in Scotland under the new constitutional arrangements has been recognised by successive administrations in Edinburgh. Since 2007, along with Scottish Opera, Scottish Ballet and the country's two major orchestras, the NTS has been funded directly by the devolved Scottish government, a clear signal that the national companies are seen as both ambassadors for, and custodians of, Scottish culture.

Trish Reid
Kingston University, 2014

Notes

1   McMillan, J., *Scotsman*, 4 July 2011.
2   Booth, L., *New Statesman*, 19 February 2001.
3   Hunter, A., *Daily Express*, 23 August 2010.
4   Archibald, A., 'History in Contemporary Scottish Theatre' in
    I. Brown, (ed.), *The Edinburgh Companion to Scottish Drama.*
    Edinburgh: Edinburgh University Press, 2011, pp. 85–94.
5   Harvie, J., *Fair Play: Art, Performance and Neoliberalism.*
    Basingstoke: Palgrave, 2013, p. 1.
6   Fisher, M., *Guardian*, 8 November 2012.
7   Sierz, A., *In-Yer-Face Theatre: British Drama Today*. London: Faber
    and Faber, 2000, p. 68.

Caledonia

Alistair Beaton
with lyrics by Alistair Beaton
(some based on ballads of the time)

Caledonia was first performed at the King's Theatre, Edinburgh, on 21 August 2010, in a co-production between the National Theatre of Scotland and the Edinburgh International Festival.

The cast, in alphabetical order, was as follows:

Reverend Francis Borland	Paul Blair
Robert Blackwood	Tam Dean Burn
King William of Orange	Cliff Burnett
Joost	David Carlyle
James Balfour	Alan Francis
Mrs Paterson	Frances Grey
William Paterson	Paul Higgins
John Erskine	Neil McKinven
Ensemble	Robert Melling
Roderick Mackenzie	Matthew Pidgeon
Ensemble	Morna Young

Nameless of the Earth, MPs, Merchants, Subscribers, Clerks, Councillors, Sailors, Colonists, Servants and all other parts played by the Company.

Director	Anthony Neilson
Designer	Peter McKintosh
Composer/Musical Supervisor	Paddy Cunneen
Musical Director	Robert Melling
Lighting Designer	Chahine Yavroyan
Sound Designer	Nick Sagar
Movement Director/Assistant Director	Anna Morrissey
Casting Director	Anne Henderson

Preface

Caledonia is a story of greed, folly and mass delusion. In that respect it is a very modern tale. But it is also a darkly tragic and fitfully heroic tale of its time.

In the 1690s, Scotland – still an independent nation despite a shared crown with England – decided it wanted to be a colonial power. That great Scottish visionary, charmer and financier William Paterson was the moving spirit behind the decision to set up a colony on the Isthmus of Panama. He dreamed that Scotland would thereby control the trade between East and West and virtually overnight be transformed from a small, poor nation into one of the world's major economic powers. There was every reason to believe him: this was, after all, the man who just a few years earlier had founded the Bank of England. The atmosphere was also propitious: the growing popularity of that recent invention, the joint stock company, persuaded people that there were new and virtually risk-free ways of making vast amounts of money.

Paterson's plan for a Scottish colony was greeted with nationwide enthusiasm. Subscription books were opened in Edinburgh and Glasgow and within weeks the Scottish people had invested a vast proportion of their wealth.

The vision may have been soaring, but the execution was prosaically bad. Virtually every danger had been underestimated. Perhaps two thousand settlers died from disease, hunger and skirmishes with Spanish troops. Nor had Paterson reckoned with the implacable opposition of King William and the English Parliament. Despite sending two mighty fleets, Scotland was soon forced to abandon the colony, which in a moment of grandeur and hope, had been named Caledonia.

The catastrophe left Scotland fatally weakened and led a few years later to the end of Scotland as an independent nation. Following the Treaty of Union with England in 1707, cartloads of money were sent to Scotland to pay off the shareholders of the Company that had been responsible for the disaster.

Every history play has to strike a balance between historical truth and dramatic truth. To make the subject work as a play I had to simplify some incidents, change the order of some events, and create a mixture of invented and historically real characters. What is astonishing though, is how many of the details of the story strike a chord with today's world of finance without my having to alter a word. This echo of today extends even to Paterson's use of lavish hospitality to win over the Great and the Good.

That is why *Caledonia* is a Scottish story, an international story, an ancient story, and a modern story.

Alistair Beaton

Principal Characters

William Paterson
Roderick Mackenzie
James Balfour
Robert Blackwood
John Erskine
Mrs Paterson
Reverend Francis Borland
Robert Pennicuick

A chorus of the Nameless of the Earth

Other Characters

Innkeeper
Members of the Parliament of Scotland
First Serving Maid
Second Serving Maid
Serving Boy
The Marquis of Tweedale
Sergeant-at-Arms
King William of Orange
Joost
Town Crier
Flunkey
Foreign Merchants
Servant to William Paterson
Various Servants
Directors of the Company of Scotland
Lionel Wafer
Clerks
Subscribers
Drunks
Councillors of the Colony
James Smyth, Merchant
Servant to James Smyth

Poor Girl
Sailors
Lookout
Colonists
Captain Aguillon
Gravediggers
Ship's Boy
Servant to Balfour and Blackwood
Banker

Act One

Curtain up or lights up on **Paterson**, *dictating to an* **Innkeeper** *who proceeds to follow him obsequiously round the room, writing everything down.* **Paterson** *is thinking up his order as he goes. To one side of the stage stands* **Mackenzie**, *a leather-bound ledger under his arm. Hanging from the set (which should be constructed to permit climbing) downstage left and downstage right are the miserably attired* **Nameless of the Earth**. *They silently observe the action. For the other characters on stage, the* **Nameless** *do not exist.*

Paterson   I want it to be just right, do you understand? Everything . . . just right.

Innkeeper   Of course, Mr Paterson. I have reserved the private dining room on the first floor.

Paterson   Very good.

Innkeeper   And as to the menu, we can offer –

Paterson   Yes, yes, thank you. We will have . . . um . . . five pound of herring.

Innkeeper   Very good, Mr Paterson. Five pound . . . of . . . herring.

Paterson   Three lobsters. No, better make that four. Four lobsters.

Innkeeper   Four lobsters.

Mackenzie (*anxious*)   Mr Paterson.

Paterson (*ignoring* **Mackenzie)**   Oh, we should have some soup, should we not?

Innkeeper   We do a very fine lambshead broth.

Paterson   Lambshead broth? Hmmmm . . . let us have something finer. Something . . . grander.

Innkeeper   Pottage of venison?

Paterson   Very good. Pottage of venison. Two large tureens.

Innkeeper   Two large tureens . . . pottage . . . of venison. Were you aware, Mr Paterson, that the Ship Tavern is renowned for its eel and oyster pie?

Paterson   Is it now? Then we shall have the Ship Tavern's eel and oyster pie. And plenty of it.

Innkeeper   Eel and oyster pie . . .

Paterson   And two ducks.

Innkeeper   Two ducks.

Paterson   Two ducks. Is that enough? Make that three ducks!

Innkeeper   Three ducks.

Paterson   And five chickens with gooseberries.

Innkeeper (*now struggling to keep up*)   Five chickens with goose –

Mackenzie   I hope you're aware of the price of chickens, Mr Paterson?

Paterson (*to* **Innkeeper**)   Should we not also have some veal collops. Yes, why not? Veal collops, lots of veal collops.

Innkeeper   A few . . . pounds of veal collops?

Paterson   Very good. With a plate or two of sparagrass.

Innkeeper   Veal collops, sparagrass . . .

Paterson   A sleeve of mutton.

Innkeeper   Sleeve of –

Paterson   Mutton.

Innkeeper (*flustered*)   Mutton. Sleeve of mutton.

Paterson   And two dozen bottles of your very finest claret.

Mackenzie (*shocked*)   Mr Paterson!

Innkeeper   Finest claret . . .

Paterson   Then we will want fruit, cheeses, bread, ale, brandy.

Innkeeper   Fruit . . . cheeses . . .

Paterson   French brandy.

Innkeeper   French, of course, Mr Paterson, for you, sir.

Mackenzie   This will cost a large sum of money, Mr Paterson.

Paterson   I think that will be all. Oh. Tobacco and pipes.

Innkeeper   Tobacco . . . and pipes . . .

Paterson   If you excel yourself, you will be well rewarded. And a shilling each for the serving boys. If they do not spill the soup. Come along Mackenzie.

Paterson *heads towards the door.* **Mackenzie** *follows, shaking his head.*

Innkeeper   Yes, Mr Paterson. Thank you, Mr Paterson. We look forward to receiving you and your guests.

Paterson   Yes, yes. Goodbye. (*Makes to leave.*)

Innkeeper   Oh, Mr Paterson, sorry. I nearly forgot. Number of guests. We can accommodate up to forty. How many will you be?

Paterson   Six.

Innkeeper   Six?

Paterson   Aye. Six.

Innkeeper   Six?

Paterson   Aye. Six.

Innkeeper   Of course, we're grateful for your business, Mr Paterson. But . . . are you quite sure? I mean, all that food and drink for . . . six.

Paterson   I am quite sure.

Innkeeper   Well . . . those must be mighty hungry men, Mr Paterson. And mighty thirsty.

Paterson   They are, sir, they are. They're Members of Parliament.

Paterson *and* **Mackenzie** *leave.*

The **Nameless Of The Earth** *climb down onto the stage, singing. The* **Innkeeper** *shucks off his outer clothing, revealing the same rags as the* **Nameless**, *whom he joins.*

Song No. 1   The Nameless of the Earth

Nameless   *It must be nice*
So nice
Nice to have the money
To order up a duck
Or chicken
Or veal.
To sit down to a meal
And have enough to eat
Oh what a treat
To have enough to eat.

Clothes stands are rolled on with articles of **MPs**' *clothing, which they put on. Two of the* **Nameless** *adopt the dress of* **Serving Maids** *while one dresses as a* **Serving Boy**.

Nameless   *All history is written by the winners*
No place for us poor sinners
Unknown
Unsung
The nameless of the earth. Despised, forgotten,
Of humble birth
Of little worth.
Although
We know
That history is written by the winners
We never give up hope
The nameless of the earth
All live in hope.

First Nameless   *So let us have a play*
In which the nameless of the earth
Will have a role.

Second Nameless *A little play encompassing*
Each immortal soul.

Paterson *enters.*

Third Nameless   *And here's the lovely actor*
Who agreed to play the lead

Fourth Nameless *Oh yes, I like the look of him*

Fifth Nameless   *He's exactly what we need.*

Food is laid out.

Nameless   *Aye, every now and then*
The nameless of the earth can still be heard
Can dream at least
Of one day being invited to the feast.

Scene Two – The Ship Tavern, Edinburgh

Five of the **Nameless** *are now* **MPs***, rather aware of their own importance. As they take their seats at table* **Paterson** *enters. The* **Serving Boy** *stands discreetly to one side.*

Paterson   Gentlemen. Welcome. What a pleasure it is to have your company. Your . . . esteemed company.

There is a murmur of satisfaction. The **Serving Maids** *withdraw.*

Paterson   I know you are dedicated men. I know how hard you work on Scotland's behalf. And I know it can't be easy, sitting up there in Parliament Hall day in day out listening to the endless blather of the Scottish aristocracy – those perfumed peacocks who neither see nor sense the tide of history.

They nod and smile, recognising the picture.

First MP   True enough, true enough.

Paterson   They resent you, gentlemen. Like you they may be members of Parliament, but they are the past, and you are the future. *We* are the future. Men who understand the meaning of money. Men who can do so much for this nation. If only we're allowed to change the old way of doing things.

Second MP   I never realised that Scotland was so close to your heart, Mr Paterson.

Third MP   Aye, you've spent a great part of your life abroad, have you not?

Second MP (*citing a heinous offence*)   Much of it in England.

Paterson   Should a man be blamed for leaving his native land in the hope of making his fortune?

Second MP   No, but –

Paterson   You think I could have founded the Bank of England without ever leaving Scotland, do you?

First MP   No need to boast, Mr Paterson. We all know how important you are. We just wonder why you've left behind all your fashionable friends in London in order to come back and scheme and plot amidst the stinking streets of Edinburgh.

Paterson   Because my country needs me. What has Scotland presently got to offer the world? Go on, gentlemen. Tell me.

Underscoring ends. **Paterson** *looks at the* **MPs** *challengingly. For a few moments there is silence around the table.*

Fourth MP   Fish.

Paterson   Fish?!

Fourth MP   Aye. It is my belief that the abundance of fish in Scotland is divine compensation for the lack of sunshine.

Paterson   Very well. Fish. What else?

The two **Serving Maids** *leave.*

Fifth MP   Hides.

Third MP   Coal.

First MP   Salt.

Fourth MP   Whisky.

Second MP   And knitted hosiery. We sell to England prodigious quantities of knitted hosiery.

Paterson   Oh, damn your knitted hosiery, sir. Scotland will not become great through the exporting of socks. A few rickety carts trundling down to England loaded with knitting is not going to do much for us. The advancement of overseas trade. That is what'll save Scotland from its present miserable condition.

Fourth MP   It is not so easy. Other countries will not permit us to trade with their colonies.

Paterson   Then Scotland must have colonies of its own.

Second MP (*laughs*)   You were aye a bit of a dreamer, Mr Paterson.

Paterson   We all dream, do we not? It's what you do with your dream, that's what matters.

First MP (*dismissively*)   Yes, but the idea of a Scottish colony . . . really, sir . . .

Paterson   The English have colonies. The Spanish have colonies. The French have colonies. The Portuguese have colonies. The Dutch have colonies. Even Denmark has colonies. Why should not Scotland have its colonies?

Third MP   Because Scotland's too poor. And too small. Do you mean to tell me that a nation of a million souls can conquer the globe?

Paterson   It's not conquest that I have in mind, sir. It is trade. Trade. The great civilising force of the future. And in a few days' time you'll have your chance to vote for the bill that will make it all possible.

Fourth MP   Oh, you want our votes, eh? I thought maybe you did. (*Looks at others, chuckles knowingly.*)

Paterson   I do. Yes, I do. Listen. Why has England been so successful in overseas trade? Because of the East India Company – and all the powers that have been given it by the English Parliament. Now it's our turn to do the same. When the Bill comes before you next week, I ask you to vote to establish Scotland's very own joint stock trading company. The Company of Scotland. Financed by private investment, protected by the state. Give this company powers. Grant it monopolies. Free it from the burden of taxation.

First MP   And will your new company stop the harvests from failing? (*Takes a big mouthful of food.*) Three years in a row we've had famine. Failed harvest after failed harvest.

The **Serving Maids** *enter with more food.*

Paterson   If we had the wealth, we could import food. And what now offers the fastest, most certain path to wealth? The joint stock company. There's no greater instrument for creating wealth. It's the most ingenious of all modern inventions.

First MP   To my mind, when there's a sudden fashion for new financial instruments, it is time to close your purse. There's aye some clever fellow who claims he's found a new road to riches. Some of us would prefer to risk our money in a more pleasurable manner.

Fifth MP   Like a wee game of cards.

First MP   Like a wee game of cards.

Paterson   Ah, but I can take away risk.

First MP   How would you do that?

Paterson   In the past, a man would invest in one ship going on one voyage. If that ship failed to return, he would lose everything. Now the risk is spread . . . you are not investing in a single voyage. You're investing in a company. A joint stock company set up by Parliament itself. A company that's as powerful as the nation itself. A company with its own ships. A company with its own colonies.

Fifth MP (*warming to the idea*)   A Scottish colony. 'Tis a bold idea.

Second MP   It may be worth . . . considering.

First MP   Aye, after all, Paterson, we're men of the world. We're not against earning the odd shilling.

Paterson   Yes, and when the sands of history are shifting, that's when a man of the world can make a fortune. And at the same time, benefit his native land. Wealth for one. Wealth for all, that's what I'm offering. We are entering a new age. Men will trade not only in goods but in company shares. Buying and selling. Selling and buying. Making money out of money. Trade will increase trade. Money will beget money. This is the simple idea that is going to transform the world. What I offer you, gentlemen, is nothing less than wealth without end.

There is a moment's silence. The **MPs** *accept* **Paterson**'s *ideas, tentatively at first.*

Song No. 2   Trade Begets Trade

First MP   *Trade begets trade . . .*

Fourth MP   *Money makes money . . .*

Third MP   *Wealth creates wealth*

Second MP   *Riches from riches*

Fifth MP   *Piled upon riches*

First MP   *To the end of the world.*

They embrace the idea.

All MPs   *Trade begets trade*
        Money makes money
        Wealth creates wealth
        Riches from riches
        Piled upon riches
        To the end of the world.

First MP   I am with you, Mr Paterson.

Third MP   So am I. A man needs to move with the times. You can be assured I will vote for the Bill. Scotland will have its trading company!

Second MP   I will speak to the motion.

First MP   Aye, it'll need some fine speech-making if we're to win the debate.

*The other **MPs** murmur their agreement.*

Paterson (*thoughtfully*)   I've been thinking . . . a debate. Do we really need a debate? Do we want some wheezing and decrepit old aristocrats telling Parliament that a joint stock company is not in their interests?

Fourth MP   The King would expect there to be a debate.

Paterson   The King is four hundred miles away.

Second MP (*shakes his head in disapproval*)   Aye, we have an absentee monarchy in this country.

Paterson   Isn't that the best kind? Especially with our own Parliament just up the road?

Fifth MP   I suppose . . . I mean, if the king's attention were elsewhere at the time.

Paterson   The King's attention is forever elsewhere. Yon Dutchman has never even set foot in Scotland, why should he start now? No, the King will leave everything to Tweedale, as he always does. Do not trouble yourselves with a debate, gentlemen. Be bold. Be brave. Be the messengers of a new world.

The music returns, now in a mood of religious fervour.

All MPs   *Trade begets trade*
    Money makes money
    Wealth creates wealth
    Riches from riches
    Piled upon riches
    To the end of the world.

A splendidly dressed **Tweedale** *is flown in* (*or enters*). *The* **MPs** *leave.* **Paterson** *leaves or goes to the side of the stage and observes.*

Scene Three – Parliament Hall, Edinburgh

A Sergeant of Arms *enters, bearing a sceptre. Lose music.*

Sergeant   This session of the Parliament of Scotland is hereby holden and begun at Edinburgh upon this the twenty-sixth day of June, one thousand, six hundred and ninety five, presided over by his grace the Marquis of Tweedale, Lord High Chancellor of Scotland.

Tweedale *looks around a little confused. The* **Sergeant** *looks up, whistles or signals, and a parliamentary Bill flies in, festooned with seals and ribbons.* **Tweedale** *reads from it.*

Tweedale (*reads*)   His Majesty understanding that several persons are willing to engage themselves with great sums of money in a trade to be exercised from this Kingdom, does hereby grant unto them a monopoly on trade to Asia, Africa and America, together with exemption from all taxation for a period of twenty-one years.

MPs (*off or recorded*)   Hear! Hear!

Tweedale   The said persons shall form a joint stock trading company, which shall be known as the Company of Scotland.

MPs (*off or recorded*)   Hear! Hear!

Tweedale   This Company is hereby empowered to equip, fit, set out and navigate ships from any of the ports and places of this Kingdom, in warlike or in other manner to any Lands, Islands, Countries or places in Asia, Africa, or America, and there to plant colonies and build Cities, Towns and Forts.

MPs (*off or recorded*)   Hear! Hear! Hear!

Tweedale   The passing into law of this Bill shall be accompanied by the creation of a Scottish bank in whom all men may place their trust. The directors of this new Company shall be those named in the Bill.

MPs (*off or recorded*)   Hear! Hear! Hear!

Tweedale *snaps his fingers.*

Tweedale (*peevishly*)   Sceptre!

He touches the Bill with the sceptre.

Sergeant   The Bill is touched with the royal sceptre and becomes law.

The **Nameless** *change clothes to become directors of the Company of Scotland.* **Tweedale** *hands the sceptre back. A few bars of music are heard as* **Tweedale** *flies out or leaves.*

Scene Four – Paterson's office, Edinburgh

Mackenzie *enters, carrying a ledger, places it on a high desk or table or lectern and prepares to write.* **Balfour** *and* **Blackwood** *enter, each with a glass of red wine in his hand.*

Balfour   Here's tae us, wha's like us, gey few and they're aw deid!

Blackwood   Aye, it's time to celebrate all right.

Balfour   Scotland! Scotland will conquer the globe!

Mackenzie (*coughs to attract their attention*)   Gentlemen, Roderick Mackenzie at your service. If you would kindly sign the Company articles (*holds out quill*).

Balfour   Aye, all in good time, sir, all in good time. (*Raises his glass to* **Blackwood**.) To the Company of Scotland!

Blackwood   The Company of Scotland!

Mackenzie   Each director of the company is required to sign the articles.

Balfour   Oh, very well, very well.

Mackenzie   Here, please. Just below Mr Paterson's name. (*Signs.*)

Mackenzie   Thank you, Mr Balfour. (*Gives quill to* **Blackwood**.)

Blackwood   Is it my signature you want?

Mackenzie (*wondering at the stupidity*)   Yes.

Blackwood   Here?

Mackenzie (*with forced patience*)   Yes.

Blackwood *signs.*

Mackenzie   Thank you, Mr Blackwood.

Erskine *enters.*

Balfour   Mr Erskine. Will you join us in a glass?

Erskine   A small one. I am here to sign the articles, not carouse late into the night. (*Signs.*)

Borland (*entering*)   I am glad to hear it. (*Signs.*) You will have a glass of water for me, I hope?

Blackwood (*puzzled*)   A glass of water?

Balfour (*pouring another glass of wine*)   Scotland! Scotland will rule the world.

Mackenzie (*without looking up from ledger*)   Do you think that's maybe a wee bit ambitious, Mr Balfour?

Balfour   Aye well, let's rule bits of it.

Erskine   Which bits? That's the question, is it not?

Balfour   Big bits.

Paterson (*enters*)   Gentleman, it is time to make plans.

Erskine   Good. Here we are, directors of this new company of yours, Paterson, and we don't even know where you plan to establish the first colony.

Blackwood   It'll be somewhere overseas.

All *turn and look for a moment, wondering whether* **Blackwood** *is as stupid as that sounded.*

Erskine (*to* **Paterson**)   We're thinking of the East Indies, are we not?

Balfour   Aye, the East Indies, that's where we should be heading. Or Africa. Or the Caribbean. Or all three!

Erskine (*to* **Paterson**)   The Act has been passed. Now's the time to decide where we trade, where we plant our first colony.

Paterson   All in good time, Mr Erskine. There are ships to be built. Men to be hired. Supplies to be bought. All this will require a great deal of money. Most of it will have to come from English investors.

Blackwood   English investors, that's a good idea. It will require a journey to England.

Erskine   I believe that's generally where the English are to be found, Mr Blackwood.

Paterson   London will be the foundation of this endeavour. It's there I intend to start.

Blackwood   Oh, it's a grand place, London.

Balfour   Only because it's full of Scots. (*Pours himself another glass.*)

Erskine (*to* **Paterson**)   You will have a target sum in mind?

Paterson   Yes.

Erskine   And . . . ?

Balfour (*thinking he's being ambitious*)   I suggest you aim at raising one hundred thousand pounds.

Paterson   I will raise more than that.

Balfour   That's the spirit, sir! Two hundred thousand!

Paterson   More than two hundred thousand.

Balfour   Yes! You're a great man, Mr Paterson. May the good Lord bless you and the Company of Scotland.

Erskine (*coldly, to* **Paterson**)   So how much do you have in mind?

Paterson   Three hundred thousand.

Balfour (*triumphantly*)   Three hundred thousand!

Mackenzie (*looks up sharply*)   Three hundred thousand?

Paterson   I want us to build a trading fleet that'll be the envy of the world. Not those sorry excuses for ships that Scotland presently possesses. I mean great ships, mighty ships, as mighty as those of the Dutch. Ships that will be looked on with awe. Ships that speak of wealth. Ships that make a man's heart race. Ships that will have men rushing to invest. We'll open a subscription book in London. It will not take long to raise what we need. The money always follows the money.

A **Servant Boy** *and* **Girl** *prepare* **Paterson** *for the journey.*

Mackenzie   It will have to be carefully accounted for, Mr Paterson. There must be no irregularities. We have Scotland's reputation to protect. Every last penny must be recorded in these ledgers.

Paterson (*laughs*)   Oh, Mackenzie, Mackenzie. It is good we have made you our Company Secretary. It will let you give full rein to your anxiety. Every Company needs a man who worries about the detail.

Erskine   The English will rush to invest in a Scottish Company trading overseas, will they? They will trust us?

Blackwood   They will certainly trust Mr Paterson. Everyone trusts Mr Paterson.

Erskine   Let us hope so.

Blackwood   The man who founded the Bank of England? I don't think there is any doubt upon the matter. How could they not put their money in the hands of a man who once ran a bank?

Balfour   Very good point, Mr Blackwood, very good point.

Erskine   You do not think the English merchants will see us as a threat?

Paterson   They may. Or as an investment. Never underestimate the lure of an investment, Mr Erskine. (*To* **Mackenzie**.) Well, don't just stand there, man, you and I are leaving for London.

Paterson *leaves.* **Balfour** *and* **Blackwood** *perform a skippy little dance and reprise the previous number, this time in a skittish version.*

Song No. 3   Trade Begets Trade (Reprise)

Balfour & Blackwood   *Trade begets trade*
Money makes money
Wealth creates wealth
Riches from riches
Piled upon riches
To the end of the world.

Balfour *and* **Blackwood** *dance off in the opposite direction from* **Paterson**. **Mackenzie** *readies himself for the journey.*

Erskine   He plays his cards close to his chest, that man.

Mackenzie   Mr Paterson knows what he's doing.

Erskine   He has no doubt told you about where we are to found our colony?

Mackenzie   No.

Erskine   Really?

Mackenzie   I said no, Mr Erskine.

Erskine   This secrecy. What is the purpose of it?

Mackenzie   If it were to become public knowledge, other nations might send their ships there before us.

Erskine   He doesn't trust us to hold our tongues?

Mackenzie   Why should he?

Erskine   There must be trust. I don't do business with men I don't trust.

Mackenzie   Then you must do gey little business, Mr Erskine.

Erskine   What if he doesn't know? What if that's his secret? That he doesn't even know where this colony is to be?

Mackenzie   Och, now you're being silly, Mr Erskine. (*Turns.*) Mr Paterson! Wait for me!

Mackenzie *hurries off after* **Paterson**. **Erskine** *leaves.*

Scene Five – the Streets of London (alternatively a coffee house)

A dance routine. **Investors** *thrust / throw banknotes at* **Paterson**, *while* **Mackenzie** *nervously collects the stray notes. While this is happening,* **Three Nameless** *enter downstage and sing.*

Song No. 4   When You've Founded A Bank

First Nameless   *Regardless of rank*
When you've founded a bank
Society opens its doors
And those in high places
with big smiling faces
Are suddenly down on all fours.

Second Nameless   *Though your mind may be blank*
Once you've founded a bank
It's like leading a lamb to the slaughter.
Old men in fine breeches
Will make lovely speeches
And leave you alone with their daughter.

Third Nameless   *Now let us be frank*
When you've founded a bank
Society pays you attention
You are keenly awaited
And greeted and feted
And end up with quite a nice pension.

They all three do a little dance. **King William** *enters, dressed for hunting. He lingers upstage while* **Joost**, *a handsome young courtier enters, carrying a cushion with rings and jewellery. He goes over to observe* **Paterson**. *The dance ends. The* **Nameless** *leave.* **Paterson** *is left breathlessly scrambling around stuffing banknotes into his pockets.* **Joost** *stares at this undignified scene for a moment or two.*

Joost (*disdainfully*)   The King commands you to attend upon him.

Paterson *dusts himself down, straightens his clothing.* **Mackenzie** *leaves.*

Scene Six – the Court of King William, London

King William *examines himself in the long mirror, coughs, fusses, examines his hunting outfit.*

Joost   Your Majesty. Mr William Paterson.

William *coughs again, ignores* **Paterson**, *fusses with his clothing. He takes a ring, tries it on, discards it.* **Joost** *offers him another choice.*

William (*without turning round*)   I'm about to go hunting.

Paterson (*bows slightly*)   Your Majesty.

William   I do so love hunting. Do you hunt much yourself, Paterson?

Paterson   Hunting is not something in which I indulge, Sire.

William   How very odd. (*He and* **Joost** *exchange glances in confirmation of the oddity.*) And life in Scotland? Is it bearable?

Paterson   It suits me well enough, Sire.

William   I have never been to Scotland. Tell me, is it true that to avoid the lice a gentleman must go to bed wearing gloves and stockings? (*Exchanges exaggerated looks of horror with* **Joost**.)

Paterson   That is to overstate the case.

William   Still, you must miss the pleasures of London life.

Paterson   I am happy to live in Scotland for the foreseeable future. A man has an attachment to the land of his birth.

William   And the purpose of your visit to England?

Paterson   I believe your Majesty is apprised of the purpose of my visit.

William (*his mood no longer playful*)   Yes. You are absolutely right. We are. You have opened subscription books here in London for this new Scotch Trading Company. And you have already raised three hundred thousand pounds. In just two weeks.

Paterson   In twelve days. To be precise. Sire.

William   Such a large sum in such a short time. Our men of wealth must love you very dearly.

Paterson   They trust me, Sire. I have experience in raising capital for new enterprises. The Bank of England. The Hampstead Water Company. The Southwark Corporation for the supply of –

William   Yes, that's the problem. You make people believe in you. We do not like it. You have a persuasive tongue. We have nothing against your tongue, sir. It is a most accomplished instrument. You may do with your tongue what you will.

Joost *giggles.*

William (*contd.*)   Unless your tongue begins to damage English trading interests.

Paterson   I can assure your Majesty that –

William The shareholders of the East India Company are unhappy. They do not want to see English wealth draining away to Edinburgh. And we certainly don't wish to see Scottish colonies set up in competition to English colonies. I want no distractions from the war with France. I have been ill served in Scotland. That old fool Tweedale exceeded his powers. This is what happens when I don't personally take command. I should go there myself. But I do not want to go to Scotland. It does not appeal. The weather. The filth. The drink.

Paterson   Your subjects in Scotland would be greatly heartened were Your Majesty pleased to go there.

William   I have sufficient problems at home. No King should have two Parliaments. One is more than enough. Two parliaments and one king. Two independent nations under one crown. Only the people of these islands could have devised such a regrettable constitutional settlement. Sooner or later there must be union between England and Scotland. It is obvious.

Paterson   The people of Scotland cling fiercely to their independence.

William   But I will not permit them to damage English trade. And I think the English Parliament is likely to feel the same. And now I am going hunting. Come along, Joost. (*Leaves.*)

Joost (*as he passes*)   Lik mijn reet.

Paterson   What?

Joost   Lik mijn reet.

Paterson   Sorry, I don't speak Dutch.

Joost   How very fortunate for you. (*Leaves.*)

Scene Seven – a London street or square

Paterson *alone on stage. A* **Town Crier** *enters, ringing a handbell. Behind him comes a* **Liveried Flunkey** *pushing a wooden wheelbarrow. As the* **Town Crier** *speaks,* **Paterson** *reluctantly empties his pockets of money into the wheelbarrow. Near the end, the* **Flunkey** *points at a pocket and* **Paterson** *takes out the last few notes he has missed.*

Town Crier   Hear ye! Hear ye! Hear ye! It is hereby solemnly resolved by the Sovereign Parliament of England and Ireland that the Directors of the Company of Scotland by raising monies in England under pretext of a Scotch Act of Parliament are guilty of a High Crime and Misdemeanour. It is further resolved that a Committee be appointed to prepare the impeachment of Mr William Paterson. (*Leaves. Off.*) Hear ye! Hear ye! Hear ye!

The **Servant** *with the wheelbarrow also leaves.*

Mackenzie (*entering*)   So, our Company is attacked in its swaddling clothes and strangled in its infancy.

Paterson   No.

He clicks his fingers and a **Servant** *enters with a trunk.*

Mackenzie   But they will impeach you.

Paterson   They threaten to. But that's only to frighten off the investors.

Mackenzie   It has succeeded. All the monies pledged have been withdrawn. We have raised not one penny. The investors are terrified.

Paterson   The English investors are terrified.

Mackenzie (*looks at trunk*)   You leave for Scotland?

Paterson   No. I leave for Amsterdam. And Rotterdam. And Hamburg. And Bremen. And Lübeck. The English are not the only people on this earth with money to invest.

Mackenzie   But . . . I mean . . . King William . . . . . He will hear of it. He will not like it. He has diverse interests. Interests and influence.

Paterson   Yes. But money also has influence.

Music.

Servant (*to audience*)   We will now pander to popular prejudice by offering a short and faintly anachronistic scene in which a number of foreigners are caricatured in an unacceptable manner. Any members of the audience who find this offensive may ask for their money back. Though they will not get it. Thank you. (*Picks up trunk and leaves.*)

Scene Eight – the capitals of Northern Europe

A few bars of appropriate national music announce each caricature as he opens a window or emerges through a door. The **French Merchant** *has a beret and a baguette, the* **German Merchant** *has sausages and wears Lederhosen, the* **Dutch Merchant** *wears clogs, carries tulips, and is perhaps dressed as a windmill, the* **Danish Merchant** *is dressed as a Viking. They dance and sing.*

Song No. 5   The International Language

Paterson   *Everybody speaks the language of money*
It's the international language.
And that's why we all get on

Foreign Merchants   *Jawohl.*
Bien sur.
Ja.
Jawel.

Paterson   *Everybody speaks the language of money,*
That's why we all get on.

Foreign Merchants   *That's why we all get on.*

Paterson   *Oh yes, that's why we all get on.*

Foreign Merchants   *That's why we all get on.*
Oh my, how we all get on.

They dance. Music changes or suddenly ceases as **Joost** *enters.*

Joost   King William has been informed that representatives of a Scotch trading Company are travelling the Continent endeavouring to raise money. (*The merchants put on an act of baffled innocence.*) His Majesty has commanded me most expressly to notify Your Magnificences that if you enter into business with these men his Majesty will regard it as an affront to his royal authority and (*heavily*) he will not fail to resent it. (*Leaves.*)

There is a clap of thunder and they gasp in fear. The **Foreign Merchants** *go to* **Mackenzie** *and take back their bags of coins.*

Merchants   Sorry!

They slam shut the doors or windows.

Paterson *stands there head bowed as* **Mackenzie** *looks on anxiously.*

Mackenzie   Let's go home, Mr Paterson.

He does not reply.

Mackenzie   All doors are closed against us. The King will never allow Scotland to have its colonies. It was a noble dream, Mr Paterson, but that's all it is now. A dream.

Blackout.

Scene Nine – a room in Paterson's house, Edinburgh

It is comfortable but restrained. In one corner a large globe of the world. **Mrs Paterson** *is directing* **Two Male Servants** *who are carrying in a piece of furniture covered by a cloth. A* **Servant Girl** *is standing watching.*

Mrs Paterson   Over there.

The **Servants** *place the piece of furniture where she indicates.*

They remove the cloth. It is a brand new day bed. She steps back to consider it.

Mrs Paterson   A wee bit more to the left. (*Pause.*) No, more to the right. (*Pause.*) No, back where it was. Yes. That'll do it.

*The **Servants** make to leave.*

Mrs Paterson   It doesn't look right.

*The **Servants** go back to the day bed.*

Mrs Paterson   Ach no, it's fine. Leave it where it is. It just needs the new cushions.

*The **Domestic Servants** withdraw.*

Mrs Paterson   Well where are they, then? Where are the new cushions? Come along, lassie, don't just stand there looking glaekit.

Servant Girl   Sorry, Mrs Paterson. They're in yon kist.

Mrs Paterson   Bring them here, then.

Servant Girl   Yes, Madam.

Mrs Paterson   And will you stop calling it a kist? It's not some farmworker's box for storing oats. It's a French linenfold coffer. In walnut.

Servant Girl   Yes, Madam. (*Takes out the brightly coloured cushions, unwrapping them from paper.*) Oh, they're so bonnie.

Mrs Paterson *points at the day bed. The **Servant Girl** places the cushions on the day bed. **Mrs Paterson** assesses them. They make a bold splash of colour in an otherwise dark and simple room.*

Off: Dogs bark. Rattle of a carriage. Horses neigh. Male voices shouting orders.

Servant Girl   The maister! The maister is hame! I will go help.

Mrs Paterson   Go on then!

The **Servant Girl** *leaves.* **Mrs Paterson** *hurriedly checks her appearance in the mirror.*

She goes back to the cushions, rearranges them to her satisfaction. **Paterson** *enters purposefully, carrying a leather satchel.*

Mrs Paterson   Will . . .

He crosses to her, picks her up, whirls her round, kisses her.

Mrs Paterson   So, it went well?

Paterson   No. It went badly.

Mrs Paterson   So why then are you so cheerful?

Paterson   Aha, that is for you to guess. (*Looks at the day bed.*) What in the name of God is that?

Mrs Paterson   It's a reposing bed.

Paterson   A what?!

Mrs Paterson   A reposing bed. For a rest during the day. Look. It has straps here. So you can adjust it. It's all the rage.

Paterson   Hmmm . . . To my mind, a bed is for sleeping in at night. Among other purposes.

Mrs Paterson   But I bought it for you.

Paterson   I don't want it. (*Realises he's being too harsh.*) Sorry. I mean, it looks very nice. By all means let's keep it. (*He takes out a manuscript from his satchel.*) But at this moment I have reading to do.

Mrs Paterson   Will you not rest after the journey?

Paterson   No. I cannot.

She takes the manuscript, looks at it. He tries to take it away from her. She dodges him, walks away and reads it out.

Mrs Paterson (*reads*)   A new Voyage and Description of the Isthmus of America, giving an account of the Author's abode there . . .

Paterson   Give it to me. Please.

Mrs Paterson (*Dodges away from him and reads.*) . . . the form and make of the country, the Coasts, Hills, Rivers, Beasts, Birds, and Fish . . .

Paterson   I will thank you to –

Mrs Paterson (*reads*)   The Indian Inhabitants. Their Features, their Customs, their Language. With remarkable Occurrences in the South Sea and Elsewhere. By . . . Lionel Wafer.

He tries to take it away from her. They are now in a sort of embrace. She teases him, holding the manuscript out of reach.

Mrs Paterson   And who is this Lionel Wafer? It's a damned strange name for a man.

Paterson   He is a surgeon. A sailor. A traveller in Central America. This is his journal. Not yet published. I will finish reading it tonight.

Mrs Paterson   Must it be tonight?

Paterson   Yes.

Mrs Paterson   Judging by your mood, you raised all the money.

Paterson   I did not raise any money. The King has blocked us at every turn. The money will have to be raised in Scotland. In its entirety.

Mrs Paterson   Is that possible?

Paterson   Aye. If I can but light a flame that will burn in the heart of every Scot from the Borders to the Orkneys.

Mrs Paterson   And can you?

Paterson   I believe I can. With God's help. And perhaps a little help from Mr Wafer.

She looks at him, she looks at the manuscript, she looks back at him. It dawns on her.

Mrs Paterson (*with growing excitement*)   Will . . . ? . . . Is this

where you are to found your colony? . . . It is, isn't it? This is
where you plan to found your colony.

Paterson   Give me back the manuscript!

Mrs Paterson   Is it?!

Paterson   Yes. (*Pause.*) On all of God's earth, I cannot imagine
a more propitious place. The manuscript. Please. I cannot sleep till
I've read it to the end.

She hands it back to him.

Mrs Paterson   Then you must read it to the end. Goodnight,
Will.

*She kisses him and withdraws. She gets to the door, turns, waits.
He is already staring at the manuscript. He looks up.*

Paterson   Oh. Sorry. Goodnight.

Mrs Paterson   Goodnight.

She leaves.

Underscoring.

Paterson *lays out the manuscript on a desk or table. He picks up
a few pages, paces, reads. He crosses to the big globe, spins it
gently. He puts a finger on it and it stops turning.*

Scene Ten – the Offices of the Company of Scotland

Paterson *remains where he was as the scene transforms into a
meeting room in Edinburgh. Three of the* **Nameless** *are getting
dressed up while a long wooden table with quills and pens is set
up, with a row of seven chairs behind it. The Coat of Arms of the
Company of Scotland flies in.*

Underscoring continues.

First Nameless   Who are we now?

Second Nameless   I think we're on the board of directors.

First Nameless   Is that right?

Third Nameless   Aye. We're directors of the Company of
Scotland. We get to decide everything.

First Nameless   But I don't know anything.

Third Nameless   That doesn't matter.

First Nameless   Do we get paid?

Third Nameless   Oh aye.

They are finally dressed as **Directors** *and are joined by* **Balfour,**
Blackwood, Erskine *and the* **Rev. Francis Borland,** *a Church
of Scotland Minister. To one side a* **Servant** *hovers discreetly. The*
Directors *solemnly take their seats.* **Paterson** *makes his pitch.*

Paterson   Gentlemen. I can reveal where our colony is to be
founded.

There is a murmur of anticipation.

Paterson   I propose that we send a fleet to Central America. A
Scottish expedition to occupy the Gulf of Darien. (*Pointing at
globe.*) Here. The narrowest part of the isthmus of Panama that
links North and South America. On one side, the Atlantic. On the
other, the Pacific. Two great oceans separated by one tiny neck
of land. Across this tiny neck of land we build a trading road.
Linking the two oceans. At a stroke, the whole shape of world
trade is transformed. The journey to Asia is halved. The time and
expense of navigation to China – halved. To Japan – halved. To
the Spice Islands – halved. The sale of European goods – doubled.
And for every journey across that isthmus the merchants of the
world will pay us a levy . . . Scotland will control the flow of
commodities from east to west. And from west to east. We will be
the proprietors of this land called Darien. We shall give laws unto
both oceans. We shall be the arbitrators of the commercial world.

Lose music. A silence descends.

Erskine   Mr Paterson. This is a vast undertaking.

Paterson   It is, Mr Erskine, it is.

Erskine   The Spaniard will not like it. The Dutch will not like it. The English will not like it.

Paterson   That is possible.

Erskine   We will need to build a mighty fleet. Well armed.

Paterson   Aye.

Balfour   It's a bold plan. A bonnie plan. I like it, Mr Paterson, I like it.

Erskine   It is an expensive plan. Impossibly expensive. We have scarce any funds.

Paterson   We will have. I promise you. We will have.

Erskine   How?

Borland   The Good Lord will provide.

Blackwood   Tell us more about the Gulf of . . . what's it called again?

Erskine (*irritated*)   Darien.

Blackwood   Yes. Darien. (*To neighbour.*) It's called Darien.

Erskine   Have you ever been there, Mr Paterson?

Paterson   As you know, Mr Erskine, I've voyaged extensively in the Americas.

Erskine   But not set foot in Darien itself.

Paterson   No.

Erskine   No, I thought not.

Paterson   But I've spoken to those who have. And I have documents. (*Handing them over.*) Letters. Affidavits. Reports from travellers. (*Lowers his voice to emphasise importance of confidentiality.*) Among them, this manuscript. Lent to me by the author in person. It must be read by nobody but yourselves. (*Hands over a manuscript.*)

The **Directors** *glance at the manuscript.* **Blackwood**
appropriates it.

Erskine   Lionel . . . Wafer?

Paterson   Yes.

Erskine   It is somehow not a name that inspires confidence.

Blackwood   It says here (*Reads.*) 'The country I am going to
describe is the narrowest part of the Isth . . . the Isth . . . the
Isth-mus of America.' It's a bugger of a word that. Isth-mus.

Borland   Who is Lionel Wafer?

Paterson   A most respectable and reliable gentleman, who has
visited Darien and knows it well. Would you like to meet him?

Blackwood   Is he here?

Paterson   Indeed. (*Nods to* **Servant**.)

The **Servant** *leaves.*

Blackwood (*to neighbour*)   He is here.

Erskine   You're full of tricks, Mr Paterson.

Servant (*enters*)   Mr Lionel Wafer.

Wafer *enters.* **Paterson** *shakes him by the hand.* **Erskine** *takes
the manuscript and looks at it.*

Paterson   It is good of you to attend here today.

Wafer   Well, you said that if I came to Edinburgh you'd –

Paterson (*interrupting*)   Yes, yes. Now these gentlemen would
like to know more about the land you call Darien.

Wafer   Gentlemen. I am at your service.

Balfour   Tell us everything. Everything. The landscape, the
features of the place. Is it mountainous? Is it flat? Is it wooded?

Wafer   There are low mountains. Some wooded. Where the
River Darien meets the sea there's a fine bay with deep water.

Paterson   It affords a good anchorage?

Wafer   It's a first class anchorage.

Erskine (*looking at manuscript*)   Now wait. Now just wait. (*Reads.*) 'The shore of the isth-

Blackwood   Isthmus. It's pronounced isth-mus.

Erskine (*irritated*)   Yes, thank you Mr Blackwood. 'The shore of the isthmus is partially drowned, swampy, mangrove land, where there is no going ashore but up to the middle in mud.'

Wafer   Some of the coast is like that.

Paterson   But much of it is not?

Wafer   Much of it is not.

Blackwood (*nods, turns to others*)   Much of it is not.

Borland   The land. Is it fruitful?

Wafer   Yes. The natives grow plantains in great abundance. There also grows a fruit called a banana.

Blackwood   A what?

Wafer   A banana.

All Directors (*in wonderment, to audience*)   A ba-na-na.

Borland   Do the natives consume strong liquor?

Wafer   They make a drink of fermented maize. They drink large quantities of it and are very fond of it. It makes them belch very much. And in their drink the men are very quarrelsome.

Blackwood   Tis the right place for a Scottish colony.

Balfour   The women. Tell us about the womenfolk, Mr Wafer.

Borland   Why? Why would you wish to know about the womenfolk?

Paterson (*to* **Wafer**)   I gather they wear no clothes?

Borland   What?

Wafer   Ordinarily, they wear no clothes.

Balfour   None at all?

Wafer   They have but a small piece of cloth . . . in front of their . . . in front. And tied behind with a thread.

There is a stirring of embarrassment and ill-concealed interest.

Blackwood   Is it a strong thread? (*To a neighbour.*) It'd have to be a strong thread.

Borland   There must be ministers on this expedition. To save our people from licentiousness.

Erskine   There may not be an expedition. It is most unlikely that money can be raised for such a venture. And why have others not built a trading road across the isthmus?

Blackwood (*to himself*)   Isth-mus. Isth-muss . . . Maybe I've got it wrong. Isthm-us . . .

Erskine   Will you be quiet, sir!

Borland   The relation between the sexes? Do they marry, or do they just . . . breed like dogs?

Blackwood *goes back to looking at the manuscript.*

Wafer   They marry. But the women are little better than slaves to their husbands. Though you would never know it, because they do their work so readily and cheerfully. They observe their husbands with a profound respect and duty upon all occasions.

Balfour   So their culture is quite advanced?

Erskine   I doubt that these travellers' tales are an adequate basis upon which to consider founding a colony. And if it is so wonderful why has it not been occupied by the Spaniard?

First Nameless (*as Councillor*)   Aye, why has it not been occupied by the Spaniard?

Second Nameless (*as Councillor*)   It's a very good question.

Blackwood (*looking up from manuscript*)   You know what's bothering me? What's bothering me is this: why has it not been occupied by the Spaniard?

All turn to give him a withering look.

Erskine   Will the Spanish take kindly to a rival colony set up in their midst?

Borland   We will drive them out. Those idolatrous Papish hordes shall be put to the sword.

Paterson   The Spanish are not in Darien itself. And if they do come at us, we will be well armed. We'll be prepared. Men will fight and die to defend our colony, because it is our future.

Erskine   Hmmmm . . . I cannot decide if your confidence be bluff, or truth, or simply a means of deceiving yourself.

Paterson *is for a moment on the back heel.* **Balfour** *takes the manuscript.*

Paterson   Mr Wafer has not yet spoken of the gold, have you, Mr Wafer?

Erskine   Gold?

Paterson   Gold.

All Directors (*turning like automatons to the audience*)   Gold!

Borland   There is gold in Darien?

Wafer   Yes. Mines of gold. And also in the rivers.

Balfour (*excited*)   Yes. Look. It says here, it says here . . . where is it? Yes . . . here. (*Reads.*) 'We passed by a river where men were gathering gold.'

Erskine   Gold . . .

All Directors (*to audience*)   Gold!

Balfour   So there is gold to be panned from the rivers? How wonderful, how marvellous. Gold in the rivers!

Paterson *has wandered over to the manuscript sheets, he picks one out, slides it over to* **Blackwood**, *his finger on a paragraph.*

Wafer   Yes. In fact, one of the rivers in the South is called the Gold River.

Blackwood (*reading the part indicated*)   'Gold dust is washed down the rivers and gathered by the natives in great quantity.' You have witnessed this?

Wafer   Yes. The men use gold to make ornamentations for themselves.

Borland   So the men wear clothing?

Wafer   No.

Borland   How then do they wear ornamentations of gold?

Blackwood   In their hair, I expect. Wee gold clips in their hair, eh, am I right? Like lassies.

Wafer   No. The men fashion a vessel of gold, like the extinguisher of a candle, which they wear upon the penis, close to the pubes. They keep it there with a string going about their waists.

Erskine   Ye Gods.

Wafer   They leave the scrotum exposed, having no sense of shame with reference to that.

Blackwood   Must be awful in the winter. Do they have a winter?

Wafer   They have a rainy season.

Blackwood   Well, you wouldnae want to go out in the rain dressed like that, would you?

Borland   We must take the gospel to these poor wretches.

Paterson   I believe Mr Wafer has brought back with him an example . . .

Wafer   Yes. Yes, indeed.

He takes out a cloth, carefully unwraps it. Inside it is a solid gold penis gourd. He holds it up. It is surprisingly large.

Erskine   Oh, my heavens.

Balfour   It is . . . it is . . . it is . . .

Blackwood   Big.

Balfour   Gold.

Wafer   Yes. Solid gold.

It is passed around.

Erskine   Gentlemen. Please! Let us not get carried away. However alluring the prospects of a colony in Darien, we have no funds. (*Takes the penis gourd, hands it to* **Wafer***, who wraps it up again.*) Mr Paterson, you have been to London, Hamburg, Amsterdam . . . And have raised how much for the Company?

Paterson   Next to nothing. No matter. We will raise the money in Scotland.

Erskine (*in disbelief*)   All of it?

Paterson   Aye. It can be done.

Erskine   Can it?

Paterson   It can be done if it is done at speed, so people have no time to discover doubt. Each man must fear that if he doesn't subscribe, he will lose forever the chance of great riches.

Balfour   That's how it worked with the Bank of England, is it not, Mr Paterson?

Paterson   Just so. In founding the Bank of England we allocated only six weeks from the opening of the books, and our funding was finished in nine days. You see, if a thing go not on with the first heat, the raising of a fund seldom succeeds.

Erskine   And why should that be?

Paterson   Because, Mr Erskine, the multitude are commonly led more by example than by reason.

Erskine And you believe this is possible even though you failed to raise funds abroad?

Paterson I didn't fail. The money was there. The English cheated Scotland of its due.

As **Paterson** *speaks, the* **Nameless of the Earth** *drift in, and his speech effectively becomes a speech to the audience / the people of Scotland. At some point, Saltires are brought in, perhaps paraded down through the audience and up on to the stage.*

Paterson The English imagine we can do nothing without their help. But this is not true. Not if we believe in Scotland. Not if we believe in ourselves. Why should other countries have their colonies and not Scotland? Why should Scotland be left out? Are we more stupid than they? Less enterprising? Less ingenious? Less hard-working? I think not. It can be done. It can be done. (*Underscoring creeps in.*) This will be a national endeavour. A source of pride for every Scot. A promise of wealth for every subscriber. A promise of greatness for Scotland. Overnight this poor small nation will join the ranks of the rich and mighty. If we but act wisely and boldly, trade will increase trade, and money will beget money, and the trading world shall need no more to want work for their hands, but will rather want hands for their work. (*Pauses, then delivers his inspirational clincher.*) In Darien, gentlemen, I offer you the door of the seas and the keys of the universe.

Balfour, **Blackwood** *and* **Borland** *sing.* **Paterson** *goes over to* **Wafer** *and pays him off.* **Wafer** *leaves.*

Song No. 6   Let Scotland's Name

> *Let Scotland's name*
> *Across the world resound*
> *To foreign lands*
> *Where riches abound*
> *One pound today*
> *Tomorrow will be ten*
> *And Scotland will*
> *Be mighty once again.*

Erskine *takes* **Paterson** *to one side while* **Balfour**, **Blackwood**
and **Borland** *and the other* **Directors** *leave.*

Erskine   I observe that Darien has become a wonderfully
patriotic undertaking.

Paterson   I don't take your meaning, Mr Erskine.

Erskine   You're no nationalist, Mr Paterson. You're more at
home in the drawing rooms of London, or Amsterdam or Berlin
than you are in the coffee houses of Edinburgh. But to persuade
the people to invest, you're waving the flag of St Andrew at them.
How else are you going to raise these vast sums of money in a
small poor country? I won't say I'm not impressed. You're a very
persuasive man.

Paterson   It is in the interests of the people of Scotland.

Erskine   That's why you're doing it, is it? For the people of
Scotland?

Paterson   For myself and for the people of Scotland. Our
interests are the same.

Erskine   Are they?

Paterson   History will prove me right.

Erskine   Oh I'm not too interested in history. I'm interested in
getting rich. Much the same as you are. But I know the risks. Do
you think the people of Scotland know the risks?

Paterson   Yes.

Erskine   You've made it clear to them have you?

Paterson   I can't offer certainty. Some things are in God's hands.

Erskine   Oh yes. A great deal will be in God's hands. But no
doubt you'll have had a word with him. A clever Scot aye gets the
kirk on his side. (*Leaves.*)

Scene Eleven – a Protestant Church

Borland *steps up into the pulpit.*

Borland   Galatians Chapter Six Verse Seven: 'Be not deceived. God is not mocked. For whatever a man sows, that shall he also reap.' (*Fixes the congregation.*) I look around me and I see sin. I see sin and I see sinners. Aye, in this very congregation. I know you. The Lord knows you. He knows about your profaneness and your immorality, oh aye, he kens every detail. He sees your excessive drinking and your tippling and your fighting and your cursing. He hears you when you take the Lord's name in vain. He makes note of each abomination, and carefully enters the perpetrator's name in the ledger of eternal damnation. Whatever a man sows, that shall he also reap . . . . . But what if a man sows goodness, as the farmer sows his crops? So that there be not famine in the land? This nation has seen famine, like unto the great famine that was in the days of Abraham. When Isaac dwelt in the land of Gerar, and sowed in that land. But Isaac was blessed with a plentiful harvest. He received an hundredfold of what he had sown. And I believe that soon, the people of Scotland will receive an hundredfold for what they will sow. Aye, they will take their little wealth and see it grow, and the people of Scotland will wax great, as the nation waxes great. And the Lord will bless this nation and its great enterprise abroad and will bless all those who sow, for they shall reap. They shall reap an hundredfold.

Scene Twelve – the House of Mrs Purdie, High Street, Edinburgh

Mackenzie *enters as a tall stool and desk are set up on which is placed a large leather bound entry book.* **Mackenzie** *sits at it and keeps a record.* **Paterson** *enters and stands near him.*

Mackenzie   Edinburgh, the twentie sixth day of February, 1696. At the House of Mrs Purdie, in the North side of the High Street, over and against the Cross. (*Reads.*) Pursuant to an Act of Parliament, entitled Act for a Company Trading to Africa and the

Indies, we, the under subscribers, do each of us become obleidged for the payment of the respective sums subscribed by us subject to the rules and constitutions of the said Company.

Ordinary Merchants *enter, stand around and seem reluctant to sign up.* **Mackenzie** *holds out the quill to them. No takers. He looks questioningly at* **Paterson**.

Mackenzie   Mr Paterson, you said –

Paterson   Shush.

Mackenzie   But we've been here nigh on an hour and nobody has yet –

Paterson   Patience, Mackenzie, patience.

Silence for a few seconds. Gasps from the crowd as the **Duchess of Hamilton** *enters.*

First Subscriber (*approaches the ledger and signs*)   Anne, Duchess of Hamilton and Chasterault. One thousand pounds.

Second Subscriber   Margarett, Countess of Rothesse. Two thousand pounds. (*Signs.*)

Third Subscriber   Lady Hope of Houpetoun. Three thousand pounds. (*Signs.*)

There is a growing sense of competition amongst the **Subscribers**.

First Subscriber (*coming back to the ledger*)   Anne, Duchess of Hamilton and Chasterault. For her son Murdoch, one thousand pounds.

Second Subscriber (*coming back to the ledger*)   Margarett, Countess of Rothesse. For her son Thomas, Earle of Haddington. Two thousand pounds. (*Signs.*)

Third Subscriber (*coming back to the ledger*)   Lady Hope of Hopetoun. For her nephew Hopetoun. Three thousand pounds. (*Signs.*)

Fourth Subscriber   David Lord Cardross. Five hundred pounds. (*Signs.*)

Fifth Subscriber   John Lord Glenorchy. Two thousand pounds. (*Signs.*)

Sixth Subscriber   James Byres, Merchant in Edinburgh. Two hundred pounds. (*Signs.*)

Paterson (*calmly*)   You see, my dear Mackenzie. The aristocracy still have their uses. Where the aristocracy go, others follow. God knows why, but they do. (*Smiles, bows as Duchess of Hamilton leaves.*) Your Grace.

Seventh Subscriber   Thomas Campbell, butcher in Edinburgh. Two hundred pounds.

Paterson   You see?

Paterson *continues to watch. Music. In a choreographed sequence the subscribers announce their investment to* **Mackenzie**.

One   Colin Campbell of Arkinlass. Five hundred pounds.

Two   John Swinton of that Ilk. One thousand pounds.

Three   Robert Douglas, Soap-Boiler in Leith. One hundred pounds.

Four   Andrew Broune, watchmaker in Edinburgh. Two hundred pounds.

Five   William Callender, merchant in Falkirk. Three hundred pounds.

Six   The Incorporation of Shoemakers of Edinburgh. One hundred pounds.

Seven   Frederick Corser, merchant in Dundee. Five hundred pounds.

Eight   George Cruickshank junior, merchant in Aberdeen. Fifty pounds.

Nine   James Dunbar, Baillie of Inverness. One hundred and eighty pounds.

Ten   George Stirling, Doctor of Medicine. Two hundred pounds. (*Signs.*)

Eleven   Sir Archibald Stevenson, Doctor of Medicine. Six hundred pounds. (*Signs. Nods contemptuously at Seventh Subscriber.*)

Twelve   Mr James Gregory, Professor of the Mathematicks in the College of Edinburgh. Eight hundred pounds.

Thirteen   In the name of the Good Town of Edinburgh, the Lord Provost of Edinburgh. Three thousand pounds. (*Signs.*)

Fourteen (*competitively*)   Lord Provost John Anderson, in the name of the City of Glasgow. Three thousand pounds. (*Signs.*)

Song No. 7   Let Scotland's Name (Reprise)

Subscribers   *Let Scotland's name*
Across the world resound
To foreign lands
Where riches abound
One pound today
Tomorrow will be ten
And Scotland will
Be mighty once again.

First Nameless As Subscriber   Was Scotland ever mighty?

Second Nameless As Subscriber   I don't think so.

First Nameless As Subscriber   No, I thought not.

The **Subscribers** *leave.* **Balfour**, **Blackwood** *and* **Borland** *enter, joining* **Paterson** *and* **Mackenzie**. *All others leave. The mood is one of awe rather than triumphalism.*

Paterson   How much, Mr Mackenzie?

Mackenzie   Four hundred thousand pounds.

Blackwood   Four hundred thousand pounds?

Mackenzie   Yes. Four hundred thousand pounds.

Blackwood   Four. Hundred. Thousand?

Paterson   Aye.

Balfour   It is more than half the nation's wealth.

Paterson   Aye.

Mackenzie   It is near enough five times the annual revenue of government.

Paterson   Aye.

Borland   The Lord has smiled upon us. There will be prayers of thanksgiving in every kirk across the land.

Balfour   Four hundred thousand. That sits nicely on the tongue, does it not? Four hundred thousand.

Blackwood   It's a hundred thousand more than three hundred thousand.

All stare at him in their can-he-really-be-this-stupid look.

Blackwood   What we'd hoped to get in London. It's a hundred thousand more than that. We've done better.

Balfour   Oh, right. Well, Scotland aye does better, when we put our minds to it.

Blackwood   Four . . . hundred . . . thousand . . .

Paterson   Yes. (*Silence.*) Gentlemen we are now more powerful than the state.

They contemplate this in silence for a moment.

Paterson   And now, gentleman, it is time for action. There is much work ahead.

Murmuring agreement, they leave.

Paterson   Oh, Mackenzie. A word with you.

He waits for the others to go.

Paterson   A small practical matter . . . at the moment sterling is not a strong currency . . .

Mackenzie   Indeed it is not . . .

Paterson   This weakness of sterling is but a temporary phenomenon, though? Would you not say?

Mackenzie   It can scarcely fall much further.

Paterson   Precisely my view. So. We shall transfer a portion of the Company's assets into Sterling. And when Sterling recovers, we shall transfer it back and make a profit for the company.

Mackenzie   Is that wise, Mr Paterson? No one can absolutely guarantee that the English pound will recover. It might just keep going down and down. There are no guarantees when it comes to currency fluctuations, Mr Paterson.

Paterson   A man can be too careful, you know.

Mackenzie   But to raise all this money, Mr Paterson, with such success, and then to gamble with it. Is that not . . . a step too far?

Paterson   No, no. Now listen, have you ever met James Smyth?

Mackenzie   The London merchant?

Paterson   Yes. A very reliable man.

Mackenzie   A very young man.

Paterson   Young and reliable. And with a shrewd sense of business. I shall charge him with conveying the money to London.

Mackenzie   Have the other directors of the company been consulted?

Paterson   What? Oh, they will have no objection. And we'll limit it to say . . . what shall we say? Twenty-five thousand pounds?

Mackenzie   That is a substantial proportion of our reserves.

Paterson   Yes, and in a few months, when Sterling recovers, then our reserves will be greater than ever before.

Mackenzie   If you say so, Mr Paterson.

Paterson   I do, I do!

From off comes the growing sound of drunken singing. **Paterson**
turns in the direction of the singing. **Mackenzie** *shakes his head
and leaves the other way.*

Scene Thirteen – a street in Edinburgh

Song No. 8   Come Rouse Up Your Hearts

Drunks (*off*)   *Come rouse up your hearts*
                        Come rouse up anon
                        And think of the wisdom of old Solomon
                        And heartily join with our own Paterson
                        To bring home shiploads of treasure.

Four Drunks, *all of them obviously poor, weave slowly and
drunkenly across the stage.*

Drunks   *Come rouse up your hearts*
                        Come rouse up anon
                        And think of the wisdom of old Solomon
                        And heartily join with our own Paterson
                        To bring home shiploads of treasure.

Paterson *looks in the direction of the departing drunks.*
Mrs Paterson *enters.*

Mrs Paterson   You're a national hero, Mr Paterson.

Paterson   So it would seem.

Mrs Paterson   Does it make you feel proud?

Paterson   In a way.

Mrs Paterson   Does it make you feel afraid?

Paterson   A little.

Mrs Paterson   You've set the whole country aflame.

Paterson   I think I have. (*Turns to look at her.*) You do believe in
this venture, don't you?

Mrs Paterson   I believe in you.

Paterson   I hear some . . . reservation.

Mrs Paterson   It will be dangerous.

Paterson   Of course.

Mrs Paterson   You'll make enemies.

Paterson   Courage will be needed. It will be hard. But it can be done. It can be done. It is the pursuit of paradise on earth. All men need to believe in paradise. Some believe it's for the life hereafter. I believe it can also be here on earth. (*Pause.*) You know I will be going with the expedition, don't you?

Mrs Paterson   You've never been one to let other people take all the risks.

Paterson   I will be gone for some long time.

Mrs Paterson   Yes . . . . . as will I.

Paterson (*taken aback*)   Where are you going?

Mrs Paterson   The same place as you.

She takes him by the arm and they walk.

Mrs Paterson   And in our cabin there will be a reposing bed.

Blackout.

Paterson *and* **Mrs Paterson** *leave.*

Scene Fourteen – a workshop in Edinburgh

Underscoring as the stage erupts into purposeful and optimistic busyness. Upstage of the main action we see images of big sailing ships being constructed.

Mackenzie *enters with a shoal of* **Clerks** *following him. Papers are exchanged, signed etc., with* **Mackenzie** *frequently intervening to check something or to sign something off. Huge ledgers are carried about, opened up, filled in, closed, carried off.*

Mackenzie   A contract has been drawn up with Thomas Brown of Edinburgh for one hundred iron spades.

First Clerk   At one shilling and nine pence each.

Mackenzie   One hundred large stocklocks.

First Clerk   At eight pence each.

Mackenzie   One hundred lesser stocklocks.

First Clerk   At four pence each.

Mackenzie   Two hundred chamber doorlocks.

First Clerk   At ten pence each.

Mackenzie   One hundred felling axes.

First Clerk   At one shilling each.

Paterson *enters, sweeps across the stage, followed by* **Balfour** *carrying rolls of plans and piles of documents.*

Paterson   The Endeavour?

Balfour   One hundred and thirty tons. Ten guns.

Paterson   Cost?

Balfour   One thousand eight hundred pounds.

Paterson   Build it.

Balfour   Yes, Mr Paterson!

They leave.

Third Clerk   Mr Robert Arlington to obtain four hundred fishing lines of one hundred fathom in each line.

Second Clerk   William Gray to purchase sufficient amounts of smiths' hammers, anvils, forehammers and bellows.

First Clerk   A letter to be written to Glasgow for patterns of the following particulars: Wooden bowls.

Mackenzie   With their lowest prices.

First Clerk   Horn spoons.

Mackenzie   With their lowest prices.

First Clerk   Smoothing irons.

Mackenzie   With their lowest prices.

First Clerk   White-iron candlesticks.

Mackenzie   With their lowest prices.

Paterson, Balfour *and* **Blackwood** *cross the stage.*

Paterson   The Dolphin?

Blackwood   Two hundred tons. Twenty guns . . . No, no, wait, eighteen guns. Sorry.

Paterson   Cost?

Balfour   Two thousand and fifty pounds.

Paterson   Build it.

They leave.

James Smyth *enters, sharply dressed. He is followed by his* **Servant**. *He crosses to* **Mackenzie** *who is engrossed in bookkeeping.*

Smyth   Ah, Mackenzie, here you are. Had the devil of a job finding you. You are Mackenzie, are you not?

Mackenzie   Mr Mackenzie, aye. We have met.

Smyth   Yes. And what an honour it was. And is. And is.

Mackenzie   You will have come about the money that is to be transferred into sterling?

Smyth   How right you are.

Mackenzie   Wait here.

Mackenzie *produces several large keys, goes over to a black cast iron chest and laboriously opens it, making sure that* **Smyth**'s *prying eyes cannot see inside. He takes out leather pouches of banknotes, closes and carefully locks the chest.*

Mackenzie   You have an armed escort for the journey to London?

Smyth   Armed to the teeth. No footpad shall have the Company's money, that you can be sure of.

Mackenzie   I'm delighted to hear it. Your instructions are to deposit the money in a sterling account at the Bank of England within twenty-four hours of your arriving in London. If you'll but sign here. And here. And here. And here. And here. And there.

Smyth (*sarcastically*)   Can't be too careful, eh?

Mackenzie   No, you can't.

Smyth (*signs, takes the money*)   Done.

Mackenzie   God speed, Mr Smyth. Goodbye, sir.

Smyth   Goodbye.

Smyth *tosses the leather bags to his* **Servant** *and swaggers off. The* **Servant** *follows, watched balefully by* **Mackenzie**.

First Clerk   Virginia tobacco pipes, two thousand.

Second Clerk   Plaiding hose, four hundred pair.

First Clerk   Fish hooks general purpose, five thousand.

Third Clerk   Cod hooks, three thousand.

Second Clerk   Haddock hooks, three thousand.

Third Clerk   Two hundred and fifty bob wigs.

First Clerk   Six hundred periwigs.

Second Clerk   Thirty dozen pairs of fine loom stockings.

Third Clerk   Forty dozen pairs of kid gloves.

First Clerk   Sixty dozen pairs of woollen gloves.

Second Clerk   One thousand three hundred and eighty Bibles.

Mackenzie   With their lowest prices.

They all write carefully in ledgers.

Song No. 9   Make A List

The Nameless   *When there's nothing must be missed*
Make a list
Make a list
Get the world around you under your control.
To make sure that you exist
Make a list
Make a list
A list will help to satisfy your soul
Your hungry Presbyterian soul.

It's the poetry of profit
That will earn you your reward,
Diligence and detail will
Endear you to the Lord
When the Day of Judgment beckons
The punishment is swift
And your best hope of salvation
Is frugality and thrift.

It's the poetry of order
The romance of neat accounts
The road to heaven's measured out
In very small amounts.
If your ledger's neat and tidy
You may conquer all your fears
While the jingling of your coin
Becomes the music of the spheres.

Paterson, **Balfour** *and* **Blackwood** *enter.*

Paterson   The Unicorn?

Balfour   Three hundred and twenty tons. Forty guns.

Paterson   Cost?

Blackwood   Eight thousand six hundred pounds.

Paterson   Let it be built.

They leave.

Mackenzie   Sixty horsemen's swords at seven shillings per piece and forty mounted guns at twenty shillings per piece.

First Clerk   Ordered.

Mackenzie   Dr Munro to proceed to Aberdeen to inform this committee as to the cheapest prices of barrelled codfish.

Second Clerk   He has been told.

The scene gets busier and busier. Maybe instead of remaining on stage the **Clerks** *run in and out.*

First Clerk   John Drummond at his discretion to buy two hundred cows for the Company's use.

Second Clerk   Robert Watson to provide fifteen tons of the best cured pork he can find.

Third Clerk   Daniel Lodge to provide three hundred oxen the best he can find to be slaughtered at Leith.

Paterson, **Balfour** *and* **Blackwood** *enter.*

Paterson   The St Andrew will cost?

Balfour   Eleven thousand five hundred pounds. It is three hundred and fifty tons and will carry forty-eight guns.

Paterson   Good. And the Caledonia?

Balfour   She will cost fifteen thousand pounds.

Blackwood   Six hundred tons and fifty-six guns.

Paterson   Let them be built!

They leave.

Second Clerk   Thomas Campbell to provide sixty tuns of good quality cured beef, seven and a half tuns of suet, ten tuns of cheese and ten tuns of butter.

First Clerk George Clark to provide twelve tuns of Spanish salt, ten barrels of mustard seed, twenty barrels of the best vinegar.

Second Clerk And forty barrels of brandy.

Third Clerk And fifty barrels of claret.

First Clerk Strong claret!

Third Clerk Strong claret.

The Nameless *When there's nothing must be missed*
Make a list
Make a list
Get the world around you under your control.
To make sure that you exist
Make a list
Make a list
A list will help to satisfy your soul
Your hungry Presbyterian soul.

It's the poetry of order
The romance of neat accounts
Marking out the course of life
In very small amounts.
If you keep the wages modest
You may conquer half the world
And the neatly folded flag
Will be triumphantly unfurled . . .

Blackout.

Scene Fifteen – the new offices of the Company of Scotland

Paterson *enters with* **Mackenzie** *in tow.*

Paterson How long will it take to load supplies on to the ships?

Mackenzie Mr Paterson. There is a matter which –

Paterson How long?

Mackenzie   I have estimated three weeks, but –

Paterson   Three weeks is too long.

Mackenzie   I have this morning received information concerning –

Paterson   Can it be done in two weeks?

Mackenzie   I am not sure. But there is another matter –

Paterson   I will personally check the condition of the food supplies before the fleet sails.

Mackenzie   Mr Paterson, you may not be allowed to do that!

Paterson   Not allowed? Not allowed? Mackenzie, what are you talking about? I want to check supplies once they are loaded. I don't want to find it's all been so badly stored that half of it's rotten before we even get there. And furthermore –

Mackenzie (*explodes*)   Mr Paterson! The money you sent to London has gone!

Paterson   What?

Mackenzie   The money you sent with Mr Smyth. To be held in sterling. It was never invested. Mr Smyth is thought to be somewhere on the Continent. With twenty-five thousand pounds of the Company's money. Which we are unlikely ever to see again.

Paterson (*dazed*)   He did not convert it into Sterling?

Mackenzie (*shouts*)   Mr Paterson. It has been embezzled. Stolen. Gone.

Paterson   Am I to understand that – ?

Mackenzie   Your reliable Mr Smyth is a common thief.

Paterson   Do the directors know?

Mackenzie   Yes, they know.

Paterson   I will speak with them. (*Leaves followed by* **Mackenzie**.)

Mackenzie (*leaving*)   And they will speak with you.

Scene Sixteen – a coffee house in Edinburgh

We discover the **Directors** *including* **Borland**, **Erskine**, **Blackwood** *and* **Balfour** *in the midst of a planning meeting.*

Erskine (*with document*)   So, we are agreed? These seven men will constitute the council which will rule the Colony?

Directors   Agreed.

Erskine   Each Councillor to be given shares in the company to the sum of one thousand two hundred pounds sterling. Agreed?

Directors   Yes, agreed.

Erskine   Each colonist will be given fifty acres of fertile land for cultivation. Gentlemen to be given a hundred acres. Councillors to be given a hundred and fifty acres. Agreed?

Directors   Aye. Yes.

Paterson (*entering*)   Gentlemen, what is this about the stores? It has always been clear that the loading of the stores will be supervised by me. I propose –

Borland   We may not wish to know what you propose, Mr Paterson.

Blackwood   I find this very difficult to admit, Mr Paterson, but our faith in you . . . is . . . well, it is . . . damaged.

Balfour   And you know how much I admire you, but to entrust such a sum . . .

Borland   Without consulting us.

Blackwood   Without consulting us.

Erskine   We will keep this information from the public. A new call on funds will have to be made. We shall say it is because of the great success of the previous call.

Paterson   I wish to discuss the provisions. And how they are stored. As a councillor, I have the right to –

Balfour   You are not a Councillor.

Paterson (*incredulous*)   I am not a Councillor?

Balfour   I am sorry. We cannot have the colony ruled by men who are careless with the Company's money.

Paterson   Careless? I was not careless, Mr Balfour. I was working to enrich the Company.

Borland   By taking risks. No fear of risk. That is your weakness, Mr Paterson.

Paterson   Do not lecture me, Mr Borland. Your abilities are too modest to permit you to lecture William Paterson. And who is to be councillor in my stead?

Erskine   I am.

Paterson   You? You? (*To others.*) You have chosen Erskine as a Councillor?

Balfour   Aye, we have.

Paterson (*to* **Erskine**)   You who've shown so little belief in this undertaking?

Erskine   I have an investment to protect. From incompetent men.

Balfour   We all have investments to protect.

Blackwood   Aye. That's why we have put Mr Erskine in charge of the supplies. Your proposed inspection will not be necessary.

Paterson *grabs the list, looks at the names.*

Paterson   These are our councillors? These are their names?

Erskine   Yes.

Paterson *laughs.*

Paterson (*in mocking disbelief*)   Major James Cunningham? He is to be a Councillor of the Colony?

Blackwood   He's a most reliable and upright gentleman.

Paterson   James Cunningham has never been out of Scotland!

Balfour   He is a true patriot.

Paterson   He knows nothing about ships. He knows nothing about trade. And his military experience is restricted to taking part in the massacre of Glencoe.

Borland   The man is a pillar of the kirk.

Paterson   Oh, and is that intended to be a recommendation?

Borland   Do not speak thus, Mr Paterson!

Paterson (*reads*)   John Montgomerie?! Good God. Are you mad?

Balfour   His uncle is Lord of the Treasury.

Blackwood   I like his uncle a great deal, actually. Very nice man. Has a most beautiful house near Inverness. With very fine hedges.

Paterson   Robert Jolly . . .

Balfour   Ship's captain.

Paterson   Retired ship's captain! He hasn't commanded a ship for twelve years. William Vetch. No qualifications whatsoever.

Borland   His father and I studied divinity together.

Paterson (*stares at document*)   You have made Robert Pennicuick Commodore of the Fleet?!

Erskine   I know him well.

Paterson   Oh. Then you will know he is a lover of strong drink. That he is hated by the men under his command. How many servants did he insist on taking? . . . Come on, tell me! . . .

Balfour   None at all.

Blackwood (*blurts it out*)   Five. (*Realises.*) Sorry.

Paterson   Only five. You are fortunate.

Erskine   Stop this, Mr Paterson.

Paterson   You fools.

Balfour   The Board of Directors appointed the best possible people.

Paterson   The Board of Directors appointed its friends. Behind my back. These are decisions you will long regret.

Erskine   We remain grateful to you, Mr Paterson. It's your vision that has made this noble undertaking possible. Of course we realise that you will no longer wish to sail with the expedition. But your counsels will be greatly valued here in Edinburgh and when the fleet returns –

Paterson   I do not think you know me well enough, Mr Erskine. When the fleet sails, I will be aboard it.

He leaves. The **Directors** *leave from the opposite side.*

Scene Seventeen – a piece of land overlooking the port of Leith.

Off. Crowd noises.

Song No. 10   Let Scotland's Name (Reprise)

Singers (*off*)   *Let Scotland's name*
Across the world resound
To foreign lands
Where riches abound

One pound today
Tomorrow will be ten
And Scotland will
Be mighty once again.

The melody continues as underscoring, or maybe continues to be sung as if coming from far away. **Paterson** *and* **Mrs Paterson** *enter, ready for the journey,* **Servants** *carrying luggage.*

Mrs Paterson   Listen. You hear them?

Paterson   Yes.

Mrs Paterson   They are gathering in their thousands to watch the fleet set sail. Everywhere. On Castle Hill. On Caltoun Crags. Never has Leith seen so many people.

Mackenzie (*entering*)   Mr Paterson. Mrs Paterson. You must hurry. It will take time to get through the crowds. There's more want to go than there are places. They're finding dozens of men hidden in the ships and removing them by force. There's men pleading and begging to be allowed to go, clinging to the ropes and timbers till the very last moment. Beacons are to be lit all the way up the east coast to mark the progress of the fleet. The country has known nothing like it, Mr Paterson. Nothing.

Paterson   We will be there shortly.

Mackenzie   As soon as possible please, Mr Paterson. (*Leaves.*)

Paterson   My dear?

He holds out his arm. She takes it. They leave followed by the **Servants**. *The cheering crowds get louder. Church bells. Then this dips as a* **Poor Girl** *appears and sings.*

Song No. 11   Auspicious Day

Poor Girl   *On this auspicious day*
The valiant Scots display
Their colours to the world.

Chorus   *The door of the seas*
The keys of the universe.

Poor Girl   *May Neptune favour them*
With wind and tide
And may the Lord provide
Protection from the storm.

Chorus   *The door of the seas*
The keys of the universe.

Poor Girl   *The St Andrew*
                       The Endeavour
                       And the Dolphin all set sail
                       Caledonia sets sail
                       And the Unicorn sets sail.
                       All ships and men
                       Directed by the hand of God.

Chorus   *The door of the seas*
                       The keys of the universe
                       The door of the seas
                       The keys of the universe
                       Will be ours
                       Will be Scotland's
                       Will be ours.

Poor Girl   *And so our country's darkest night is gone*
                       And Scotland stands
                       To greet a glorious dawn.

As the music soars to match the vision of the closing words, a
Spanish Soldier *enters downstage left. He watches silently for a
few seconds, then turns and leaves.*

Chorus / Poor Girl *Our country's darkest night is gone*
                        And Scotland stands
                        To greet a glorious dawn.

Blackout.

Interval.

Act Two

Scene One – on board the Caledonia

Members of the **Crew** *turn the capstain or pull on ropes.*
One **Sailor** *takes the solo part, while everyone else joins in the chorus.*

Song No. 12   Sea Shanty

Sailor   *A sailor lad from Aberdeen*
          Was handsome tall and strong

Crew   *Hey, hey, hey, high, ho.*

Sailor   *He met a whore from Amsterdam*
          And swived her all night long

Crew   *Now there's fire down below*

Sailor   *He swived that whore from Amsterdam*
          And never got a kiss

Crew   *Hey, hey, hey, high, ho.*

Sailor   *But ever since he swived her*
          He's afraid to take a piss

Crew   *'Cause there's fire down below.*
          Fire down below me lads, Fire down below.

Sailor   *A gentleman from London*
          Was so scraggy and so thin

Crew   *Hey, hey, hey, high, ho.*

Sailor   *She didn't even notice*
          When he tried to slip it in

The **Rev. Borland** *appears upstage of them, Bible in clasped hands, and in blissful ignorance smilingly observes. They don't notice his presence. He sways to the music.*

Crew	*But there's fire down below.* *Fire down below, me lads,* *Fire down below.*
Sailor	*A farming man from Inverness* *Preferred his whoories cheap*
Crew	*Hey, hey, hey, high, ho.*
Sailor	*If they asked for too much money* *He'd go off and find a sheep.*
Borland	*frowns, a bit worried, but doesn't quite get it.*
Crew	*And there's fire down below.*
Sailor	*A Church of Scotland Minister* *Was riding with the hunt*
Crew	*Hey, hey, hey, high, ho.*
Borland	*gets it.*
Sailor	*He wasn't hunting deer* *What he was hoping for . . . was . . .*

*The **Sailor** has caught sight of **Borland** and stops singing.*
***Borland** gazes fiercely at him for a few seconds. The **Crew** realise what's going on and jump into the chorus.*

Crew	*And there's fire down below.*

***Borland** stands staring a moment longer and then turns in disgust and walks off. The **Crew** pause till he has gone, then they all tip-toe off, singing in a loud whisper.*

Sailor	*A Church of Scotland Minister* *Was riding with the hunt*
Crew	*Hey, hey, hey, high, ho.*
Sailor	*He wasn't hunting deer* *What he was hoping for was . . .* (mouths) *cunt.*

They leave.

Music.

The ship is now under full sail. **Paterson** *appears, followed by* **Erskine***.*

Paterson   No, Mr Erskine, I do not get seasick.

Erskine   But I do, Mr Paterson, I do.

Paterson   Ah, well. Worry not. (*Cheerfully.*) In my experience the first six weeks are the worst.

Erskine *runs to the side of the ship, leans over and retches.*

Paterson   That is a terrible waste of food, Mr Erskine, a terrible waste. We're short enough of rations as it is.

Erskine (*weakly*)   You're not a man of great sympathies, are you?

Paterson   The voyage does not appear to incommode my wife. If a mere woman can cope, I'm sure you can too.

Erskine   Your wife is no mere woman.

Paterson   In any case, a little seasickness is nothing. It's the flux and the fever you need to be afraid of.

Erskine *runs to the side again, retches.*

Paterson   Dear, oh dear.

Mackenzie *appears.*

Paterson   Mackenzie. How fares our Captain this fine morning?

Mackenzie   I wish we had sailed upon the Endeavour. There is much to be said for a ship's captain who is sober for at least a few hours a day.

Paterson   I agree. But not being a Councillor . . . well, I'm in no position to choose which ship we sail in.

Mackenzie   It's a shame and a scandal how you have been treated, Mr Paterson. Without you, this whole venture –

Paterson   Yes, yes. (*Sees* **Erskine** *approaching.*) Voided to your heart's content, Mr Erskine?

Erskine   Mr Paterson, since we have little choice but to spend many weeks together in cramped and difficult circumstances, might it be wiser if you chose not to mock those afflicted by seasickness?

Paterson   Oh, Mr Erskine, you would deprive me of what small pleasures are left to me?

Erskine   Now listen, sir, and listen well. I believe in this expedition.

Paterson   Oh? Why then did you not take the trouble to ensure that the food was stored properly? Only three weeks into our voyage and the men already on reduced rations? A quarter of our stores are rotted. It was foolishness. And it need not have happened. I told you how the supplies needed to be stowed, Mr Erskine, I told you! I have experience of such things. And did you listen? Did you?

Erskine   No, I did not. It was my fault. I am sorry.

Paterson (*surprised*)   Oh . . . well, it is a strong man who admits to his errors. But I am puzzled, Mr Erskine. It doesn't seem to me that your heart has ever fully been engaged in this endeavour.

Erskine   It was not, to begin with. You persuaded me. I was not convinced. And you persuaded me. After the matter of James Smyth and the missing funds, well, I could no longer see you as Councillor. But that is the sort of man you are, Paterson. You have ideas. You have vision. You have courage. And then you go too far. Always one step too far, Mr Paterson. That is why I am on board. To protect you from yourself.

Paterson   (*bows slightly*)   How kind of you.

Erskine   Let us work together, sir. For the sake of Darien. For the sake of Scotland.

He holds out his hand. **Paterson** *stares at it for a moment, then takes it.* **Pennicuick** *appears.* **Erskine** *leaves.*

Pennicuick   Paterson! Good morning!

Paterson   Captain Pennicuick. What a pleasure. We are making good progress?

Pennicuick   Well enough, sir. By my reckoning we are some twenty leagues ahead of the rest of the fleet.

Paterson   It is a tribute to your navigational skills, Captain.

Mackenzie *stifles a laugh.* **Pennicuick** *shoots him a sharp glance.*

Pennicuick   What mean you by that?

Paterson   I mean that you have difficulty reading the navigation tables.

Pennicuick   Arrant nonsense, sir.

Paterson   I have watched you. All I can say is that I am grateful for the first mate. He seems to be competent in the use of the astrolabe. So they'll never make *him* a captain, eh?

Pennicuick   It's time for my breakfast. (*Makes to leave.*)

Paterson (*quietly*)   Is that what you call it?

Borland *enters.*

Borland   Captain Pennicuick. Do not go.

Pennicuick   But I have need of my breakfast.

Borland   We all know what your breakfast consists of Captain. Half a bottle of rum.

Pennicuick   That is not true, sir. That is absolutely not true. It is normally half a bottle of brandy. (*Laughs at his own joke.*)

Borland   Your men are out of control. They sing lewd and profane songs.

Pennicuck   They are sailors, Reverend. Their lives are hard. Harder than yours has ever been. Or ever will be. They are at sea for months at a time. Of course their songs are lewd. So would yours be if you hadn't swived a woman in three months . . . Aye, well in your case, maybe the argument doesn't quite hold up. Now if you'll excuse me . . . breakfast. (*Leaves.*)

Borland   Mr Paterson. The men seem to respect you . . .

Mackenzie   They do, Mr Borland, they do.

Borland   So if our Captain will not admonish them, you must do so, Mr Paterson. These men must be chastised for their dissolute behaviour. The Lowlanders are bad enough. But the Highlanders are yet worse. They keep themselves to themselves, drinking their abominable usquebaugh and no doubt secretly muttering their hocus pocus and pledging loyalty to the Pope in Rome.

Paterson   There is something you must know, Mr Borland. I am not greatly concerned about a man's religion.

Borland   Not greatly concerned?!

Paterson   Like you, sir, I am glad we have thrown off the chains of Rome. Many died to make that possible. But I observe that those who are ardent in pursuing their own religious freedom are often equally ardent in denying it to others.

Mackenzie   Mr Paterson, take care.

Borland   Do not speak of freedom, sir. Man is too base to be permitted the burden of freedom. Such is the furious rage of man's corrupt nature that unless severe punishment be appointed and malefactors controlled, it were better that man live among brutes and wild beasts than among men.

Paterson   I have higher hopes for mankind, Mr Borland. You should know, sir, that Darien will not merely be a little Scotland. It will be a better place.

Borland   Better than Scotland?

Paterson   Aye, a better world. Where men may worship as they please, without fear of persecution.

Borland (*intimate*)   You are not . . . you are not a freethinker, are you, sir?

Paterson   I care not what I am called. I only know that no man should be tortured and persecuted for the sake of his faith.

Borland   I will hear no more of this. (*Leaves.*)

The **Nameless** *as* **Sailors** *enter with buckets and long-handled scrubbing brushes or mops. They pour out liquid and begin to wash and scrub the decks.*

First Nameless   I never really wanted to play the part of a sailor.

Second Nameless   Oh, I suppose you wanted to be King William, did you?

First Nameless   Aye, King William, that'd have done me fine.

Third Nameless   You could never be a King William. Look at you.

Second Nameless (*looks at* **First Nameless**) He's right you know.

Fourth Nameless   I'd like to play a rich man in Edinburgh. You know, one of them who spends all day in coffee houses telling people why it's only right and proper he earns about two thousand times what I do.

First Nameless   That'd be nice.

Second Nameless Aye, that'd be nice.

They continue swabbing the decks. **Mrs Paterson** *enters.*

Mrs Paterson   Oh, that smell of vinegar again. It's worse than the smell below decks. Well, almost.

Paterson   It keeps the fever at bay.

Mrs Paterson   Does it? Since leaving Leith fourteen men have died. And one of the Councillors is gravely ill.

Paterson   Fourteen is fewer than you'd expect for a voyage of this duration. But I would still have them wash down the decks with vinegar every day. Unfortunately the men know they can get away with twice a week. They have no respect for our captain. And why should they?

Mrs Paterson   Will, have you considered . . . ? If this Councillor should die . . . ?

Paterson   How mean you?

Mrs Paterson   If he should die, they are obliged to elect a replacement.

Paterson   They will want me? Is that what you mean to say?

Mrs Paterson   It is. You have been proven right on so many things. In their hearts they know it. They know that their safety depends on men like you. Men whose vision is not clouded by stupidity. Or by drink. Men who are where they are because of merit, not because of rank or connections. I hope you will write in your journal how they have treated you.

Paterson   My journal should not be a litany of complaint.

Mrs Paterson   But history must know the truth.

The **Sailors** *stop swabbing the deck.*
Lighting change.
Music.
The ship is becalmed.
Paterson *sits writing in his journal. The* **Sailors** *come downstage and become the* **Nameless***.*

Song No. 13   The Nameless of the Earth (Partial Reprise)

First Nameless
All history is written
By those who can write
Can read and can write
So history
Is normally
Black and white.

Mrs Paterson
And then
It's written by men

All Nameless & Mrs Paterson
And so we fear
That we may disappear
Unknown
Unsung
The nameless of the earth
Despised
Forgotten

Of little worth
Yet hoping that our voices can
be heard.
Hoping that every now and then
The nameless of the earth can
still be heard
Can dream at least
Of one day being invited to the
feast.

During the last few lines of the number, the **Sailors** *carry on a dead body sewn into a sailcloth. Behind comes* **Pennicuick** *with prayer book and then the* **Rev Borland**, *open Bible in his hands. The body is committed to the deep.*

Borland   Most merciful father we beseech thee of thine infinite goodness to give us grace to live in thy fear and love and to die in thy favour, that when the judgement shall come we may be found acceptable in thy sight through the love of thy Son, our Saviour, Jesus Christ. Amen.

The **Sailors** *disperse.*

Pennicuick   Tis the second one, today, Mr Borland. Could we not maybe combine them, so as to . . . you know . . . save time . . . ?

Borland   We have just buried a Councillor of the Colony, Captain. I will thank you to show a little respect.

Pennicuick   Aye, you're right.

Borland   Although, of course, every man is equal in the sight of God.

Pennicuick (*unconvinced*)   Aye. (*Pause.*) Would you care for a wee brandy? No, no, I suppose you wouldn't.

Borland   Your constant tippling is an abomination, Captain.

Pennicuick   An abomination?

Borland   Yes.

Pennicuick   Is it that bad?

Borland   Yes, it is.

Pennicuick   Aye, well, I'd better get back to my cabin. For a wee abomination. (*Leaves.*)

Music.

Borland *remains on deck.* **Erskine** *enters.* **First Councillor** *enters.* **Mackenzie** *enters, carrying a foolscap leather-bound book.*

Mackenzie   Gentlemen, following the death of one of your fellow Councillors, you are obliged under Chapter Seven of the constitution of the Company of Scotland, to agree upon a replacement forthwith.

There is an awkward silence.

Borland   I suppose we're meant to appoint Paterson, are we?

Mackenzie   The choice is yours gentlemen, not mine. Perhaps you'd prefer Captain Pennicuick?

Borland   That is an ill-judged jest, Mackenzie.

Erskine   Aye, but it reveals a truth, does it not? As everybody is aware, I have had my difficulties with Mr Paterson. But he has experience. And knowledge. And has been the moving spirit of this enterprise.

Borland   I have no doubt as to the competence of the man. But will he uphold the word of God?

Erskine   That is your job, Mr Borland. I propose that we appoint Paterson.

First Councillor   I agree.

Erskine   We will better be able to control the man.

Borland   Maybe . . .

Mackenzie   So it is agreed?

Erskine   Yes.

First Councillor   Yes.

Borland   Aye . . . well . . . all right.

Mackenzie   Mr Paterson is appointed Councillor of the Colony of Darien.

All leave except **Mackenzie**. **Paterson** *enters and he and* **Mackenzie** *shake hands warmly. They leave. Time passes. Music.*

The **Sailors** *appear. There follows a movement sequence, slow and languid, a sense of time hanging heavy in the hot air as the ship moves slowly.* **Paterson** *enters, watches the sailors in silence for a moment.*

Paterson   Men. Can I say a few words to you?

They groan and show reluctance to listen.

Paterson   It's nigh on four months since we left home. It's been hard. It is hard. You've all left behind family, and friends, sweethearts.

Second Sailor (*points to another sailor*)   *He* hasn't! (*Laughter.*)

Paterson   Every voyage is hard. I know that. I've sailed half around the globe in my time. Seen storms and shipwrecks. Looked starvation in the face. Smelt the stench of death below decks. Watched men die. Watched many men die. So it is on every voyage. And yet . . . this voyage is different. Aye, it's full of dangers, I never said otherwise. But think what awaits us. A new land. A new life. A life of plenty. An escape from want. An escape from famine. To a new land waiting to be tamed. By us. We will find ourselves in one of the most healthful, rich and fruitful countries upon earth, situated between two vast oceans, which means Darien can become the emporium for the treasures of half the world. Men, you will be rich. You will be the rich and famous sons of Scotland. In centuries to come, you will be remembered as the men who created a new Scotland. A Scotland of wealth and power and confidence. All founded upon the land of Darien, where glory awaits you. Glory – and gold. So be brave as I know you are. Bold and brave. My men. And with you I will share not only the gold, I will share with you the dangers. This is my word.

Song No. 14   Time To Be Bold

First Sailor	*Time to be bold, me lads,* *Time to be bold,* *Time to think of better times to come.* *Think about the gold, me lads,* *Think about the gold,* *Think about the women and the rum.*
Second Sailor	*Maybe we'll find fortune*
Third Sailor	*Maybe we'll find fame*
Fourth Sailor	*Maybe we'll find nothing* *And wish that we were hame*
Fifth Sailor	*Maybe we'll meet Spaniards* *And we'll find out how they feel* *About taking in their bellies* *A length of Scottish steel*
Sixth Sailor	*Maybe we'll meet natives* *In a land that time forgot*
First Sailor	*But maybe they'll have women* *Who'll be hungry for a Scot*
All Sailors	*Aye we're sure that there are better times to come.*
First Sailor	*So think about the gold, me lads.*
All Sailors	*Think about the gold.* *And could we have another round of rum?*
Lookout	Land ahoy!

Music.

Scene Two – Darien

*Lighting change as we go into an impressionistic rendering of
a romantic paradise. On the sound track we hear rowing boats,
shouted commands, surf. Then exotic tropical rainforest sounds –
insects, birds, frogs, toads, other animals.*

Borland *leads the hymn-singing.*

Song No. 15   What Should We Do But Sing His Praise

Borland & Others   *What should we do but sing His praise*
                         Who led us through the watery maze
                         And brought us safe ashore?
                         To God above we give our thanks
                         And praise him evermore.

Paterson   And now, by virtue of the powers granted unto us, we
do here settle, and in the name of God establish ourselves. And we
do name the city which we here shall build New Edinburgh.

Cheering.

Paterson   And we do name the fort which we shall here build
Fort St Andrew.

Cheering.

Paterson   And for the honour and the memory of the most
ancient and renowned name of our Mother Kingdom, we do and
will from henceforth call this country of Darien by the name of
Caledonia.

Cheering.

Paterson   And ourselves and our successors, by the name of
Caledonians!

Prolonged cheering. **Borland** *tries to impose his will. But the
atmosphere is raucous.*

Borland   We will now sing . . . we will now sing . . . We will
now sing Hymn number . . .

A **Colonist** *launches into a song.*

Song No. 16   Come Rouse Up Your Hearts (Reprise)

Colonist   *Come rouse up your hearts*
Come rouse up anon . . .

Others *join in.* **Borland** *is forced to give up.*

Colonists   *And think of the wisdom of old Solomon*
And heartily join with our own Paterson
To bring home shiploads of treasure.
Come rouse up your hearts
Come rouse up anon
And think of the wisdom of old Solomon
And heartily join with our own Paterson
To bring home shiploads of treasure.

We go into a choreographed scene of multiple discoveries.
Awe-struck and excited **Colonists** *report and exchange*
information about what they have seen.

Mackenzie   There are cedar trees in great abundance.

Erskine   And also mahogany.

Mackenzie   And lignum vitae and yellow sanders.

First Colonist Two leagues hence we met about twenty Indians
with bows and lances.

Second Colonist   But when we approached, they unstrung their
bows in token of friendship.

First Colonist   One of us gave us this. (*Shows a penis cover.*)

Second Colonist   It is gold!

Erskine   Gold?! Let me see . . . Yes, I believe it is gold!

Mackenzie   Gold!

Second Colonist   What use do they make of such a thing?

First Colonist *holds it over the front of his trousers. There is*
ribald laughter.

Mackenzie   Did you have to give them anything in return?

First Colonist   We gave them a hat, a wig and a Bible.

Second Colonist   One of them spoke a few words of Spanish. As far as we could understand, they do not love the Spaniard. They are pleased that we are here.

First Colonist   I saw a river. It may be the river where they pan for gold!

All   Gold!

First Colonist   There are wild hogs!

Second Colonist   That may be eaten! And a kind of partridge. And fish in the rivers. This big!

First Colonist   And a large bird with a pouch under its throat where it can store the fish it catches.

Second Colonist   The natives call it a pec-ilan.

First Colonist   A pel-ican!

Second Colonist   Yes.

The **Rev. Borland** *arrives. They ignore him or do not notice him.*

Erskine   The ground is fertile and rich. They grow cocoa, for the making of chocolate.

Mackenzie   They also grow vanilla. And sugar cane. And maize.

Erskine   And oranges.

Mackenzie   And oranges.

First Colonist   Plantains. Yams.

Third Colonist (*arriving*)   The women wear no clothes! The women wear no clothes!

All   Hooray!

First Colonist   Where are they, where are they?

Second Colonist   Is it far?

First Colonist   Did you bring me one?

Second Colonist   Any nice young virgins to be had? I don't want one that's been swived by a Spaniard.

Third Colonist   Aye, let's hope there's enough virgins to go round.

Borland (*scandalised*)   You filthy immoral degenerate creatures! Sinners! Sinners, all of you! Sinners! Think not that you can escape God's wrath by coming to this place. This is Scottish soil now. Christian soil!

Pennicuick *emerges, a bottle in his hand and blearily observes.*

Borland   And let me tell you, in case you do not know, it is the local custom that if a man debauches another man's wife, they thrust a briar into the passage of his member, and turn it round a dozen times.

Colonists *all wince noisily.*

Borland   Aye, that will make you hesitate, though eternal damnation should make you hesitate yet more.

Pennicuick   Well said, Reverend.

Borland   And you, Captain Pennicuick are a disgrace. A drunken disgrace to the name of Scotland.

Pennicuick   You see that briar you just talked about? Why don't you stick one up your pious Presbyterian arse?

The conflict is defused as **Paterson** *enters purposefully with maps. He is followed by* **Erskine.** **Paterson** *spreads out the maps. They sit down on barrels / packing cases.* **Borland** *remains a little apart from the others.*

Paterson   There is a natural harbour . . . here. On one side of it there's a peninsula of flat sandy ground, of about thirty acres in extent. There we shall build our capital city.

Pennicuick   Let me see, let me see. Oh aye, excellent, excellent.

Erskine   And to defend it?

Paterson   We must build a fort. But before that we shall erect a battery of fifteen heavy guns. They can both defend the city from the land and also command the harbour entrance.

Pennicuick   Yes, good. Good.

Mrs Paterson *joins them. All except* **Paterson** *look a bit put out.*

Paterson   Now. At its narrowest part this little peninsula here is only two hundred paces wide.

Erskine   We make a cutting through it!

Paterson   Exactly. A deep cutting to let in the sea. Our capital city will thus be on an island, and safe from attack on all sides. Once this has been established, we will survey the isthmus and plan the building of our trading road to link the two oceans.

Mrs Paterson   Huts for the sick. That is the first thing. Land must be cleared and huts built for those who are sick.

Mr Paterson   You are right. Mr Erskine. Will you take command of the building of these huts?

Erskine   I am already in command of building the fort.

Mrs Paterson   Yes, and now you are being asked also to be in command of building the huts.

Erskine   Has Mrs Paterson been appointed Councillor? I was not aware she was empowered to give commands. To men.

Paterson   Think of it as a suggestion, Mr Erskine. And then do it.

Borland (*intervening*)   We will need to keep a firm grip on the morals of the men in this place.

Mrs Paterson   You've always been an ambitious person, Mr Borland.

Mackenzie (*comes running, excited*) Mr Paterson, Mr Paterson! (*Struggling to get his breath.*) There is a French sloop in the bay. They are sailing to Jamaica tomorrow. They can take our letters. From there they can be put on a ship bound for Bristol. With luck and a fair wind Edinburgh will have news of us in only three months from now!

Paterson   That's excellent, Mackenzie. Well done. Tell everyone they have half a day to write to their loved ones. Let those who are lettered help those who are not. As for us, we have reports to write. Reports that will bring cheer to every man and woman in Scotland.

Scene Three – Darien

Music.
Darkness.
Music.
The sound track is now the rainforest at night – threatening and sinister. Strange howls and screeches. It is dark, and raining heavily. By the light of an oil lamp two **Gravediggers**. *As day begins to break we see a short row of simple wooden crosses. The two* **Gravediggers** *leave. The sounds change. Steam rises from the jungle. Sheltered under an awning are* **Erskine,** **Pennicuick** *and* **Paterson***, squinting at a map. The rain thunders down. Each entry of the* **Gravediggers** *marks a time jump in the conversation.*

Paterson   It should have been built by now, Mr Erskine.

Erskine   The land is difficult to build upon.

Paterson   As I told you it would be. You have chosen the wrong spot.

Pennicuick *pours himself a brandy, thereby discovering the bottle is empty.*

Erskine   Captain Pennicuick and I think it the best spot.

Paterson   It's a swamp. A morass. You couldn't even grow anything there, far less build a fort upon it.

Pennicuick   It has easy access for the ships.

Paterson   Is that your only concern?

Pennicuick   No. I'd like some more brandy. (*Shouts.*) Boy!

The **Gravediggers** *enter carrying a simple wooden cross, which they hammer into the ground.*

Erskine   They need to work faster.

Paterson   You want the men to work faster? In this heat? This humidity? Without proper rations?

Pennicuick   We'll unload a few more barrels of salted pork.

Paterson   It's uneatable. Not fit for dogs. It's green and stinking and riddled with maggots.

Pennicuick   Give it to the Highlanders. Better than boiled oats, eh?

Paterson   I notice your own fare does not include rotting pork.

Pennicuick   Indeed it does not. If the men want decent food, they must get on with clearing the land and planting.

Paterson   They are weakened by disease. Made ill by this unrelenting rainfall. The land is not so easily cleared as once we thought.

Erskine   And whose fault is that? Who made us believe we were coming to an earthly paradise?

Paterson *looks away. The* **Gravediggers** *enter carrying a simple wooden cross, which they hammer into the ground.*

Paterson   Why are all the supplies being kept on board the ships?

Erskine   So that they remain dry.

Paterson   No. The Councillors are sitting in the ships controlling the supply of food. And keeping the best for themselves.

Pennicuick   Why, would you want us to keep the worst for ourselves? (*Laughs at his own wit. Waves a glass in the air.*) Boy!

The **Gravediggers** *enter carrying a simple wooden cross, which they hammer into the ground.*

Pennicuick   Now just hold on, Mr Paterson. You want us to leave our cabins and sleep in yon half-built huts among the noxious vapours of the mangrove swamps?

Paterson   It's what I'm going to do henceforth.

Erskine   You are being foolish.

Paterson   The men need leadership. They will respond. We have suffered setbacks. They can be overcome. It can be done. It can be done. (*Gets up to go.*)

Pennicuick   I will have more brandy. Boy!

The **Boy** *arrives, pours out a very large brandy.*

Pennicuick *leaves, followed by* **Erskine**. **Paterson**, *alone on stage, takes in the wooden crosses, turns comes downstage. Contemplating failure – or perhaps trying to drive the thought away – he stands in the rain until he is soaked.*

Scene Four – the Company Offices, Edinburgh

Off: a horse galloping. **Balfour** *and* **Blackwood** *look up. A* **Messenger** *enters, big leather knapsack over one shoulder. He hands* **Blackwood** *and* **Balfour** *packages in heavy oiled paper. With trembling hands* **Blackwood** *opens a sheaf of letters. He reads.*

Blackwood   They are safe. They are well.

Balfour   Thanks be to God.

Balfour *tears open other letters. They exchange news of the contents.*

Blackwood   They made landfall in Darien exactly as planned. No ships lost. Only twenty-eight men dead on the voyage over.

Balfour (*reading*)   The land is fertile and fruitful!

Blackwood (*reading*)   The climate is benign!

Balfour (*reading*)   They are building a fort to be known as Fort St Andrew!

Blackwood (*reading*)   And a capital city to be known as New Edinburgh!

Balfour *turns to the* **Horseman**.

Balfour   Convey this news to Parliament. Tell the Lord High Chancellor that Scotland has an empire!

The **Horseman** *bows briefly and leaves.*

Balfour   Oh, what a day, what a day for Scotland. May God bless this country. And God bless you, Mr Blackwood! (*Emotional, he embraces* **Blackwood**, *then feels embarrassed and steps back stiffly.*) Sorry, sorry. Got a wee bit carried away.

Music begins. **Tweedale** *appears in full regalia.*

Tweedale   Let us give thanks to Almighty God that the Darien expedition has been crowned with success! Let there be prayers said in every church in the land. A service of thanksgiving in St Giles Cathedral. Let all Scotland rejoice. Let riders be sent to every corner of the land to promulgate the happy news. Let the guns of the Half Moon battery be fired across the North Loch. Let bonfires be lit at Holyrood and at the Netherbow port. And tonight, tonight issue an order that candles are to be displayed in every window in the High Street.

Song No. 17   Oh Caledonia

Singers (*off*)   *Oh Caledonia*
Your glory we proclaim
Soon all mankind
Will recognise thy fame
An end to poverty
An end to shame
Dear Caledonia
We praise thy name.

Lights go down and we see the High Street of Edinburgh with candles in the windows. Church bells ring out. Cheering crowds in the distance.

Scene Five – Darien

Off: for a few moments the previous song may continue. **Paterson** *enters followed by* **Erskine**.

Paterson   How often do I have to tell you? Once we start trading, all will be well. We did not choose Darien for its beauty or its ease. We chose it because it is our key to trading across the isthmus.

Erskine   We did not choose Darien. You chose Darien, Mr Paterson. You told us there would be gold, and what have we found so far? A few bits and pieces of native ornamentation – some of it unmentionable in polite circles. You did not tell us about the mangrove swamps. Or the disease. Or the heat and the humidity.

Paterson   Did you think you were coming to a piece of Scotland, Mr Erskine? Did it not occur to you that the climate might be different? You are part of this now, remember, Mr Erskine. We are in this together.

Erskine   Aye, I know. But men are dying of the fever every day. There is weariness. There is despair. Hope can only take you so far, you know. It is a commodity that is not endless in its supply. Except in your case.

Paterson   We always knew it would be hard at the start. We always knew that men would die.

Erskine   And did you say that to them?

Paterson   They knew! They know. These men have fled famine and starvation. They know the meaning of danger. But this is danger with the possibility of a great and glorious outcome.

Erskine   Glorious . . . (*shakes his head*).

Mackenzie *enters.*

Mackenzie   We have conversed with the Indians. Not without some difficulty I must confess. Some speak a few words of Spanish, but . . . well, my Spanish is not of the best. But they also have a language of gesture. It is most ingenious.

Erskine   Will you come to the point, Mr Mackenzie?

Mackenzie   Do you know how they express the passing of time? It is thus: (*performs a mime of his hand crossing the sky, and ending with his head against the pillow of his hands*). That is a day and a night. Twenty-four hours. And we have established how many days' march it is to cross from here to the Pacific Ocean.

Erskine   How many?

Mackenzie   This many.

Paterson *watches in fascination as* **Mackenzie** *laboriously performs the mime of six days.*

Erskine (*mutters*)   Oh, in heaven's name.

Paterson   Six?

Mackenzie   Six.

Paterson   Only six days' march to traverse the peninsula! Did you hear that Mr Erskine?

Erskine   Aye.

Mackenzie   It is good news. Excellent news.

Paterson   Even Mr Erskine will acknowledge that. Think. If the isthmus can be crossed through the jungle in only six days, imagine . . . once we have cleared a trail . . . goods can be transported swiftly . . . we will look back on our early difficulties and wonder why we ever had a single doubt.

Erskine *stares bleakly at him.*

Scene Six – the Court of King William

William *arranges hair and clothes in mirror, trying on different articles of clothing, helped by* **Joost**.

William   Well, who would have thought it? The Scotchmen have landed, eh? And thriving, I hear?

Joost   So we are informed, your Majesty. There is much rejoicing in Edinburgh.

William   I suppose that means 'much drinking' . . . ?
Not that one. The blue one. Do pay attention, Joost. This 'colony' of theirs. It is engaged in trade?

Joost   That is certainly what they intend.

William   Shall we leave the Spaniard to deal with them, shall we, Joost? That would be convenient.

Joost   The Spanish have ships on the coast. And soldiers. But they hesitate to attack. The Scotchmen are likely to make a good fight of it.

William   How very tiresome of them. (*Coughs.*) So . . . we had better make sure these Northern savages do not prosper. A Scottish trading empire in the Americas, it does not bear thinking about.

Joost (*revealing a scroll*)   I have had a proclamation prepared, Sire.

William   Ah, you are useful. Read it out, then, read it out.

Joost   His Majesty's subjects are hereby commanded not to enter into any correspondence with the Scots Colony in Darien . . .

William   Good, good.

Joost   Nor to trade with them, nor to give them any assistance of any kind, whether of arms, or ammunition, or provisions or any other necessaries whatsoever.

William   Very good.

Joost   Any vessel of the English nation entering a port belonging to the Scots colonists will be in contempt of His Majesty's command, and the perpetrators will at their utmost peril be made to answer for it.

William   Hm. Yes. That will do it, I think. (*Signs it.*)

Scene Seven – Darien

A **Boy** *is alone on the beach. Maybe another* **Colonist** *performs a simple dance during it.*

Song No. 18   The Lonesome Sea

Sailor Boy   *There was a Scottish ship*
And she sailed in the morn
And the name of that ship
Was the mighty Unicorn
Oh, she sailed upon
That lonely, lonesome water
Oh, she sailed upon that lonely sea.

Up stepped a cabin boy
Saying what'll you give to me
If I climb to the topsail
In a show of bravery?
If I climb above
That lonely, lonesome water
If I climb above that lonely sea.

The captain said to him
Oh, I have some gold
And I will give a sovereign
To a lad that's truly bold
And who'll climb above
That lonely, lonesome water
Who will climb above that lonely sea.

Instrumental break.

So the cabin boy climbed up
And he overcame his fear

And when he reached the top sail
All the crew began to cheer
As they sailed upon
That lonely, lonesome water
As they sailed upon that lonely sea.

And they wondered if he'd fall
From the rigging to the deck
For they knew that if he did
He would surely break his neck
As they sailed upon
That lonely, lonesome water
As they sailed upon that lonely sea.

But the boy came safely down
And the captain kept his word
And the cabin boy was cheered
By everyone on board
As they sailed upon
That lonely, lonesome water
As they sailed upon that lonely sea.

Instrumental break

And that night the cabin boy
To his shipmates softly said
Oh I fear I have the fever
By the morning he was dead
And they dropped him in
That lonely, lonesome water
They dropped him in that lonely sea.
He was buried in
That lonely lonesome water
He was buried in the lonely sea.

The **Boy** *leaves.* **Paterson** *emerges from one of the huts, followed by* **Mrs Paterson**.

Paterson   This is foolishness. You are not well. There is no need for you to sleep in these huts when you can be in the ship's cabin. It is healthier there.

Mrs Paterson   You sleep in the cabin, I will also sleep in the cabin.

Paterson   I cannot do that.

Mrs Paterson   Then nor can I.

Paterson (*enraged*)   This is an order, woman!

Mrs Paterson   Will. You know that never works with me. (*Walks away.*)

Mackenzie *enters, followed by a French sea captain,* **Aguillon**. **Paterson** *looks up.*

Mackenzie   Mr Paterson. This is Captain Aggy-on

Aguillon (*corrects pronounciation*)   Aguillon.

Mackenzie   Aggy-on.

Aguillon Alexandre Aguillon. Master of the Saint Philippe.

Erskine *arrives, listens.*

Mackenzie   Just dropped anchor in the bay.

Paterson   William Paterson. Councillor of the Scottish Colony of Caledonia.

Aguillon (*mocking*)   Caledonia, eh? Is that what you call it?

Erskine   You are trading on this coast?

Aguillon   Yes. But not with you.

Paterson   Why not? We have need of many items. Victuals above all.

Aguillon   Your King has issued a proclamation forbidding any man to trade with your Colony. He is not a man who easily forgives those who ignore his wishes.

Mackenzie   This cannot be true. Can this be true? Mr Paterson?

Paterson *is stunned.*

Aguillon   Why would I lie about this?

Paterson   It is what I feared. I feared it.

Aguillon   What you should fear more is the Spaniard. They know about your settlement here.

Mackenzie   But they lack the strength to attack us.

Aguillon   You are not aware they have three ships of fifty guns each newly come from Spain.

Paterson   You have seen these?

Aguillon   I have. And there is a second Spanish fleet at Carthagena, consisting of three sail: one of fifty guns, one of thirty guns and one of twenty-four guns. You should be prepared for an attack.

Paterson   I am grateful. Thank you, Captain.

Mackenzie   There is more.

Aguillon   The Indians say the Spaniards are marching from Panama towards Darien. With a great number of men. Their advance party has already reached Toubacanti. That is only a day's march away.

Erskine   The Indians. They lie all the time. They change sides all the time. They are not to be relied upon.

Aguillon   This is not my experience. That is all I have to tell you.

Mackenzie   You will stay? Eat and drink with us?

Aguillon   No, I will weigh anchor while the wind is still fair. It's an interesting bay you have chosen for your harbour. Easy to sail into but given the prevailing winds on this coast, not easy to sail out of I would think. I have heard the Spanish tried occupying this place some two hundred years ago. I wonder why they decided to leave? (*Makes to leave.*)

Paterson   Wait. You're a man who's taken risks in his life. Nobody need know that you have traded with us. You have victuals on board?

Aguillon   Yes. But you have nothing of value to offer me in return.

Paterson   Yes, we do. Of course we do. Mackenzie?

Mackenzie   I'm sure we can offer items that –

Paterson   There is certainly trade to be done between us.

Aguillon   Mr Paterson. I have seen what you have to offer. And I must tell you I have no interest in acquiring three hundred wigs. Nor five hundred pairs of knitted hosiery. Nor even two thousand slightly mildewed Scottish catechisms. It may surprise you to know that in Catholic France there is no great demand for Protestant prayer books. Good day, gentlemen. (*Makes to go.*)

Paterson   One moment. You came ashore merely to provide us with information? From the goodness of your heart?

Aguillon   In a way. You see, my grandfather came from Scotland – but wisely chose to live in France. Your colony is a ridiculous venture, but I have no desire to see you wiped out. I fear I am a foolish and sentimental man. Though being only one quarter Scottish, not as foolish and sentimental as yourselves. Good day to you. (*Leaves.*)

The three men absorb the information in silence.

Paterson   We could be attacked at any time. And the fort is still not built, Mr Erskine.

Erskine   If we get the twelve-pounders mounted on the escarpment, and complete the defences to the landward, then –

Paterson   We should certainly do that. And with all haste. But I have another suggestion. You may find it too bold.

Erskine   I may not.

Mackenzie   What is it?

Paterson   The Spanish will have spies along the coast. They will know that we are fortifying the town. So what will they least expect?

Erskine   What?

Paterson   They will least expect *us* to attack *them* . . . If we fall
upon their vanguard at Toubacanti we can defeat them by force
of numbers alone. When King William hears that we can defeat
the Spaniard in battle he will soon realise that we are now a
trading nation alongside England, a trading nation and a military
power, and no royal proclamation is going to put an end to us. Mr
Mackenzie. Make an announcement. Let the entire colony know
that Caledonia stands ready to fight! Let the *world* know that
Caledonia stands ready to fight!

Scene Eight – a living room in Edinburgh

Early morning in a darkened room.

Blackwood *and* **Balfour** *are found slumped over a table, amidst
empty bottles and glasses and remains of food. A* **Servant** *enters,
opens the shutters, clears up a bit. Light floods in.* **Balfour** *and*
Blackwood *groan and stir.*

Servant (*to audience*)   Ladies and gentlemen. There now
follows a bit of a cliché: two Scotsmen with a hangover. This
is to illustrate the even-handedness of the play. Having unfairly
portrayed the English, the French, the Dutch, the Germans and the
Danes, it seems only right and proper to do the same for the Scots.
Thank you.

Blackwood   What hour is it?

Servant   Ten.

Blackwood   Bring us coffee.

Balfour   Chocolate. Cups of chocolate.

Blackwood   Coffee.

Balfour   Chocolate.

Blackwood   Coffee.

Servant   I'll bring both, eh?

Balfour   Ten o'clock . . . We'll be late for the Company meeting.

Servant   Few are stirring in the town, sir. Last night all of Edinburgh was celebrating. We saw off the Spaniard, sir, did we not? I hear they are striking special silver plate to mark the Scottish victory at the Battle of Toubacanti.

Blackwood   Aye, aye, a great victory. Coffee.

Balfour   And chocolate.

Servant   Yes, sir. (*Leaves.*)

Blackwood (*derisively*)   Great victory. The Battle of Toubacanti. It was a but a skirmish. Three Spanish dead and two Scots.

Balfour   That is a victory.

Blackwood   Aye, maybe, but it scarcely merits a night of revelry and rioting. And it was all but four months ago. Who knows what may have happend since? The Spaniard may be more powerful than we thought.

Balfour   It was we who declared it a victory.

Blackwood   People were in need of good news.

Balfour   Yes. (*Looks at bottles.*) How many bottles of claret did we drink last night?

Blackwood   Well, I had two and . . . and you must have had three. (*Counts the empty bottles.*)

Balfour   Mr Blackwood, that makes five.

Blackwood   Yes.

Balfour   How many empty bottles are there?

Blackwood   Six. Oh. I see what you mean. You must have drunk four. Where's my coffee?

Balfour   I do not comprehend how you can swallow yon abominable heathenish liquid.

Blackwood   Coffee fuels the intellectual discourse of our nation, Mr Balfour.

Balfour   Intellectual discourse? When did you last take part in intellectual discourse, Mr Blackwood?

Blackwood   Um, let me see . . .

*The **Servant** enters with a cup of coffee and a cup of hot chocolate and places them on the table.*

Balfour   Hmmm. Now listen. We know Toubacanti was not the great victory that the rabble believe it to be. But it will enable us to make another call for funds.

Blackwood   Aye, that's true. There'll be no shortage of investment now.

Servant *withdraws.*

Balfour   We'll not let the English strangle our colony with their embargo. We'll equip and provision a second fleet. A fleet even mightier than the first. And if it sails from the Clyde instead of from Leith the voyage will be shortened by three weeks, maybe four.

Blackwood   It can reach Darien in . . . in . . . a little over two months.

Balfour   Very good, Mr Blackwood, very good. In no time at all you'll be able to count up to six.

Blackwood   We will make the nation proud of our heroic lads fighting overseas.

Balfour   Aye, soon enough the people will have more good news than they know what to do with.

They simultaneously reach for their coffee and their chocolate and sip.

Balfour & Blackwood   Ahhhhh.

Scene Nine – a hut in Darien

Paterson *is talking to the* **Colonists**, *several of whom are writing down what he says.*

Paterson (*dictating*)   One of . . . the . . . most fruitfullest . . . . spots of ground . . . on . . . the face . . . of the earth.

First Colonist   Are we obliged to write this exactly as you say it, Mr Paterson?

Paterson   No. If instead you wish to tell them about the swamps, and the fevers, and the depredations, and the hunger, then by all means, tell them. Tell them that we bury a dozen men a day. Tell them that New Edinburgh is but a row of straw huts. Tell that Fort St Andrew is but a half-built palisade placed upon a stinking marsh. Let tales of death and disaster circulate in Scotland. Let them think that we are half-drowned rats not worth saving. Let all of Scotland know that the Spaniard is more powerful than we thought and may soon attack us in overwhelming numbers. And when because of your wretched accounts of our great endeavour they decide to build no more ships and our needful supplies are not sent and we succumb to hunger and despair, come to me and say you are proud of what you wrote.

First Colonist   Sir, I only wish to recount the truth of our situation.

Paterson   The truth? The truth? Damn you and your truth. Your truth won't warm your grave. Let me have the truth of your courage. The truth of your resolution. The truth of your faith in God. The truth of your faith in Caledonia.

First Colonist   Yes, sir.

Second Colonist   Sir, many of us are unlettered. If somebody could –

Paterson (*pointing at* **First Colonist**)   He'll write your letters for you. (*To* **First Colonist**.) Will you not?

First Colonist   Yes, sir.

Paterson   And you'll know what to say, will you not?

First Colonist   Yes, sir.

Paterson *walks away. They wait until he is out of earshot.*

First Colonist (*quietly*)   Tell me what you truly want to say and I will write it for you.

Second Colonist   Thank you. Say . . . write this down . . . I . . . I don't know if I will see my homeland again. We live on two pounds of flour a week. That's two pounds by the Company weighing, which means one pound only.

Unnoticed by them **Pennicuick** *approaches.*

First Colonist   Slow down, slow down.

Second Colonist   And the flour must be sifted to remove the maggots . . .

Pennicuick   What are these lies?

They try to hide the letter. **Pennicuick** *snatches it, reads it.*

Pennicuick   Lies, lies.

Second Colonist   They are not lies, captain. The flour we are given is full of maggots.

First Colonist   Aye, and sometimes there's no flour at all and we get a handful of dried peas instead and when we boil them up we have first to skim the worms off the top.

Third Colonist *comes over and joins them.*

Second Colonist   And for all this short allowance we are every man daily turned out to work with hatchet, or pick-axe, or shovel, and continue until night. Sometimes we work all day up to the top of our breeches in water.

Pennicuick   You are grown soft.

Third Colonist (*pulling shirt off shoulder*)   Look, just take a look at that, Captain . . . My shoulder is so wore with carrying burdens that the skin has come off it and grown full of boils.

Pennicuick (*turns away in disgust*)   I do not wish to know about your boils, sir. They stink. I suggest you all get back to work.

Third Colonist   What do you know of work, Captain? You who lie at ease in the cabins of your ships. You and the other Councillors.

Second Colonist   Not Mr Paterson.

Third Colonist   Not Mr Paterson, no. But all the rest of you. Keeping the best food and drink for yourselves.

First Colonist   Why is a man who is sick and obliged to stay within the huts given no food?

Second Colonist   The governance of this colony has been compassed about with lies.

Third Colonist   We should not have come here. It is not probable that one Scotsman in twenty could live here, the place is unwholesome.

Second Colonist   Three hundred graves, Captain Pennicuick. Three hundred graves. And every day a dozen more.

They begin to gather round him, threateningly.

First Colonist   Three hundred graves.

Third Colonist   Three hundred graves.

It becomes a sort of chant perhaps reinforced with pre-recorded voices. **Paterson** *has appeared at one side. He watches and listens.*

Colonists   Three hundred graves. Three hundred graves. Three hundred graves. Three hundred graves. Three hundred graves . . .

Triumphal music from the next scene creeps in.

Scene Ten – a hill overlooking the Clyde estuary

Triumphal music.
Balfour *and* **Blackwood** *watch the second fleet depart. Off: cheering.*
Blackwood *points and checks off the ships in a ledger as each one is sighted.*

Blackwood   The Rising Sun.

Balfour   She's a beauty.

Blackwood   She is that.

Balfour   She cost us a pretty penny of course. More than the rest of the fleet put together. We can be proud, Mr Blackwood, we can be proud. A second great fleet to join the first. Does it not make your heart beat a little faster?

Blackwood   Aye, it does. Look. The Hamilton. She's a beauty too.

Balfour   A fine sight, a fine sight. All in all a glorious sight. Enough to stir the heart of the sourest Scot, and God knows there are plenty of them about. I never knew the Clyde could look so bonny. Almost as bonny as the Forth. Who'd have thought it, eh?

Blackwood (*points*)   And there comes the Bo'ness.

Balfour   Aye, look at yon ships. Bearing one thousand three hundred men, women and children on their way to a new and better life.

Blackwood   And look, over there, the Hope.

Balfour   Four mighty ships, Mr Blackwood, four mighty ships. Carrying the spirit of Scotland. When they reach Darien and join up with the first expedition we will be as powerful a presence in the Americas as any nation on the face of the earth. Darien will bring wealth, and power and glory to Scotland. Never again will we have to bend our knee to the English. The Lord God has smiled upon this little nation of ours, and made us great.

Blackwood   We are blessed, Mr Balfour, we are blessed.

They leave.

Scene Eleven – Darien

On Darien **Erskine,** **Pennicuick** *and* **Paterson** *are locked in grim conflict.* **Paterson** *is ill.*

Paterson   You are giving up! You are all giving up on me. You are like mice. Did you think our great endeavour would be easy? Did you? Where's the fight in you? What are you made of? Milk and curds? Dear God, why am I surrounded by poor weak feeble creatures such as you?!

Erskine   How can we build a trading colony if nobody will trade with us?

Pennicuick (*drinking*)   Erskine's right. The King's proclamation has finished us. But it allows us to abandon the Colony with our honour intact.

Paterson   You cannot have intact what you never had to start with.

Pennicuick   By God, Paterson, you're a rude bugger. (*Holding up an empty glass.*) Boy! More wine! Where is that boy?

Paterson   He is dead.

Pennicuick   Oh.

Erskine   We'll receive no more provisions from home. No more ships. No more help. They're afraid of the King. Scotland has given up on us.

Paterson   We don't know that. Ships may be on their way.

Erskine   I'll tell you what ships are on their way. Spanish ships. Seven of them, standing off the coast. And a Spanish army approaching by land.

Pennicuick   If we surrender now, we may still escape with our lives. What we cannot do is just sit here waiting and hoping. With so many men dead. So many ill. So many suffering.

Paterson   Since when did you care about the men?

Pennicuick   You're not looking so well yourself, Paterson.

Erskine   We have to leave.

Pennicuick   Aye, if the Spanish press home and attack we're all dead. Let us capitulate with honour. (*Empties his bottle.*)

Erskine, **Pennicuick** *and the other* **Colonists** *leave.* **Paterson** *is shaking and sweating. He falls to his knees.* **Mrs Paterson** *enters, kneels down beside him.*

Paterson   It can't be done. It can't be done. It can't be done.

Mrs Paterson   Will . . . it is all right. We will go home.

Paterson   Where I shall face shame and dishonour.

Mrs Paterson   All you have done, you've done with honour. There is no shame.

Paterson   It can't be done.

Mackenzie *appears. He waits, watches.*

Mackenzie (*gently*)   Mr Paterson . . . Mrs Paterson . . . I am sorry . . . The Spanish have landed. Their commander will grant us safe passage. But we must leave now.

Slowly **Paterson** *and* **Mrs Paterson** *get up and leave. As* **Mackenzie** *leaves, upstage of him a huge graveyard of crude wooden crosses is revealed.*

In a ghostly faint form we hear singing off.

Song No. 19   Time To Be Bold (Reprise)

Sailors   *Time to be bold, me lads,*
                         Time to be bold,
                         Time to think of better times to come.
                         Think about the gold, me lads,
                         Think about the gold . . .

Scene Twelve – the Port of Leith/Edinburgh

Nine of the **Nameless** *enter, half-singing, half-whispering. Each is carrying a wreath.*

Song No. 20   Trade Begets Trade (Reprise)

The Nameless   *Trade begets trade*
Money makes money
Wealth creates wealth
Riches from riches
Piled upon riches
Unto the end of the world.

Paterson *enters, head bowed.*

The **Nameless** *each declare the name of the ship, as a wreath is thrown into the sea for each ship.*

First Nameless   The Unicorn. Abandoned in New England.

Second Nameless   The St Andrew. Abandoned in Jamaica.

Third Nameless   The Dolphin. Lost to the Spanish.

First Nameless   The Endeavour. Sunk in the Caribbean.

Second Nameless   The Hope. Wrecked off Cuba.

Third Nameless   The Bo'ness. Surrendered to the Spanish.

First Nameless   The Duke of Hamilton. Sunk in Charleston Harbour.

Second Nameless   The Rising Sun. Sunk in a hurricane with the loss of all hands.

First Nameless   The Caledonia. The only ship to return to Scotland.

Blackwood (*entering*)   The climate was to blame.

Balfour (*entering*)   The English were to blame.

Mackenzie (*entering*)   The Spaniard was to blame.

Erskine (*entering*)   William Paterson was to blame.

Paterson   I know. I know.

Their gaze follows him as he leaves.

Scene Thirteen – St Giles Cathedral, Edinburgh

Borland *appears in the pulpit. His voice echoes round the cold stone walls.*

Borland   The General Assembly of Church of Scotland has taken to heart the many tokens of God's displeasure that are gone forth against this land. We see with sadness the blasting of the undertakings of this nation in the colony of Caledonia, together with the loss of two thousand of our countrymen . . . and a great part of the nation's treasure. We have cause to infer that our sins must be great and heinous in the sight of God. And great has been God's punishment. I saw the suffering. As our ships fled Darien I went below decks among the sick to visit them in their sad and dying condition, their noisome stench choking and suffocating. Malignant fevers and the flux swept away great numbers. I saw with my own eyes and heard with my own ears the last tormented moments of wretched sinners as they prepared to enter through the gates of hell. Too late for regrets. Too late for repentance. Each man paying for his mortal mistakes, as Scotland must now pay for hers. Surely it is a sign of God's wrath that a second great fleet should have been sent to Darien when the colony had already been abandoned and that it too should have been destroyed upon the high seas. It is obvious to every discerning eye that this land is filled with wickedness and abominations among persons of all ranks and degrees. And instead of repenting of our sins and renewing our engagements unto God, the most part of our people have given themselves over unto jollity and wantonness. Upon all these considerations this Assembly has thought fit to declare for the nation a day of solemn fasting and humiliation and the exercise of sincere and unfeigned repentance for the sins that abound in our land.

Scene Fourteen – the offices of the Company of Scotland

In a ritualised sequence, the **Directors** *of the Company round on* **Paterson***.*

Balfour   I want my money back, Mr Paterson.

Erskine   I want my money back, Mr Paterson.

Blackwood   I want my money back, Mr Paterson.

Borland   I want my money back, Mr Paterson.

Mackenzie   Mr Paterson, I have not been paid.

Balfour   My business is destroyed, Mr Paterson.

Erskine   Your reputation is destroyed, Mr Paterson.

Blackwood   Our future is destroyed, Mr Paterson.

Borland   Scotland is destroyed, Mr Paterson.

Mackenzie   And I have not been paid.

Balfour   I want my money back, Mr Paterson.

Erskine   I want my money back, Mr Paterson.

Blackwood   I want my money back, Mr Paterson.

Borland   I want my money back, Mr Paterson.

Mackenzie   And I have not been paid.

Paterson*, defeated, walks off as they stare after him.*

Scene Fifteen – The Court of King Willam

The **King** *is having tea. He is clearly unwell.*

Joost   Mr William Paterson!

Paterson (*bows*)   Your Majesty.

William   You never really go away, do you Paterson? How long now since you set forth on your foolish adventure in Panama?

Paterson   Nigh on four years, Sire.

William   And here you are. A failure. A wretched man who brought disaster upon his wretched land. I assume you live here in London now?

Paterson   No, Sire. In Scotland.

William   How very brave of you. Do the common people not wish to do terrible things to you?

Paterson   The common people do not present a problem, Sire. The shareholders of the Company of Scotland present a problem.

William   Ah.

Paterson   They are a barrier to the union of our two nations.

William   Why?

Paterson   Many of them sit in Parliament. If they feel cheated, they will vote against any treaty of union.

William   But they were not cheated by me, Mr Paterson, they were cheated by you. Thanks to you they lost every penny. Scotland is finished as an independent nation. Don't they know that?

Paterson   I know it, Sire. I know Scotland cannot prosper as an independent nation. We need the financial power of England. That is the lesson of Darien.

William   Oh, I thought the lesson of Darien was don't give your money to bankers.

Paterson   Sire. The treaty that is being envisaged requires Scotland to take on a part of England's national debt. It is a vast sum. It is an unbearable sum to impose upon Scotland. It means union with England will never be accepted. They will not swallow it, Sire.

William   They must. I may not live to see it, but I already know that union is inevitable.

Paterson   It is not, I assure you, Sire. There may still be years of negotiation ahead before union comes about. During that time, Scottish resentment against England can only increase. His Majesty's embargo on trade with our colony dealt us a fatal blow.

William   Oh come, come. Darien was simply the wrong place to go. You are looking for an excuse. How easy it is for you Scots always to blame the English.

Paterson   Your Majesty must understand that others may tell him what he wishes to hear. From me he will hear only the truth.

William   I cannot allow Scotland to escape its share of the national debt. The English Parliament would not countenance it.

Paterson   There may be another way to solve it, Sire.

William   How?

Paterson (*tentatively*)   Well . . . if England were to offer a cash sum . . . A sum that is equivalent to Scotland's share of the national debt . . . That could be . . . helpful.

William   Why should England do that? It makes no sense. We are meant to take from Scotland with one hand and give it back with the other?

Paterson   You would not be giving it back to Scotland, Sire. Not exactly.

William   So to whom would we be giving this . . . 'cash sum'?

Paterson   To the directors and shareholders of the Company of Scotland. To compensate those who lost their money in the Darien venture.

William   Why?

Paterson   Many of them wield great influence. Indeed, many sit in the Scottish Parliament. If they are compensated, they will be inclined to favour a treaty of union. And vote for it.

William   You are proposing a bribe.

Paterson   I am proposing compensation.

William   I am to compensate them for every penny of their losses, is that what you propose?

Paterson   Yes. Plus interest.

William   Plus interest?

Paterson   Yes. Everything they lost. Plus fifty per cent. Sire.

William   You are very bold, Paterson. Are you not?

Paterson   Your Majesty wishes to see England and Scotland united as one nation. Does he not?

William (*thinks*)   The Company of Scotland . . . I am told you have plans for new colonies?

Paterson   I have.

William   If the English Parliament agrees to your proposition . . .

Paterson   Your Majesty will put it to them?

William   I may. But following union, we cannot allow the Company of Scotland to continue. Any treaty would have to ensure the Company of Scotland is dissolved.

Paterson   I would find that most regrettable.

William   I suspect you will get over it. You will always devise some new scheme to make money, Paterson, I know the sort of man you are. With every passing day I encounter more and more men such as you.

Paterson   I beg your Majesty not to dissolve the Company of Scotland.

William   It is decided.

Paterson   But –

William   Do not argue with me, sir. Your shareholders will be compensated, they will help to bring about union, and your wretched trading company will be closed down. Not another word from you, sir, not another word! Joost. Hunting. I fear I am too ill.

Paterson *bows as* **William** *and* **Joost** *leave. He straightens up with a smile of triumph on his face.*

Scene Sixteen – a street in Edinburgh

A cart laden with banknotes, gold and silver coin is pulled onto the stage, protected by English Dragoons. Coins and notes spill out on to the ground.

Song No. 21   They Sent It Up From London

The Nameless   *They sent it up from London*
                      With soldiers either side
                      The money
                      The money
                      The money
                      The money always follows the money
                      And poverty has no place left to hide.

                      The directors all make money
                      The investors all make money
                      Oh and we almost forgot to mention
                      William Paterson
                      Pleads poverty
                      And gets a pension.
                      How nice to have a pension.

                      A few years later
                      The money that's left over
                      Is handed to a brand new institution . . . .

A **Banker** *from the early eighteenth century comes on, makes a little formal speech.*

Banker   And so in conclusion, to our investors I would say this: to no establishment could our money and trust be with more propriety confided than to our eminent offspring . . . the Royal Bank of Scotland.

The Nameless   *They brought it through the high street*
                      One sunny day in June
                      The money
                      The money
                      The money always follows the money
                      And he who pays the piper calls the tune.

*A **Piper** enters and plays a lament as the gold is shovelled and the banknotes unloaded.*

The Nameless   Thomas Dalrymple, planter. Dead of the fever.

Charles Hamilton, midshipman. Dead of the flux.

Jacob Yorkland, volunteer. Dead of the flux.

James Davidson, planter. Dead of the fever.

Henry Charters, volunteer. Dead of the flux.

Adam Hill, planter. Dead of the flux.

Walter Eliot, midshipman. Dead of the fever.

David Henderson, sailor. Dead of the flux.

Andrew Brown, cabin boy. Drowned.

Lieutenant Hugh Hay.

Robert Gaudie, planter.

James Montgomerie, sailor.

John Malbon, merchant,

Margaret Paterson, wife of William Paterson.

The music dies.

*The **Piper** withdraws. **Paterson** crosses the stage, head bowed, carrying a single wooden cross. The **Nameless** whisper/chant the next song.*

Song No. 22   Make A List (Reprise)

The Nameless   *When there's nothing must be missed*
Make a list
Make a list
Get the world around you under your control.
To make sure that you exist
Make a list
Make a list
Make a list . . . .

George Menzies, planter.

Walter Johnson, surgeon's mate.

John Aird, planter.

Henry Grapes, trumpeter.

Peter Telfer, planter.

John Burrell, sailor.

Daniel Martin, sailor.

Lieutenant James Inglis.

William McClellan, boy.

Song No. 23   Trade Begets Trade (Reprise)

Paterson   *Trade begets trade*

All   *Trade begets trade*

Paterson   *Money makes money*

All   *Money makes money*

Paterson   *Wealth creates wealth*

All   *Wealth creates wealth*
Riches from riches
Piled upon riches
To the end of the world.

Banknotes descend upon the heads of the audience. On each banknote is written the name of a colonist who died.

Curtain.

Bullet Catch

Rob Drummond

Dedicated to our friend, Ross Ramsay

Bullet Catch was first performed by Rob Drummond at The Arches, Glasgow in 2009 as part of the Behaviour Festival.

Characters

William Wonder   Rob Drummond
Charles Garth   A Random Audience Member

Co-director   Rob Drummond
Co-director   David Overend
Stage Designer   Francis Gallop
Lighting Designer   Alberto Santos Belido
Sound Designer   Ross Ramsay
Stage Manager   Deanne Jones
Arches Artistic Director   Jackie Wylie
Arches Production Manager   Abby McMillan

Author/Performer's Note

It should be stressed that each assistant was selected without preordainment from the theatre audience during the performance. At no point was a plant used.

In this text the assistant is named Lisa, after one of my more memorable volunteers. The dialogue is not necessarily directly drawn from her show alone but is intended rather as a representation of some of the many responses and dialogues which occurred organically during the run.

Much of this script occurred as written. However, due to the live entertainment feel and the rogue element of an unprepared audience member onstage, improvisation was employed throughout. Many of the most magical moments in the show occurred as a result of this approach.

[I have included in this text bracketed notes which explain and detail some of the more unusual moments.]

Scene One

BLACK BALL.

Charles Garth *enters wearing a large overcoat. He nervously surveys the crowd.*

Garth A kind, mild mannered man with no history of violence or mental illness walks into a room full of people. Not knowing anyone and not knowing what to do with himself, he takes a seat.

The man places his overcoat on the back of the seat. He becomes **William Wonder**.

Wonder One hour later he is surprised to find himself the centre of attention, and as the crowd look on in silence, he is persuaded to shoot a man in the face. How did this happen? Is it possible to persuade someone to do something they do not wish to do?

Wonder *smiles at the audience.*

Ladies and gentlemen, I require a volunteer.

But I don't want anyone up here against their will so could *everyone* please put their hand into the air.

And now if the idea of coming up on stage tonight makes you want to kill yourself, please drop your hand to your side. Thank you. If you are not comfortable talking about yourself, your life, or reading out loud in front of a group of people, please put your hand down. If you are under eighteen, for legal reasons, please put your hand down. Thanks. Being honest with yourself and – no judgement – if you've had maybe one too many drinks today, then please put your hand down. I can't have anyone up here who is even a little bit inebriated. And lastly, if you are at all uncomfortable handling live snakes then . . . don't worry because there are none in the show.

Now, I'm going to walk around the audience and make eye contact with everyone who still has their hand in the air.

Please take this quite seriously and hold my gaze because it's important I get the right person up here.

Wonder *prowls the edge of the stage making eye contact with the willing volunteers. He stops occasionally. Looks deeply into some eyes. Glances at others. Smiles at some faces. Puzzles at others. This process is careful. Deliberate. Never rushed.*

He selects three **Volunteers** *from the crowd and thanks the others for their enthusiasm. He wishes he could have used them all.*

He turns his attention to one of the three and picks up a velvet bag from a table.

Could you please confirm this bag is empty?

They confirm.

Now, I have here two white balls and one black ball.

Wonder *puts the balls into the bag.*

I want each of you to put your hand into the bag and pick out a ball, but make sure to keep your hand held tightly around it until I tell you to look at it.

They remove one ball each.

Now, I'm going to turn my back and when I do, you all have five seconds to hold your ball up so everyone can see it.

Wonder *turns his back and begins a countdown from five. When he is finished he turns back. He is now the only one in the room who does not know the location of the black ball.*

Now, I'm just going to start by asking you all a very simple question.

He turns to the **First Volunteer**.

What is your name?

Lisa   Lisa.

Wonder   Is your name Lisa?

Lisa   Yes.

He repeats this procedure with the other two **Volunteers**. *They all answer, 'Yes.'*

[On one occasion an audience member replied, 'No'. It was late in the run and I was feeling cocky so I decided to take a risk and made sure he became my assistant. That particular show went very well, but in general it is wise to avoid comedians.]

OK, so what I've done there is found a kind of a base reading – I now know what you look and sound like when you are telling the truth. Assuming, of course, you have given me the right name.

Now, what I want you to do next is extremely simple – I want you to lie. No matter what I ask you, the answer must be 'Yes.' Understand?

They all say, 'Yes.'

Good start.

As the lighting closes in so does **Wonder** *on* **Lisa**.

The answers to the following questions are always 'Yes.'

Is your name Charles Garth?

Are you forty years old?

Are we in London?

Is it 7.30pm on the 6th June 1912?

Are you a labourer in a ship yard on the Thames?

Do you have a wife and a young son?

Does your son leave a lemon drop on the dresser each night for you to find when you return from work?

Have you come to watch a magic show?

Are you on your own?

You've come to a magic show on your own?

Wonder *turns to the* **Second Volunteer**.

Is your name William Henderson?

Are you the most exciting young magician in the Commonwealth?

Are you performing a Bullet Catch tonight?

In front of an audience of two thousand?

Have you got a bad feeling about the show tonight?

Do you wake up with a bad feeling most days?

Do you find it hard to connect with people?

Do you believe that free will is an illusion?

Wonder *'notices', and smiles at, the* **Third Volunteer**.

Are you William Henderson's wife?

Do you love him?

Do you find him devastatingly attractive?

Are you pregnant with your first child?

Are you scared to watch his shows?

Are you fearful one night he will not return?

Is tonight that night?

The world opens out once more and **Wonder** *turns nonchalantly to the audience.*

OK, ladies and gentlemen, I now have a good idea of what they look like when they are lying. So, one last question and you must all answer 'Yes', no matter what the real answer may be.

Understand?

They all say, 'Yes.'

Are you holding the black ball?

Wonder *asks the question over and over, switching his attention from* **Volunteer** *to* **Volunteer**, *trying to catch them out by varying the intensity and direction of the questions. He thinks he senses something in the* **Third Volunteer**. *Stops. Asks them the question one more time.*

He takes a deep breath.

I think you are lying. Open your hand.

The hand opens. To his obvious relief, **Wonder** *is correct.*

He takes the ball from them and refocuses.

He continues to ask the question of the remaining **Volunteers***, encouraged by his good start.*

'Are you holding the black ball? Are you holding the black ball?'

Back and forth. Back and forth.

It's difficult now. He tells the **Second Volunteer** *that they are a tricky one.*

He asks the question again.

He has decided.

He could be wrong. He is sometimes wrong.

He points to **Lisa***.*

I think . . . you are holding the black ball.

Could you both reveal on the count of three.

One, two, three.

Wonder *flinches at this moment, convinced he may be wrong.*

But he isn't.

And he receives his reward in the form of applause.

Scene Two

CONTEXT.

Wonder *turns his attention to the black ball holder.*

Now, it was Lisa, wasn't it?

Lisa, my name is William Wonder, I'm a famous magician, you must have heard of me?

Lisa Yes.

The audience laugh.

Wonder Lisa, my name is William and I don't have a gun. Comforting words to hear, I'm sure you'll agree. Lisa, I don't have a gun but do you have an item on you that we could use to represent a firearm?

Lisa *offers up a mobile phone.*

[Other items including books, jewellery, inhalers and glasses cases are often proffered but by far and away the most popular is the iPhone.]

And now would you please join me on stage? I'm sure everyone will give you a warm round of applause as you make your way up.

Lisa *stands on stage.*

Don't worry.

I hate it when people are asked on stage and then made a fool of – I'm not going to do that to you. And please don't feel awkward – no one is looking at you and thinking you're standing weird or anything – they're all too concerned with themselves – we're all the same and we're all in this together with you, aren't we?

The audience all agree. 'Yes.'

Would you mind just slipping this on?

Lisa *puts on the overcoat – she now represents* **Charles Garth**.

[At this stage I sometimes comment on how I have already lied about not making them look a fool, depending on how ill-fitting the jacket appears. I always follow this up by kindly rolling up their sleeves for them.]

Does everyone know what a Bullet Catch is?

The Bullet Catch is really pretty simple. A bullet is marked and loaded into a firearm. The firearm is given to an assistant, whether predetermined or newly acquired from the audience.

Wonder *gives the mobile phone to* **Lisa**.

The assistant, carefully, takes the weapon and holds it in the safety position.

Wonder *shows* **Lisa** *the safety position, the 'gun' pointed away from her feet towards the ground and never at the audience.*

The assistant then stands on a designated spot.

Wonder *places* **Lisa** *on her spot.*

The magician takes up his position . . .

Wonder *stands opposite her.*

. . . and encourages the assistant to aim at his mouth.

Wonder *encourages* **Lisa** *to aim the phone.*

And when the magician gives the signal – sometimes verbally, but in Henderson's case by lowering his arm from above his head to his side – the assistant squeezes the trigger, sending a bullet hurtling at five hundred miles per hour towards the magician's head with a loud bang.

Wonder *drops his hand to his side and waits to see if* **Lisa** *will take the initiative and make a 'bang' noise. She does. It is comically weak. He thanks her and invites her to take a seat onstage.*

Usually this is followed by the magician staggering backwards before revealing the marked bullet between his teeth. But it doesn't always happen this way. In 1613 the inventor of the stunt, Coullew of Lorraine, was accidentally shot in the head when his assistant – who also happened to be his wife – decided to down half a bottle of absinthe before the show to calm her nerves. Arnold Buck in 1840 died when a volunteer secretly loaded nails from his pocket into the barrel of the gun. And Raoul Curran, forty years later, successfully accomplished the stunt only for an audience member to stand up, take out his own pistol and shout 'Oi, Curran, catch this.'

There's a reason this is known as magic's riskiest stunt. When William Henderson declared he was going to attempt it in London using an audience member to pull the trigger, his friend and mentor Houdini wrote to him.

Wonder *takes out a letter.*

Now, my dear boy, this is advice from the heart, don't try the damned Bullet Catching, no matter how sure you may feel of its success. There is always the biggest kind of risk that something will go wrong. And we can't afford to lose Henderson. You have enough good material to maintain your position at the head of the profession. And you owe it to your friends and your family to cut out all the things that entail risk of your life. Please, William, listen to your old friend Harry who loves you as his own son and don't do it. You have too much to lose. You are free to choose not to do this.

This last line is delivered directly to **Lisa**.

Of course, Henderson ignored this advice and one hundred years ago was killed instantly in front of two thousand people at the London Palace Theatre when kind, mild-mannered labourer Charles Garth shot him in the face.

Garth is reported to have stood stock still for a good two minutes after the shooting, presumably waiting for Henderson to get up. When the police arrived he was still clutching the weapon. They took it from him, secured it in a lock box (**Wonder** *feigns difficulty in pulling the phone from* **Lisa**'*s grasp then puts the item very carefully into an empty box and closes the lid*) and took him in for questioning.

Over the next few months Garth writes a series of letters to his sister in Manchester.

Wonder *hands* **Lisa** *a piece of paper. He leans in and instructs her of her task.*

Now, here's where I need you to help me out. Please could you read this clearly, loudly and slowly so everyone can hear – don't worry about acting too much, just read it. Is that OK?

Lisa *confirms that she understands her role and* **Wonder** *moves to the rear of the stage while the focus shifts to her.*

Lisa   Dearest Bette,

You'll have read by now what happened – the damndest thing. Please do not worry, I'm fine and well – after all, it wasn't me who got hurt, so I've no cause to complain. The Rozzers asked me all sorts of questions after the show. As if I had shot the poor bugger on purpose. It was just a horrible accident, that's all. There's one thing I can't help wondering though. Would it have turned out differently if I hadn't picked the word 'SAVE'?

Scene Three

KILL, SAVE, LOVE.

Framed pictures featuring the words KILL, SAVE and LOVE are now highlighted.

Wonder *is looking at the word SAVE.*

Wonder   Freud said that when we meet a new person – hello, my name is William – three questions instantly, in the merest of nanoseconds, register in our minds. Can I kill it, can it kill me, can I shag it? Every time we meet someone new. Do I fight, flee or make love? Every time. Kill, save, love. Don't feel guilty – we all do it. We have no control over this. We have no control whatsoever.

You see, these questions are built into our DNA – they echo back in time to the days when we were little more than animals and every encounter with another living being was life, death or procreation and nothing else. Think about that. How important would it be to pick the right person to connect with if you knew your life depended on it?

Again, this last line is pointed towards **Lisa**.

Lisa, I'd like you now to think carefully and when you are ready, speak one of these three words aloud.

Lisa *considers this deeply.*

Don't rush into it.

Lisa *picks her word. KILL.*

[The selection of the word is genuinely free each night but only two assistants have ever selected KILL at this stage. No matter the selected word, I always react like it means a lot. KILL is the rarest but easiest word to react to. I include this selection here as it is undeniably the most dramatic choice.]

OK. We'll come back to this later.

[My next line always depends on the word they had selected. If they pick KILL, I go with . . . 'I can see we have some work to do in order to make a connection.' If they pick SAVE or LOVE I say, 'I can see we've already started to develop some sort of connection. Let's see if we can test this connection to see if it's real.']

Now. Lisa.

I'd like you to stand up and pick one of these books – look at the titles and covers and maybe one will jump out above the rest – and when you've done that please sit down with it on the edge of the chest there.

What book did you choose?

Lisa   The Super Ego.

Wonder   Why did you choose that one?

Lisa   Because I think I have a tendency to be a little bit of a narcissist.

Wonder   Don't we all?

Pause. **Wonder** *turns away.*

I'd like you now to turn to any page and pick any word.

Try not to pick something too long or complicated – pick something that you know the meaning of and that everyone in the room is likely to know – try to work with me here not against me. And when you've done that please close the book.

Now, I don't want this word spoken aloud so could you please write it down on this Post-it in nice big clear capital letters so when we pass it into the audience they will be able to read it.

Thank you. And when you've done that, could someone from the far side please step onto the stage and just take the Post-it. Lisa, you keep hold of the book.

Now, you don't need to all look at it individually, just show it to a few people at a time and let it work its way round the audience being careful not to flash it towards me.

Wonder *sits nearer the assistant.*

Have you ever fancied someone at a party and made a right mess of chatting them up? Here's a handy hint – instead of going right up to them and saying, 'Hey, I really like you so eh, how's about it?' – hold off, get yourself within eyesight of them and using your peripheral vision start to mimic their body language. Before long, they'll feel an inexplicable connection to you. And when you do eventually go up and talk to them, they'll feel like they've known you for years, but they won't know why. This works. I wouldn't be married otherwise.

I used to tell people that I got into magic because I wanted to be able to amaze other people. Affect them. But I have come to realise that that is not true at all. It was so they could affect me. So they would think I was special. So I could make a connection that I found hard to make any other way.

Now, I'm going to go through the alphabet and when I hit the letter that your word begins with, I want you to scream – YES – inside your head.

Wonder *mimics* **Lisa***'s body language. She is slightly awkward. Nervous.* **Wonder** *accentuates this without it becoming unkind.*

He speaks the alphabet, quickly at first. He senses something and narrows down his search to a section of the alphabet. He reminds

Lisa *not to give any clues but simply to shout YES in her head. He narrows the letter down to two possible candidates. R and S.*

He speaks these directly to **Lisa** *one at a time, gauging her non-response each time.*

He guesses the letter. 'S'.

The audience chuckle. **Lisa** *is amazed.*

Now I just want you to visualise this word as an image.

Lisa *frowns involuntarily.*

OK. So from that reaction I can tell that this is not an easily visualised word. So it's not a noun like a sheep or a sideboard. It is more of a concept. Am I right?

Lisa *nods, embarrassed that she has given this away.*

OK, so hold that word in your mind, let it flow through you and without moving or miming just embody that word and feel whatever it means to you. And do that while I talk.

Wonder *addresses the audience while* **Lisa** *thinks.*

I think the need for the acceptance and love of fellow human beings is a powerful determinant of behaviour and some believe that it is this need that keeps humanity alive. Without it there would be no point to life. If you lose that need for human connection then you lose hope and ultimately there is no meaning to anything.

So pulling someone at a party shouldn't really be that tough.

Even if you are . . . SHY.

Lisa *is amazed. The audience gasp. And clap.*

[I usually try to integrate the chosen word into the final sentence of my monologue but sometimes just pulling the word from thin air is more incredible, especially if the assistant has tried to be clever by picking a particularly difficult word, like antidisestablishmentarianism. True story.]

Wonder *asks* **Lisa** *to read again from the card.*

Focus shifts to **Lisa/Garth**.

Lisa   Dearest Bette,

I appear to be famous. I was stopped in the street today by one of Henderson's fans. He called me a murderer. The silly thing is that I know I'm not to blame – I was only doing what I was bloody well told – but I still can't shake the feeling that there was something wrong that night. Something in Henderson's eyes that I should have recognised. This morning Samuel gave me a lemon drop and said, 'Why are you never happy Daddy?' Always looking after me that one – he takes after his aunt.

Scene Four

MIND READING.

Wonder *takes the card back from* **Lisa**. *He asks her* . . .

Wonder   Why are you never happy?

She does not know how to respond.

Sorry – it's unfair of me to put you on the spot like that. It's just, you read that so well. I've read these extracts hundreds of times but it's only when someone else reads them, and reads them well, that I can really hear them and understand them and get a sense of who Garth was, so thank you for that.

I wonder if we might try to experience something that Garth and Henderson experienced that night on stage. You see, Henderson was obsessed with a routine that dealt with the formula for happiness.

Do you want to know the secret to happiness?

Lisa   Sure.

Wonder   Sometimes knowing the secret isn't all it's cracked up to be. During the performance that night, Henderson gave away the secret to one of his tricks and people were not happy at all.

The theory states that there are seven areas of human life upon which our happiness or contentment depends. It has been demonstrated that if the majority of these areas remain 'in good working order' one feels one's life has purpose. Meaning.

Wonder *lifts some playing cards from a side table.*

Now, I am quite happy to talk about these areas because, much like Henderson, my life is pretty much in good working order. So by that logic I should be a very happy person, right?

He stares at **Lisa**. *She nods.*

That night Henderson sat Garth down on stage and asked him about his own life. Do you mind if I ask you about your own life, so we can get to know each other a little better? You don't have to talk about anything you don't want to.

Could you move up so I can sit next to you?

This is not magic by the way – this is a conversation. In many ways I find this far more difficult.

The seven areas are . . . Travel, Health, Education, Sex, Career, Ambition and Money.

So, which area would you be happy to talk about?

[In this section I always let the assistant lead the way and choose the areas they would most like to talk about. Lisa, surprisingly, chose HEALTH, which, along with SEX, is the least chosen card. She told me that she had epilepsy and that her doctors had been reticent in allowing her to fly from her home in the USA to Edinburgh at all. 'I'm not meant to put myself in stressful situations, in case I get an attack.' This declaration only served to raise the stakes in the room. I usually try to link this section back to Garth in some way and finished on this occasion by saying that he also had some health issues related to his work in the shipyards.]

Thanks for sharing, Lisa.

Now, imagine there are two people. One is laughing and one is crying. Who do you feel more connected to?

Lisa   The crying one.

Wonder   Why?

Lisa   Because I want to see if there's anything I can do to help them.

Wonder   So you like to use your positivity to help other people?

Lisa   Yes.

Wonder   Are you generally quite a positive person?

Lisa   I can be.

Wonder   But sometimes not?

Lisa   Sometimes not.

Wonder   We're all the same.

I want you now to pick a card. (**Lisa** *picks a card.*) Remember it and hold it between your hands so I can't see it.

Now, think of a memory associated with the word on that card. A time when you felt positive and full of hope and sure that there was a point to all this. A time when thoughts of the finite nature of life were far away. A time when immortality seemed possible. Or just a time you were happy.

Is there a specific time period associated with this memory? A month, year, date, time of year?

I'm going to do something 'psychics' won't do and that's make hard and fast, specific predictions, so they might not be spot on.

So, look at me.

I want you to go back to the time associated with this memory and remember what it felt like to be you at that time. And think very specifically now of the date or the time period and focus solely on that.

Wonder *writes down his prediction on a piece of paper, folds it up and places it on the table.*

Now, tell everyone the time period – not the memory itself – just the time period associated with it.

Lisa   It was 2004.

Wonder *looks at his prediction on the table. No changing it now.*

He shrugs.

Wonder   OK. Not bad. I don't always get these spot on, as I said.

Now, is there a person associated with this memory?

Lisa   Yes.

Wonder   I want you to imagine you are looking at them now – remember what it is like to be in their company. Look at me and imagine I am them. And now, using only your eyes, just draw their name on the back of this pad. All the time keeping the memory alive in your mind.

Now, names are difficult because of the different spellings and variants but we'll see how we do.

Wonder *writes his prediction and folds it on the table.*

And finally concentrate specifically on the word on the card – sorry, could you just let everyone know the name?

Lisa   It was Michael.

Wonder *sighs.*

Wonder   OK. Not spot on but never mind.

Lastly, I want you to just concentrate on the word on the card itself. Just think of that word and how it relates to the memory as a whole. And look at me.

Wonder *writes his prediction and places it on the table.*

Would you mind sharing the memory?

[Some assistants are more willing than others to share. Some speak for minutes, others for seconds but I always simply stand back and let them go, usually with touching results. Lisa told us a story about meeting her boyfriend who had subsequently become her husband.]

That's a lovely memory. Are you generally quite a happy person?

Lisa   Generally.

Wonder   Yeah. That's pretty much what Garth said too.

Wonder *picks up the first prediction.*

Now, I think having heard your story, I've got this one correct. Please hold up the card you selected.

Lisa *holds up the SEX card.*

Yes, I got this correct but the overriding feeling I got was one of love, so I wrote that as well.

Wonder *reveals his prediction. It says, 'LOVE/SEX.'*

Lisa   Yes, that makes sense. It was more love than sex really.

The audience applaud.

Wonder   And now, that name. It was Michael, wasn't it?

I'm afraid I got this slightly wrong . . .

Wonder *opens the second prediction. It says Mike.*

I wrote Mike. Does that make any sense?

Lisa   Yes. That's what I called him, but his mum didn't like it.

The audience applaud.

Wonder   And finally, the date. What did you say the date was?

Lisa   It would have been 2004.

Wonder   Ah, well, this one, I couldn't decide so I put . . .

He reveals the final prediction. '2003? 2004?'

So, I didn't fully commit to that one.

Lisa   No. It happened at a New Year's party so . . . that's amazing, yes, it would have straddled over both those years.

Wonder   Well, that explains why I was getting both years in my head. Thank you so much for sharing, Lisa. Give her a big round of applause.

The audience respond and **Lisa** *stares at* **Wonder**. *She is stunned.*

Wonder *smiles at her – they have grown closer.*

Scene Five

LEVITATION.

Wonder *reads from a piece of paper.*

Wonder   Dear Rob,

He looks at the audience and says, 'That's my real name.'

We have carried out a risk assessment and, even though you have assured us you can pull it off and that it is vital to the show, I must advise you against doing an actual Bullet Catch during the show. There are simply far too many things that could go wrong. Could you just talk about the Bullet Catch instead of doing it? It's fascinating stuff.

If you still want to do it we won't stand in your way but I will need you to sign a liability waiver. I just think it's not worth the risk.

Hope you are not too disappointed,

Kevin McCallum

Production Manager

The Traverse

Wonder *addresses the audience.*

The Traverse weren't the only ones worried about me doing this show. My own parents were horrified when I told them what I was doing. But mainly because they are religious and think that quite a lot of what I do is already fairly close to blasphemy.

My dad is a minister actually – as was Henderson's. You know, the more I learn about him the more similarities I find. If I believed in reincarnation . . . But I don't. Believe.

When I was young, I used to try to make things move. Float. Just by staring at them. Did you ever do that? We had an old side table in the front room and I remember sitting for hours trying to make it move. I don't know why I did that. I think I remember my dad saying during one of his sermons that anything was possible if you just believed enough. So I guess I was trying to test that out.

Do you believe? In anything? That there is a purpose to all this?

Lisa *considers this deeply.*

Lisa   Yes.

Wonder   What do you believe in?

Lisa   I believe in people.

Wonder   People.

Lisa   People.

[This felt like a perfect little exchange so I left it at that but this section often lasts longer. Other things people have believed in include energy, nature and science. So far no one has said God. No one has said nothing.]

Wonder *turns his attention back to the words KILL, SAVE and LOVE.*

Would you like to change your mind on the word? You are on KILL at the moment.

Lisa *thinks.*

Lisa   Yes.

Wonder   Yes, you'd like to change?

Lisa   Yes, I'd like to change.

Wonder   OK. What do you wish to change to?

Lisa   Love.

Silence.

Wonder   Are you sure?

Lisa   Yes.

Silence.

Wonder   When the table didn't move I just assumed I didn't believe enough. But it was weird because it really felt like I was believing. But the minute I started to think about believing – trying to make myself believe – that meant I didn't truly believe. You shouldn't have to think. It doesn't matter.

The sun is burning out. That is a fact. It's what stars do and no scientist would refute that. It will eventually be gone. And so will everything. It's important to believe in something (God, fate, destiny – as ludicrous as they might sound – I mean, I think we all know deep down that this is all there is. It is as simple as it seems). It is important to at least trick yourself into believing in something because if you don't you are in danger of being swallowed up by this fact.

Wonder *has lost himself. Music brings him back. He turns to* **Lisa**.

Could you take my hand?

He takes her by the hand and leads her to a side table with a tablecloth and a small box on it.

Thank you for your help so far tonight. Just stand there and take the table cloth like I do. And look at me.

Wonder *and* **Lisa** *hold two corners of the tablecloth each. The music grows. Beautiful melancholic strings.* **Wonder** *looks into* **Lisa***'s eyes and she looks back. It's not a romantic moment they share but rather a connection, one human being to another.*

The table slowly, gracefully lifts from the floor and floats upwards until the cloth is tight again. **Wonder** *invites* **Lisa** *to look underneath the cloth. She does and the table rises quickly upwards further still, until it is dancing at eye level between them. A slow waltz.* **Lisa** *looks underneath again, waves her hand over the top, searching for the secret. Searching in vain.*

She grins in delight at the miracle happening before her eyes. Shakes her head. **Wonder** *takes his hands off the table cloth completely and removes a lemon drop from the little box on top.*

He hands it to **Lisa** *while the table remains floating between them. The table slowly comes to rest.*

The music fades.

[It is impossible to do proper justice here to the beauty of this trick – it was designed by master of levitation, Dirk Losander. Clips can be found online. It always leaves the vast majority of the audience stunned.]

You can give that lemon drop to anyone in the audience as a gift.

Lisa *hands the lemon drop to an audience member.* **Wonder** *finds out their name and asks them if they liked the trick. He then asks them . . .*

Do you want to know how it's done?

Man   Yes.

Wonder   Why?

Man   Because it seems impossible.

Wonder   And you need to know?

Man   Yes.

Wonder   Would anyone else like to know how it was done?

Wonder *goes around the audience, canvassing them on why they would or would not like to know the secret.*

[The majority always want to know. Their reasons mainly fall into the sphere of frustration. 'I simply have to know!' One of the more beautiful answers involved the phrase, 'I believe in truth'. Those in the minority who do not wish to know mainly state that if you know how it works you instantly spoil the beauty. 'Sometimes it's better not to know things.' There are no wrong answers in this section. In the context any answer appears profound.]

I'll tell you what, seeing as most of you do want to know, those of you who don't – those of you who wish to remain in ignorant bliss – should cover your eyes. For the rest of you just keep watching.

The music replays. **Wonder** *dismantles and packs away the table, revealing the secret. A sad sequence somehow.*

[This has been a matter of contention amongst some members of the magic community. I accept fully that revealing the secret to a trick not of my own design is ethically fraught. However, the relationship this creates between myself and my audience, the comment on the nature of truth and depression, the moment of melancholic and profound theatre that this action makes possible, convinces me that such an act is justified in a theatre show. And anyway, they choose to look.]

After the table is packed away **Wonder** *instructs the audience members who did not look to open their eyes.*

He speaks to one of them.

Wonder   Thank you for not looking.

He turns to the majority.

Thank you for looking.

He turns his attention to **Lisa**.

Now, Lisa.

You can say no to this but . . .

I was wondering . . .

If I could have a hug?

[No one has said 'No'.]

Lisa *and* **Wonder** *hug. A moment of sheer human connection.*

Wonder *hands her the next card and asks her to read again.*

Lisa   I was called into the inquest today – I wore my good suit and bowler hat and someone took a photograph of me as I left. They're saying the shooting might not have been an accident after all. They reckon the daft sod might have planned the whole thing himself – reckon he was suffering from melancholia. You'll think me a right soft clot but I cried when they told me that. Funny thing. Don't know why.

Wonder   Why are you crying, Mr Garth?

Lisa   I'm sorry, Your Honour.

Wonder   Had you any indication that Mr Henderson was weak in the mind.

Lisa   Weak?

Wonder   That he was planning his own death.

Lisa   No.

Wonder   You signed his will, did you not?

Lisa   It was part of the show.

Wonder   You witnessed his will live on stage.

Lisa   Everyone was looking at me.

Wonder   In your opinion was Mr Henderson inebriated that night?

Lisa   Inebriated?

Wonder   Drunk. Was the man drunk?

Lisa   I don't think so.

Wonder   You are quite sure you had never met Mr Henderson before going on stage?

Lisa   Never.

Wonder   Because I'm sure you are aware that the use of stooges in these types of variety shows is well documented.

Lisa   I did not know that, Your Honour.

Wonder   Are you a nihilist, Mr Garth?

Lisa   I don't know what that is, Your Honour.

Wonder   Were you aware that Mr Henderson was a known nihilist?

Lisa   I don't know what that is, Your Honour.

Scene Six

SHATTERED.

Wonder   Why would he do it? He had everything. He was a rising star in his profession, wealthy, well-travelled, in perfect health, in love and with a baby on the way.

But in the time Henderson was performing, existential nihilism, a belief that life is without meaning, purpose or intrinsic value, was becoming the antidote to religion. And with the growing understanding of the universe, that we were just a drop in an endless ocean, that our sun would one day be gone, that free will is perhaps just an illusion . . . it's easy to see why.

Wonder *picks up a glass beer bottle and hammer. He places the bottle into a paper bag and holds it by the neck.*

So maybe it wasn't a failed trick after all but rather. . . the *ultimate* trick. He made a man, who bore him no ill will, shoot him dead, live on stage. He took control of his destiny and made an immortal mark on the world.

And maybe that's why they all did it. Risked their lives. So they could achieve some sort of immortality. We all die some time. At least they went out with a bang.

Wonder *hits the bottle with the hammer.*

Do you believe in free will? That we are free to choose what we do? That we can change the script?

Lisa   Yes.

Wonder   Can you give me an example of a free choice you have made recently?

Lisa   I came to see your show.

Wonder   And I'm glad you did. But what led you to come see the show?

Lisa   I saw it in the magazine and it looked interesting.

Wonder   And what led you to be looking at that magazine?

Lisa   I love theatre.

Wonder   And what led you to be a lover of theatre?

Lisa   My parents always took me when I was younger.

Wonder   I'm sorry for these questions, Lisa. What I'm getting at is that there is always a reason for any decision and these reasons can ultimately be traced back to your birth.

Did you choose to be created?

Lisa   No.

Wonder   Did you choose to be born?

Lisa   No.

Wonder   I don't mean to hurt you with any of this – I'm just stating the facts . . .

Scientifically, if the first variable in a chain of causality is not free then all subsequent thoughts and choices fundamentally cannot be completely free either. Cannot be.

[This theory takes longer to explain to some than others. To me it is completely rational and makes absolute sense but to some it is extremely offensive to suggest that free will cannot technically, in its truest form, exist. No one has ever truly fought me on it in the end, though. At least not on stage.]

This means we can't be held accountable for the 'bad' things we do. But neither can we feel proud or validated by our achievements.

So. Whatever happens next. It's not your fault. It's not my fault. It's just what had to happen.

Wonder *breaks the bottle and carefully takes the neck from the bag.*

He puts it neck down into a hole in a small plinth, leaving the sharp edge sticking upwards. He then covers the plinth with another brown bag making it indistinguishable to three other such upturned bags.

There then follows a silent process by which these four bags are mixed, the result being that no one in the room, **Wonder** *and* **Lisa** *included, have any idea where the broken bottle is.*

Wonder *looks at the audience.*

Does anyone need them mixed any more?

The audience laugh nervously.

Wonder   Now, Lisa, which bag is the bottle not under?

Silence.

Lisa   I have no idea.

Wonder   Of course you don't.

I'll rephrase the question if it would help.

Which bag do you choose?

Lisa   Choose for what?

Wonder   Lisa, do you trust me?

Lisa   Kind of.

Wonder   Pick one of the bags.

Lisa *points at one of the bags.*

This one?

Lisa   Yes.

No sooner has she spoken than **Wonder** *hammers his hand hard down onto the bag, crushing it completely.*

The room takes a breath. It's not the bag with the bottle.

Wonder *composes himself. That could have been bad.*

Wonder   Now, Lisa.

Which bag is the bottle under?

Lisa*, now with the knowledge of what her choice means, refuses to answer.*

It's OK, Lisa, whatever happens, it's not your fault, it's not my fault, it's just what had to happen.

Will you pick a bag for me, Lisa?

Lisa *points to another bag.*

Wonder   Are you sure?

Lisa   No.

The audience laugh nervously.

Wonder   This bag here?

Lisa   Yes.

Lisa *covers her eyes as* **Wonder** *raises his hand. He hesitates. Looks at the audience. He slams his hand down.*

He is safe.

He takes a moment to catch his breath.

Wonder   OK, Lisa. Final decision.

Two bags left.

Which bag is the bottle not under?

Long silence. **Lisa** *points at a bag. An audience member stifles a 'No!'*

No?

Do you think she should choose the other one?

The audience member says 'I don't know.'

Lisa, final decision please.

Lisa *points again at the same bag. Her hand is shaking.*

Wonder *raises his hand over the bag. The room holds its breath.*

Wonder's *hand is shaking now too.*

He tries to control it.

He pauses.

Then slams his hand down.

He doesn't yell in pain. There is no blood. He triumphantly raises the bag on the final plinth to reveal the jagged bottle.

The audience erupt in relief and pleasure.

Lisa *is almost in tears.*

[I took no joy in this reaction. As I will describe later, the audience member's safety and well-being is uppermost in my mind at all times.]

Wonder *gives her another hug.*

He talks to her and calms her down.

He makes sure she is OK.

He gives her another card to read.

She is still shaking while she reads it.

Lisa   It has been deemed death by misadventure, which is just a fancy way of saying a bloody accident as far as I can tell. His life was perfectly in order so they say suicide is impossible. I suppose they must be right. The thing is, I've been having these dreams, but not during the night, during the bloody day – wide awake dreams like I'm back there on the bloody stage. And he's asking me if I'm sure I want to go ahead. If I understand what's going to happen. And I think maybe I did understand. I think I know what it was that I saw in his eyes. You see, I've seen those eyes before, Bette.

Scene Seven

BULLET CATCH.

Wonder *has brought forward the box into which the mobile phone was inserted. He opens it up. It has transformed into a handgun.*

Wonder   This is a Glock 17, the safety is on and there are no bullets in the chamber.

Could you take that in the safety position please?

Lisa *hesitantly takes the gun and reacts to the weight.*

Yes, it's heavy, isn't it?

The safety position is with your hand around the handle, finger not on the trigger and pointed towards the ground, away from your feet. Never point it at the audience, never point it at yourself and only point it at me if I specifically ask you to.

OK. I think you know what I'm going to ask you now.

Over the past hour I've got to know you. I've got to genuinely like you and trust you. I would very much like you to be the one to fire the gun, and I think you'll be willing to help me with that.

Lisa *does not seem sure.*

[The reactions to this request have been varied. Some immediately agree and some immediately decline. On the two very rare occasions I couldn't convince the assistant to fire the weapon (even at an inanimate plate) I had to pursue other avenues such as asking the lemon drop receiver to take their place or on one ill-fated occasion asking my mum to come up and help me out. She did. She pointed the gun at my dad. I chastised her and she retreated back to her seat. True story. The vast majority react somewhere in the middle – uncertain, excited, nervous, but ultimately willing. Lisa was one of these. I NEVER ask anyone to shoot the weapon if I don't think they can handle it or if they really genuinely do not want to do it.]

I tell you what, Lisa, let's continue assuming you are going to do it and at any time if you wish to pull out you may do so. OK?

Lisa   OK.

Wonder   Now, if you are going to fire a weapon I need to have something signed.

Wonder *takes out a legal document.*

The audience laugh nervously.

That always gets a reaction but this needs to be done. This is my liability agreement with the venue – it is my legal document and at no time does it become yours – I simply wish you to insert your details into a clause here that states you will not be held liable should anything go wrong – but it is my document, not yours.

A liability agreement is read and signed by both parties.

I also need you to mark the bullet. Oh.

Wait. We don't have any bullets. What was your final decision on the word?

When last we spoke you chose love. Do you wish to change your mind?

Lisa *thinks.*

Lisa   Yes.

Wonder   You wish to change your mind?

Lisa   Yes.

Wonder   OK. What's your final choice?

Lisa   Save.

Wonder   Are you sure?

Lisa   Yes.

Wonder   OK.

Wonder *turns the three words around. KILL is blank. LOVE is blank. But on the rear of SAVE is a message. YOU WILL PICK SAVE. Two bullets are also stuck to the surface.* **Wonder** *removes these.*

It's not your fault – simply a series of events that led you to choose that word above the others. It couldn't have happened any other way.

These are eight millimetre rounds – they are small but don't let that fool you. This is the casing – this will eject from the gun when you fire it. This is the ammunition – this will be heading towards me.

Could you examine these?

Lisa *takes the bullets in her hand.*

And now mark one of them on the tip with this marker.

Lisa *makes a mark on the tip of one of the bullets.*

I now need you to confirm I am actually loading them into this magazine. The marked one first and this one on top, which will be your practice shot.

It's only fair that we give you a practice shot if you'll be firing a gun and this is it.

Wonder *reveals a dinner plate attached to a target.*

You'll be firing at this plate.

Now, I'm going to make your practice shot quite easy so you can get your aim in.

Wonder *positions her fairly close to the target.*

In a moment I'll encourage you to aim at the target, then I'll get to a safe distance and when you are ready you can squeeze the trigger. Could you show me how you intend to aim?

Lisa *aims a shaking hand at the target.*

Thank you.

Have you any gun handling experience?

Lisa   Yes. I've fired a gun before.

Pause.

Wonder   I don't know whether that's a bad thing or a good thing.

Silence.

Don't let your hand go above this line.

When you pull the trigger you will feel a kick. The casing will eject from the side and there will be a loud bang. I'll give you some ear and eye protectors. Audience, when I put my fingers in my ears you please do the same.

OK, so, do you understand the sequence? I'll chamber the round, take off the safety and hand you the gun then go over there. When you are ready just aim at the centre of the target and squeeze the trigger. Once you've done that the next round will automatically be in the chamber so please go back to the safety position. Understand?

Are you OK?

Lisa   To fire at a plate? Yes.

Wonder   Good.

Wonder *chambers the round, hands her the gun and takes his position.* **Lisa** *takes her time, aims and shoots. She hits the plate and it smashes.*

The audience suck in air. This just got very real.

Wonder *hurries to* **Lisa** *who has not put the gun back into the safety position. He lowers it for her. She apologises.*

That's OK.

Well done, how do you feel?

Lisa   OK. But that was just a plate.

Wonder *makes sure the next round is chambered.*

Now, Lisa, I need you to come and stand here.

He positions **Lisa** *in the same spot she was standing when she 'shot' the mobile phone.*

The next shot will be the same only I will be standing in front of the target and you will be aiming at my mouth. I will go over there and raise my hand – that's your cue to raise the gun. When I drop my hand that means I am ready – it does not mean shoot straight away, just that I am ready. You shoot in your own time.

Are you OK?

Lisa   Yes.

Wonder   Are you willing to do this?

Lisa   I don't know.

Wonder *leans in and whispers something in her ear.*

OK. I'll do it.

Wonder   Thank you. You don't have to do anything you don't want to. You can back out at any time.

Audience, if you didn't enjoy watching the plate and you don't think you'll enjoy this next bit then by all means, with my best wishes and full understanding, you may now leave the auditorium. People have left before, please don't be embarrassed. OK.

So everyone understands what is going to happen, then? And everyone's OK with that? Right.

Lisa *takes a deep breath.*

So. You understand the sequence? I raise my hand, you raise
the weapon. I lower my hand, you shoot when you are ready.
Audience, put your fingers in your ears when I raise my hand.

Wonder *re-secures* **Lisa***'s ear protectors. He hands her the gun
and takes his mark.*

Silence. **Wonder** *prepares.*

*He raises his arm in the air. The audience put their fingers in their
ears. Some watch through their hands, others put their heads on
the shoulders of partners. Some lean forward eagerly.*

The tension is broken by **Lisa***.*

Lisa   Are you sure about this?

Nervous laughter. But she is deadly serious.

Wonder   I'm sure.

Silence.

Wonder *focusses.*

Drops his hand.

Time stops.

Lisa *shoots.*

Wonder *falls.*

After a few seconds, during which no one has breathed, **Wonder**
*slowly begins to move. He stands up gingerly and shows the bullet
slug clamped between his teeth. He removes it from his mouth and
shows the mark on the tip to* **Lisa***, who confirms it as her own.
He takes the gun from her trembling hand and asks the audience
to give her a round of applause. He hugs her and thanks her and
helps her back to her seat in the audience.*

Wonder *puts on* **Garth***'s jacket. He is not now* **Wonder**,
Henderson, **Garth** *or* **Rob** *but rather a curious combination of
all the above.*

He takes an old letter from a drawer and reads.

[On one very special occasion I had fallen on a piece of broken dinner plate and cut my hand. By this point the blood was running dramatically down my fingers and as I read the letter it was dripping onto the floor. I remember vividly being absolutely delighted at this stroke of luck as I recited the final monologue. The cut was not deep and didn't hurt too badly but the effect was pure theatre. People afterwards asked the front of house staff how the blood effect was done. It was easy. I actually bled.]

Wonder   I know now what it was that I saw in his eyes. I have seen those eyes before, Bette. Each time I look in the mirror. I saw a sadness, deep and rooted. A hopelessness without reason. I saw it in him and he saw it in me. And he thought I would understand. And I do. (*Looking at* **Lisa**.) But I could never put a fellow through what he has put me through.

Tonight after church I found myself looking out over the bloody Thames. Don't remember even walking but there I was. And forgive me, Bette, but, for a second I thought about how easy it would be. But then I remembered little Sammy. And the lemon drop waiting for me at home.

Why did he not just stop the show and tell me? Why did he not just reach out to me? If I feel like this and if Henderson did then how many more are there out there? I feel like we must look around more. We must find each other. Because really, when it comes down to it, We Are All the Same. There is a point to all this isn't there? And it's each other.

As the lights come down **Wonder** *makes an effort to look every member of the audience in the eye.*

[The final line of the show is always delivered to the assistant and I usually make an effort to personalise it in some way, for example, by adding a reference to what they believe in. 'There is a point to all of this isn't there? And it's each other. It's people.'

After the show I always ask the assistant to wait in the bar for me. It is important to make sure they are in a fit state to re-enter the real world and not too shaken by the experience. After a chat and sometimes a drink they have always emerged feeling ultimately glad to have participated.]

The Artist Man and the Mother Woman

Morna Pearson

*Of all human struggles there is none
so treacherous and remorseless as
the struggle between the artist man
and the mother woman.*

George Bernard Shaw,
Man and Superman

The Artist Man and the Mother Woman was first performed at The Traverse Theatre, Edinburgh on 30 October 2012, with the following cast:

Geoffrey Buncher	Garry Collins
Edie Buncher	Anne Lacey
Thomas	Lewis Howden
Evelyn	Lynn Kennedy
Clara/Woman A/Woman B	Molly Innes

Director	Orla O'Loughlin
Designer	Anthony Lamble
Composer/Sound Designer	Daniel Krass
Lighting Designer	Richard Howell
Assistant Director	Marta Mari
Production Manager	Kevin McCallum
Company Stage Manager	Gemma Turner
Deputy Stage Manager	Catherine Devereux
Assistant Stage Manager	Naomi Stalker
Costume Supervisor	Kat Smith
Voice and Dialect	Ros Steen

Characters

Geoffrey Buncher
Edie Buncher, *his mother*
Thomas, *their neighbour*
Evelyn
Clara
Woman A
Woman B

Scene One

In the Bunchers' kitchen at breakfast time. On the wall there is a very old framed photo of a grinning, toothless fisherman holding a huge fish. Sunlight streams through the window. A rack of toast sits on the table. **Edie** *is opening a box that contains a new digital radio.* **Geoffrey** *enters, dressed for work, but he has obviously just rolled out of bed.*

Geoffrey   Whit's that?

Edie   My new radio.

Geoffrey   Whit's wrong wi the old ain?

Edie   It's old. And they're switching off the hingies that signalify the wavey-bobs. The soundwaves.

Geoffrey   Ay?

Edie   Aerials.

She takes the new radio over to the very old radio, unplugs the old one and passes it towards **Geoffrey**.

Edie   Here, tak this.

Geoffrey *doesn't get a proper grip of the old radio. He watches it drop to the floor.*

Geoffrey   Oops.

Edie   Geoffrey!

Geoffrey   Wis your fault.

Edie   Och, jist shut up and eat your breakfast.

Geoffrey (*stares at the kitchen table*)   Far's the jam?

Edie   Oh, you'll hiv tae open a new ain.

Excited, he opens a cupboard; inside is full of jars of strawberry and raspberry jam.

Geoffrey   Hm. Raspberry or strawberry. Raspberry or strawberry. Raspberry or strawberry.

Strawberry or raspberry. Hm. Rasp or strawb. Rasp or strawb. Rasp or strawb. Hm.

Edie   For Jesus Christ, you'd think you wis choosing a'tween firing squad or electric chair.

Geoffrey   Raspberry.

He takes a jar and sits down. **Edie** *shuts the cupboard door, annoyed at him leaving it open.* **Geoffrey** *tries to open the jam jar. He can't. He keeps trying, his face becoming red, his palms beginning to burn, but he struggles on. Meanwhile,* **Edie** *stands up, grabs the jar from him, opens it with ease and hands it back.*

Geoffrey   Oh right. Thanks.

Edie   Hm.

They sit down. **Geoffrey** *has toast,* **Edie** *reads the paper.*

Geoffrey (*having just shoved a whole slice of toast in his mouth*) Here, d'you think I could borrow some o your pot plants tomorrow for my still-lifes?

Edie   Whit? And hiv the grubby wee minks pull them apart?

Geoffrey   I'll mak sure they're nae damaged.

Edie   Hm. Duh ken aboot that. How d'you nae ask Thomas for some o his vegetables? They'd mak a good subject matter. And he's got plenty.

Geoffrey   Aye, they'd go off though. Ower four weeks, they'd definitely go off. I can water the plants, ken.

Edie   But Thomas has got so many vegetables he disnae ken whit tae dae wi them. They're coming oot his lugholes. Ken, since his wife passed. She ate an affy lot o them. An affy lot o vegetables. She wis ain o them – whit d'you call it – whit d'you call it – a vegetable fiend.

Geoffrey   Aye. And look at her noo.

Edie   Indeed.

Geoffrey (*looks at watch*)   Right. I'm off.

He grabs his bag, bicycle helmet and jacket, leans down to peck **Edie** *on the cheek.*

Edie   Come here, Geoffrey.

She licks her palm, flattens **Geoffrey**'s *hair down.*

Edie   There we go. My cheeky wee handsome.

Scene Two

Late afternoon. **Edie** *sits in the kitchen playing a card game. There's post on the kitchen table.* **Geoffrey** *comes home; looks like he's had a hard day.* **Edie** *barely glances up.*

Edie   How wis school?

Geoffrey   Sometimes I wish they'd all catch fire and die.

Edie   Ach weel. Yiv post there.

Geoffrey (*opens an envelope*)   Bank statements. Boring.

He hands it to **Edie**, *who has a quick look before tucking them away.*

Edie (*sniffs the air*)   Geoffrey? Whit's that . . . I thought I telt you tae keep your smells tae the bathroom.

Geoffrey   Ay?

He looks about him, checks the bottom of his shoes.

Och min. I've stepped in shite.

Edie   Whit? That bloody dog.

Goes to look out of window.

Geoffrey   Jist a wee bit.

Edie   Mongrel's bin digging up the gairden again. I'll wring her bloody neck.

Geoffrey   Whit's for tea?

Edie   Beef.

Geoffrey   Hm.

Edie   Ken, Thomas wis roond this morning. I couldnae get rid o him. Ended up staying for lunch an' a'. Think he's a bit lonely ken. Still adjusting. I telt him tae pull himsel' taegither. I mean, surely he cannae still be grieving his wife. She had a whore's haircut and the eyes o a gypsy.

Geoffrey (*he forces a cough*)   Think I'm getting a cough.

Silence. Moves closer to **Edie** *and coughs again.*

Geoffrey   Think I'm getting a cough.

Edie   Really.

She feels his forehead.

Weel, yiv nae a temperature. So I prescribe a hug fae your mammy.

Geoffrey *rejects the hug.*

Edie   Whit behaviour's this?

Geoffrey   I dinnae wint tae go tae school the morn.

Edie   Tough.

Geoffrey   Whit did you get at the shops?

He restlessly looks about and in cupboards. He takes a Ribena Light multipack out of the cupboard.

Whit's this?

Edie   Your Ribena.

Geoffrey   No it isnae. This is blue.

Edie   Oh, must've picked up the wrong ain.

Geoffrey   You obviously did. I'm nae drinking this. Go and get purple.

Edie   Och, surely they're all much and such.

Geoffrey   Blue's disgusting. I hate it.

Edie   Come on noo. I got your Murray Mints an' a'.

Geoffrey   I hate Murray Mints.

Edie   That's enough, Geoffrey. I'll get purple the morn.

Geoffrey   Go and get it noo.

Edie   I will not. Listen Geoffrey, you're getting bitty old for this noo. I think it's aboot time you started buying your ain Ribena.

Geoffrey   Jesus God, how wis I even born.

Edie   I'm starting tae wonder mysel'.

Geoffrey *starts banging his head against a cupboard – something he has done in moments of distress since he was a child.*

Geoffrey   I hate you I hate you I hate you –

Thomas *knocks and lets himself in. He is holding two cabbage*s.

Thomas   Jist Thomas. Oh deary me –

Edie   Hallo, Thomas.

Thomas   Hiv I interrupted something?

Edie   I'm afraid yiv walked in on some angry words. Geoffrey's got quite carried away –

Thomas   Geoffrey? D'you need tae apologise tae your mither?

Geoffrey *tuts.*

Thomas   Geoffrey . . .

Geoffrey   Sorry. I didnae mean whit I said –

Edie   Apology accepted.

Geoffrey (*looks to fisherman picture*)   I dinnae hate Murray Mints.

Beat.

I'll get my ain Ribena fae noo on.

Edie   Very weel.

Thomas   That's a lad. I bring gifts.

Offers the cabbages.

Edie   Goodness me.

Thomas   First o the season.

Edie   Affy kind.

Thomas   No problem-o.

Edie   And they'll help clear Geoffrey's blockage nae end.

Thomas   Och no, still hivvin trouble, Geoffrey?

Geoffrey (*sighs*)   When's tea ready?

Edie   Nae for a whiley.

Geoffrey   I'm going for a bath then.

Edie   Need me tae come in and scrub your back?

Geoffrey   Nae the day.

He exits.

Thomas   Oh, I certainly widnae refuse that offer.

Edie   Thomas, whit're you like. Cup o tea?

Scene Three

Breakfast time. **Edie** *is reading the local paper,* **Geoffrey** *is reading a tabloid. The radio is on in the background.*

Edie   Did you see that some manny wis eaten by a combine harvester up at Muckle Fairm?

Geoffrey   Oh nut, fa wis this?

Edie   Eh . . . says it wis . . . cannae pronounce his name.

Geoffrey   Must be fae ain o those countries.

Edie   Och weel, that's nae a bother then.

She folds up her paper, eyes **Geoffrey***'s.*

Edie   How long does it tak you tae read a cartoon?

Geoffrey   I've finished my cartoons. I'm reading something very interesting actually. Mither, apparently I'm sexy.

Edie   Course you are, deary.

Geoffrey   They've done a survey and listed the top ten sexiest professions.

Edie   I've nae interest.

Geoffrey   At number nine is teacher, and at number four – wid you believe it – is artist. So, me being an art teacher . . . I must be off the scale.

Edie   Tak it wi a pinch o salt.

Geoffrey   A' this time, I didnae realise. I'm like Lenny fae *O Mice and Men*, but wi sexy appeal instead o strength. Ken whit, I'm going tae pin it tae the staff room notice board.

Rips article out.

This'll show them.

Edie   Dinnae let it go tae your heid, dear.

Geoffrey   Aye, I see it noo. The fiery passion o the artist and the cool calm control o the teacher.

Pause.

Weel. I nivver thought I'd ivver be considered tae be sexy.

He stands up to reveal he isn't wearing any trousers.

Edie   Sexy is a bit o a strong word. And definitely nae the type o language appropriate for the breakfast table.

Geoffrey Far's my troosers?

Edie   I've jist ironed them.

The trousers sit in the middle of a neatly folded pile of ironing that sits on one of the kitchen chairs. He pulls them out of the pile with one hand, resulting in the clothes on top falling to the floor.

Edie   Geoffrey!

Geoffrey (*putting his trousers on*)   Oops.

Edie   My God, how many times? Pick it up afore you go.

Pause, as **Geoffrey** *finishes putting his trousers on. He looks at his watch.*

Geoffrey   Oh, look at the time –

Edie   Geoffrey, come here.

Geoffrey   Och whit?

Edie   Geoffrey come here. Yiv got jam.

Geoffrey *leans in closer, she pulls him even closer, and proceeds to lick the jam off his cheek.*

Geoffrey   Thanks.

Edie   Off you pop then.

Smiles and shakes her head.

Scene Four

Sainsbury's. Overwhelmed and blinded by fluorescent lighting, **Geoffrey** *finds himself at the Customer Service Desk, faced with* **Evelyn***, who is slouching, reading a magazine.*

Geoffrey (*offers his list*)   Can you get this?

Evelyn (*pause*)   Oh hiya.

Geoffrey   Can you get Ribena. Purple. Definitely purple.

Evelyn   Whit's this? A list fae the wee wife?

Geoffrey   Nut . . . the wife? I dinnae hiv a wife.

Evelyn   Sorry, I didnae mean tae assume. Life partner?

Geoffrey   D'you think someone like me could hiv a wife?

Evelyn   Here, I recognise you. Are you a teacher at the High School?

Geoffrey   Aye. Mr Buncher.

Evelyn   Buncher. Kent it. You wis my second-year art teacher. Aboot three year ago.

Geoffrey   Oh right. I dinnae quite . . . whit's your name?

Evelyn   Och it's okay. I'm nae surprised you dinnae mind, coz you spent most o the class in your cupboard greeting.

Geoffrey   Oh. I didnae ken yous kent that.

Evelyn   Wis pretty obvious.

Geoffrey   Aye weel, I'll admit I find that age group tae be particularly cruel. Very cruel indeed. Thankfully noo I'm jist assigned tae the Standard Grade and Higher classes. Ken, the ains that actually wint tae be there.

Evelyn   Aye, thinking aboot it, we were pretty harsh. Baby Buncher. That's whit we called you.

Geoffrey   I mind.

Evelyn   Coz o your greeting and that.

Geoffrey   Indeed.

Evelyn   And Barnacle Buncher.

Geoffrey   Aye.

Evelyn   Mrs Phillips came up wi that ain. Said you wis stuck ontae your mither.

Geoffrey   Anywye . . . could you –

Evelyn   Buncher Buncher, Four-Eyed Cock Muncher.

Silence.

Och, wee gudgies'll say anything that rhymes.

Beat.

You'll get your Ribena on aisle six. Onything else?

Geoffrey   Um . . . far wid a manny like mysel' acquire ain o these wife thingies?

Evelyn   Oh right, that's a bit off-topic but . . . tried the internet?

Geoffrey   Dinnae like it.

Evelyn   Speed dating?

Geoffrey   Sounds dangerous.

Evelyn   Alchies Anonymous? Far mum met my stepdad.

Geoffrey   Nut.

Evelyn   Or you could put an advert in the paper?

Geoffrey   Whit paper?

Evelyn   Depends whit type o wifie you're after.

Geoffrey   Whit type? D'you mean . . . d'you mean there's different types?

Evelyn   Ken, mental ay?

Geoffrey   Och min.

Evelyn   Here, I could set you up wi ain o my colleagues. Ken Debbie fae Meat and Fish?

Geoffrey   Debbie . . . nut, the only person I can see at Meat and Fish is that portly manny wi the ruddy cheeks.

Beat.

Oh.

Evelyn   Debbie's a really sweet quine that deserves happiness. Right weel, whit aboot a notice on the customer board?

Geoffrey   Oh right. How does that work?

Scene Five

The next day. **Geoffrey** *enters the empty kitchen. He has been painting in his shed. He speaks to the fisherman in the photo.*

Geoffrey   I've bin painting a spider plant. Ken them . . . things. I ken it's jist a spider plant and I've painted them heaps o times, but this time wis different. It almost came alive. I used tae wonder how spider plants wis called spider plants, I didnae understand, but I see it noo, I see it moving, creeping taewards its prey. D'you wint tae watch a David Attenborough wi me?

Edie *and* **Thomas** *enter.*

Edie   Will you stay for tea, Thomas?

Thomas   Oh weel, only if yiv enough.

Edie   We've plenty.

Thomas   Why dinnae I contribute ain o my prizewinning neeps tae the meal?

Edie   Lovely.

Geoffrey   Whit's prizewinning?

Thomas   My neeps. First prize at the Moray Grower's Show for three years running.

Edie   Thomas is a grower and a shower. Did you nae ken, Geoffrey?

Thomas   Aye, it's a marvellous day oot. Yous'll hiv tae come next year. There's a real buzz aboot it. It's a real adrenalin rush for the vegetable enthusiast.

The phone rings. They all look at each other.

Geoffrey   Oh. That'll be for me.

He answers the phone.

Aye?

Pause.

Aye.

Pause.

Aye.

Pause.

Dunno.

Pause.

Aye.

Pause.

Okay, bye.

He puts the phone down. Silence.

Edie   Geoffrey?

Geoffrey   Whit?

Edie   Fa wis that?

Geoffrey   Oh, that wis a wifie after a date.

Edie   A date?

Geoffrey   Oh right, aye, I've put up an advert in the Sainsbury's for a girlfriend.

Edie   You whit?

Thomas (*as he heads for the exit*)   Oh, I've jist remembered . . . I'm hivvin tea at Mrs Mahoodgie-bobs.

He exits.

Geoffrey   I wis thinking . . . if I got a lady friend it wid maybe stop the bullying. The teachers' Christmas dance is in December, and if I turn up wi a girlfriend it'll all stop. Ken, I'm fed up wi the teasing. I'm either a virgin or a practising homosexual. If anything I wish they'd jist mak up their minds.

Edie   You ken there's nothing – d'you hear me – nothing wrong wi keeping your virtue. And you ken my thoughts aboot the other.

She makes serious eye contact.

Disnae need repeating.

Geoffrey   And it's jist I get so lonely aboot here. Wid be nice tae hiv some company after you go tae bed at eight o'clock.

Edie   But yiv got a shed full o art materials.

Geoffrey   But painting the plants and the trees and the fruit is a lonely pursuit.

Edie   Weel, as for getting a girlfriend. I dinnae think so.

Geoffrey   Oh right.

Edie   It wid jist be so impractical. I mean, far wid she sit?

Geoffrey   We've got four chairs.

Edie   But I use this ain tae keep my ironing and you use that ain tae keep your school work.

Geoffrey   Oh. But I could a'wyes move my –

Edie   And then whit if you wis tae marry her? Far wid she sleep?

Geoffrey   In wi me?

Edie   Yiv got a single bed mind. Should you nae've discussed it wi me first?

Geoffrey   But I'm an independent man.

Edie   Independent, aye? The same independent manny that crawled intae his mammy's bed last night for a spooning coz he couldnae sleep?

Geoffrey   I had a bad dream.

Edie   Aw, whit a shame. Whit a shite. It's a cruel world oot there, Geoffrey. If you step intae the dating arena, they'll rip you limb frae limb. Even your pepper spray cannae help you noo.

The phone rings. **Geoffrey** *is quick to answer.*

Geoffrey   Hello.

Beat.

Speaking.

Pause.

I ken that's you, Ramsay Hamilton. Putting on a wifie's voice.

Beat.

I'll be informing the heidmaster.

He slams the phone down. **Edie** *shakes her head.*

Scene Six

Sainsbury's.

Geoffrey   Hiya.

Evelyn   Oh, hi there. Whit's up?

Geoffrey   I've got a date.

Evelyn   Really?

Geoffrey   I've got three.

Evelyn   Wowee. That's great, Mr Buncher. Weel done. The wee notice worked then?

Geoffrey   Aye. Almost too weel. I got some unsavoury calls fae my school pupils.

Evelyn   Aye, weel, you wis a bitty specific on the advert.

Geoffrey   Nervous.

Evelyn   Are you?

Geoffrey   I went tae the chemist.

Evelyn   'Don't be a fool. Wrap your tool.'

Geoffrey   I've invested in a pair o they Odour Eaters.

Takes a packet of insoles out of his pocket.

Evelyn   Oh, right.

Geoffrey   I'm nae sure aboot the exact ins and oots o dating, but I believe it may entail taking my shoes off at some point.

Evelyn   When's your first date then?

Geoffrey (*looks at watch*)   In aboot ten minutes.

Evelyn   Ten minutes? You better run hame and get changed then.

Geoffrey   I am changed.

Evelyn   Oh, right.

Geoffrey   Dae I gie her flooers?

Evelyn   Nut.

Geoffrey   Pull her chair oot?

Evelyn   Nut.

Geoffrey   Whit dae I say tae the wifies?

Evelyn   Jist normal chat.

Geoffrey   Like . . . ?

Evelyn   Jist aboot normal stuff.

Geoffrey   Like . . . a fish documentary?

Evelyn   Nae really. Whit aboot your hobbies and that. Speak aboot your painting. But ask her questions an' a'. But keep the chat light. And dinnae dwell on the negative, or mention onything you're self-conscious aboot.

Geoffrey   Like whit?

Evelyn   Like your teeth.

Geoffrey   Whit's wrong wi my teeth?

Evelyn   Or your hair.

Geoffrey   Ay?

Evelyn   Or your creepy starey eyes. Ken, it jist brings disproportionate attention tae these areas.

Beat.

Here, you could jot doon some questions you wint tae ask on some cards. Like, jist tae help if there's a lull in the conversation.

Geoffrey   Aye, okay. (*Looks at watch.*) I've got eight minutes though. I'll hiv tae dae it on the go.

Evelyn *hands him some noticeboard cards and a pen. He puts them in his jacket pocket.*

Scene Seven

Two menus and breadsticks on table.

First date. **Woman A** *suggestively slides a bread stick in and out of her mouth as* **Geoffrey** *studies the menu.*

Geoffrey   Oh. The menu looks really . . . I've nae idea whit half this stuff is. Think I'll ask if they dae chips. D'you ken whit you wint?

Woman A   Sex.

Geoffrey   Oh . . . I jist . . . Um, d'you think they serve Ribena . . .

Woman A   Nut. They dinnae.

Geoffrey   Oh right, hiv you come here afore?

Woman A   I come all the time, darlin'.

Geoffrey   That's nice. Noo, I've prepared a few questions, I hope you dinnae mind. It's my first time.

Woman A   Just when I thought I couldnae get mair aroused.

Confused and distressed, **Geoffrey** *takes question cards out of his pocket.*

Geoffrey   Um . . . question one. D'you like a bath?

Woman A   I'd love tae tak a bath wi you, fragrant candles, sensual music, oils rubbed all ower, our slippery naked bodies groaning in ecstasy –

Geoffrey   Question two . . . whit's your favourite confectionery?

Woman A   Onything I can sook.

Geoffrey   Can you narrow it doon a bitty?

Woman A   Onything long, pink and hard.

Geoffrey   Like a rhubarb and custard?

Woman A   A'right, let's jist sort something oot. We are going tae fuck our brains oot the night, ay? Else I'm jist wasting my time. See, I'm receiving mixed messages, Geoff.

Geoffrey (*silence*)   Questions three –

Woman A   Och forget it.

Second date.

Geoffrey   Question three. Whit side o the bed d'you sleep on?

Woman B   Oh.

Laughs.

Geoffrey   Och, disnae really matter, I'm rocking a single bed.

Woman B   I've got a super king size.

Laughs.

And even then there's barely enough room for me after all my doggies get in.

Laughs.

Geoffrey   You sleep wi your dogs?

Woman B   Oh, not all of them. *Laughs.*

Just Frankie and Dancer and Frisky and Ginger, they're still puppies.

Laughs.

And William at the minute, while he's got a poorly paw. And also Biscuit, while she's got demodectic mange.

Laughs.

Poor lamb.

Laughs.

I don't need an alarm clock to wake me up, just plenty of lovely doggy-woggies giving me licky-wickies when their wee belly-wellies are growly-wowly.

Laughs.

Geoffrey   D'you happen tae be free on the evening o
7th December?

Woman B   Oh, no, we're off to Doggy Santa's Christmas Grotto.

Laughs.

Geoffrey   Whit a shame.

Third date.

Clara   Geoffrey, is it?

Geoffrey (*doesn't stand up*)   Aye.

Clara   Well, it's lovely to meet you, Geoffrey.

Pause.

Okay. Have you been here before?

Geoffrey   Aye.

Clara   What d'you recommend?

Geoffrey   Dinnae ken. I've nivver got tae the ordering part yet.

Clara   Oh, right. Let's have a look . . . Mm. D'you want to tell me a bit about yourself, Geoffrey?

Geoffrey   Did you nae read the wee notice card?

Clara   Of course. You're a forty-year-old local male art teacher who enjoys long soaks in the bath and cycling from A to B.

Geoffrey   Aye, that's it.

Clara   What else?

Geoffrey   D'you like bread sticks?

Clara   Not really.

Geoffrey   Good. Dirty things.

Clara   Gluten aggravates my gut flora.

Geoffrey   You're nae fae roond here, are you?

Clara   No. I moved here to start a new, positive, chapter in my life. I dreamt of a place where I could stand in a forest and at the same time hear the crashing waves. And that dream took me here.

Geoffrey   Oh right.

Clara   I can breathe here. There's space to breathe. It just so . . . just so wonderfully . . . y'know?

Geoffrey   Nut.

Clara   Have you ever walked barefoot through a forest?

Geoffrey   Question four. Are you a tourettes person, or hiv abnormal levels o flatulence, or prone tae loud and violent sneezes or any other unsociable diseases?

Clara   Why don't we have a look at the wine list?

Geoffrey   Question five. Hiv you ivver let a dog lick your lips?

Clara   Gosh, I think I might go for a sparkling rosé.

Geoffrey   Question number – ah! Whit's your favourite cheese?

Clara   Geoffrey . . . Why all the questions?

Geoffrey   You wifies are all so confusing. I dinnae understand whit you wint.

Clara   What I want? You want to know what I want?

Geoffrey   Um . . . aye?

Clara   What do I want? You know, I've spent the past few months asking myself the same question. What I want is to breathe, and to just be. To not be judged . . . or be put down. To not be kept like a possession . . . locked in a dark place. Manipulation. Is not what I want. Bullying . . . threats. Is not what I want. What I want is something simple, honest, secure. What I want is to have fun. To laugh. But what I really want is someone to dance with. That's actually, specifically, what I'm looking for right now. Just a partner to dance with. Oh, gosh . . . It doesn't matter. I'm sorry, it's too soon. I should've known. Stupid. Sorry . . . sorry. It's too soon.

She gets up to leave.

Geoffrey   Clara. Are you free on the evening o seventh December?

Clara (*she stops, wiping her tears*)   Yes. Yes, I think so.

Geoffrey   I'll dance wi you, then. I'll dance wi you, Clara.

Scene Eight

Geoffrey *is in the kitchen marking school essays.* **Thomas** *and* **Edie** *come in from outside,* **Edie** *being supported by* **Thomas**.

Thomas   Oh good, Geoffrey, you're hame.

Geoffrey   Whit's happened?

Edie   That mongrel.

Thomas   The wee dog attacked poor Edie.

Geoffrey   Ay?

Thomas   We wis jist doon the street admiring Mrs Krimble's clematis bush.

Edie   It's a lovely big bush.

Thomas   Oh aye, it is, it is. A real feast for the eyes. And it's funny coz big ains seem tae hiv gone ooto fashion these days, abiddy's after these wee manicured bushes noo. They're labour intensive, and nae cheap.

Edie   Nae idea why.

Thomas   Nae idea why. I like a big sprawling bush mysel'. As nature intended, ken, hospitable tae wildlife. Onywye, that's by the by. We wis admiring Mrs Krimble's bush and I noticed coming up a'hind us wis the wee dog, ken, looks harmless enough, but your mither nivver noticed it until it started yappin at her ankles so of course she near fainted, but the yappin didnae stop there.

Edie   I gied it a kick.

Thomas   But that made it worse, ken. Went absolutely feel. Lucky I wis there. In all my years, I've nivver seen a dog react that wye tae a human. Honestly, the dog reacted as if you wis a right cunt.

Edie   Oh Geoffrey. I wis that feart.

Thomas   I hear yiv bin on the dating scene, Geoffrey.

Geoffrey   Aye.

Thomas   I hear you'll be seeing her again this weekend.

Geoffrey   Aye.

Thomas (*shrugs his shoulders at* **Edie**)   Bit o dancing.

Geoffrey   Okay, see yous.

Edie   Far you going?

Geoffrey   Jist oot.

Edie   But Thomas has come roond for his portrait.

Geoffrey   His whit?

Edie   He's got all dressed up look. You cannae let him doon noo.

Thomas   Weel, I wis going tae wear my al' uniform, but, I think it's shrunk. So I've worn my best T-shirt. I think it's quite flattering aboot the gut area.

Edie *and* **Geoffrey** *stare at his gut area. Pause.*

Geoffrey (*tuts*)   S'pose I've got time tae start a wee sketch.

Edie   Grand. I feel a migraine coming on. Think I'll lie doon wi a good book.

She winks at **Thomas***, prances off.*

Geoffrey *gets a sketch pad and pencil, starts drawing right away.* **Thomas** *rummages around in a carrier bag.*

Thomas   Right-o. I brought some o my finest vegetables. Thought I could perhaps pose wi them, like the Queen does wi her big gold stick.

Geoffrey   Whitivver you wint, Thomas.

Thomas   Shall I jist rest a few courgettes in my airms?

Geoffrey   If you must.

Thomas   So, whit's your eh, whit's your lady friend called?

Geoffrey   Clara.

Thomas   Clara.

Beat.

Thomas   And d'you think things might progress intae a serious relationship?

Geoffrey   Your face looks shiny.

Thomas   Oh aye, I winted tae brighten up my complexion, so I put on some o my wife's face cream. I've still nae cleaned oot her dresser drawers.

Geoffrey   Oh right.

Silence.

Thomas.

Thomas   Aye?

Geoffrey   Whit's it like tae be married?

Thomas   Oh, eh, that's a question.

He looks over to the door for guidance, but there's no sign of **Edie***.*

Thomas   Well, aye, I s'pose, I can only speak fae my experience. It has its ups and doons. But tae the extremes like. The ups are amazing, a real high. And the doons are terrible, really heartbreaking. Aye, we came close tae ending a couple o times. Mainly due tae my long hours and stress o my job.

Geoffrey   Oh, right.

Thomas   Mind that notorious washing-line trooser thief o '94.

Geoffrey   Oh aye. Mind that.

Thomas   The case took ower my life. It wis a real low point in our marriage.

Geoffrey   But you caught him, did you nae?

Thomas   Aye, but nae afore it had taken its toll. I wis a'wyes working. Barely at hame during that time and when I wis I wis nothing but aggressive towards her. Couldnae handle the drink either. I wis a man possessed.

Geoffrey   Gosh, I nivver kent.

Thomas   If I'm honest, I'd say I wis nae right in the heid during that time. Nae right. The pressure o kenning that the hale community wis being kept awake at night, nae kenning if their troosers wid still be on the line in the morn.

Geoffrey   I mind it wis Levis at first –

Thomas   Indeed, 501s.

Geoffrey   So Mum and I wernae worried. But when he started stealing troosers indiscriminately . . .

Thomas   That's when I kent I had tae get this sicko off the streets and fast.

Beat.

Oh aye, thirty-odd years on the force. I seen it a'. But it's a young lad's game. A young lad's game. If I kent my wife wis tae be taken awa so soon I'd hiv perhaps done things differently. Nae stayed on the force so long.

Beat.

Ken, spent a bit mair time . . . jist . . . holding her.

Beat.

Aye. It's a shock so it is. And an empty hoose the size o mine, jist magnifies the loneliness.

Long silence.

Thomas   But of course, hivvin said that, marriage is shite.

Geoffrey   Ay?

Thomas   Marriage is shite. Aye, it's really shite.

Geoffrey   Right weel.

Looks at watch.

I've done enough sketching.

Thomas   Yiv finished?

Geoffrey   I can finish it fae memory.

He puts the sketch pad on the table, gets his jacket and leaves.

Edie (*tiptoes in*)   How did it go?

Thomas (*examining the sketch*)   Och, I thought he'd hiv at least reduced the size o my chins.

Edie   Whit information did you get fae him?

Thomas   Are my lugs really that big?

Edie   Hush up, Thomas, you're a man obsessed. Did you manage tae put him off ?

Thomas   Aye, I did my best Edie. I did my best.

Beat.

Och, I should o shaved my nostrils.

Scene Nine

Geoffrey *and* **Clara** *dance. They aren't very good.*

Scene Ten

Geoffrey *talks to the fisherman photo.*

Geoffrey   So that's me then.

Beat.

Sewing my wild oats.

Beat.

Whitivver that means.

Beat.

Whit d'you dream o when you sleep? Coz she's entered my dreams. And she gets closer and closer, aboot tae wrap her airms aroon me, but then I wake up. And then I'm greeting coz it wisnae real. And I try tae shut my eyes and go back, but the sun is burning the curtains. Hm. I'm going tae start sleeping wi my spectacles on fae noo on. So I can see her face.

He unwraps a Murray Mint and eats it.

Och weel, my last Murray Mint.

Scene Eleven

Sainsbury's.

Geoffrey   Hiya.

Evelyn   How did it go then?

Geoffrey   Aye, good. I've got a girlfriend.

Evelyn   That wis quick.

Geoffrey   Aye, s'pose it wis.

Evelyn   Fa is she then?

Geoffrey   Clara. She's . . . nice. She's got . . . hair like . . . um . . . and eyes.

Evelyn   She sounds great. Weel done.

Geoffrey   We're going oot dancing. Like, eh, dancing classes.

Evelyn   I didnae ken you could dance.

Geoffrey   I'm trying. Maybe I'm really good but I jist dinnae ken yet.

Evelyn   I'm sure you are, Mr Buncher.

Geoffrey   She wints tae go oot for tea.

Evelyn   Oh aye. Far at?

Geoffrey   Dinnae ken. Far should we go?

Evelyn   Dunno. Whit does she like?

Geoffrey   She likes . . . dunno. She likes the wine list.

Evelyn   She likes wine?

Geoffrey   Think so. I dinnae ken aboot wine. I dinnae drink the drink.

Evelyn   You dinnae drink? Whit?

Geoffrey   Nut.

Evelyn   But you hiv tae drink, Mr Buncher. Else folk'll think you're weird.

Geoffrey   Oh, right. I dinnae wint that.

Evelyn   You could dae a wee wine course at the college. Then impress her wi your knowledge.

Geoffrey   Aye? Nut, I've nae time. D'you ken aboot wine?

Evelyn   Nut. Wish I could help, but nae idea.

Geoffrey   Ken whit, I could buy some o them tiny wee bottles o wine. Whit are they, like maternity size?

Evelyn   Aye, right enough.

Geoffrey   Maybe we could go tae the park the night and test them all.

Evelyn   Eh . . . s'pose. Aye, fuck it, get ten o them and I'll gie you money later.

Geoffrey   Och nae bother, I'll buy them.

Evelyn   In that case, get twenty.

Geoffrey   K.

Scene Twelve

Evelyn *and* **Geoffrey** *sit by the river in the park. He has his bicycle helmet on. They have a large number of mini-bottles of wine.*

Evelyn   You look like a fud wi your helmet on.

Geoffrey   Oh, far did I leave my bike? Och weel. Let's swim wi the ducks.

Evelyn   The ducks are sleeping.

Geoffrey   Ducks sleep?

Evelyn   Course.

Geoffrey   I nivver kent that.

Evelyn   Here, whit's the next wine?

Geoffrey (*picks two bottles at random*)   A pinnott grigg-io. And a cabinet suave-ington.

Evelyn   Sounds mental.

They open one each and drink.

Evelyn   Tastes the same as the last ain.

Geoffrey   Tastes like Ribena.

Evelyn   Does it?

Geoffrey   Mixed wi vinegar.

Beat.

Wait! We forgot tae feed the troll.

Evelyn   Ay?

Geoffrey   Else he'll eat us. Get some leaves and twigs.

Evelyn   This is the first time yiv bin drunk ay?

Geoffrey   Aye.

Evelyn   Nae bother. I'm glad you're nae a greeter.

Geoffrey   How many times hiv you bin drunk?

Evelyn   Too many tae mind.

Geoffrey   Oh right.

Evelyn   Officially drinking since I wis twelve. When I got my first paycheque.

Geoffrey   At twelve? I wis still in nappies at twelve. Joke.

Evelyn   Wis working for pocket money at first. Then mum stopped workin coz o her . . . problems, so I had tae work mair. Whitivver I could find. Twa paper roonds at ain point. Then worked in the newsagent's. Pickin tatties in the holidays. Washing cars. Babysitting. Walking dogs. Ken, whitivver.

Geoffrey   How did you hiv time for school?

Evelyn   I didnae. I turned up every day . . . most days, like . . .
but I wis, ken, I wis sleeping wi my eyes open. So I fucked up my
Standard grades. And then I wis going tae catch up at the college
this year, but then this job at the Sainsbury's came up. I had tae
take it. Had tae get ooto my hoose. Ken whit really fucks me off
though, I did all that for my mum and she kent I wis daeing it
for her, she asked me tae dae it. And the moment she gets hersel'
sorted she moves some fud intae our hoose. And he settled in affy
quickly. Really makin himsel' at hame. Putting up shelves far we
didnae need shelves, buying those bloody stenchin plug-ins that he
kens gies me asthma attacks, and taking ower the telly so we had
tae ask his permission. And worst of all he stairted walking roond
in his pants wi'in a fortnight. That wis jist offensive and fucking
inappropriate. Didnae feel comfortable in my ain hoose, ken. And
my mither turned intae a moose, wid dae as she wis telt, widnae
stick up for me. And ken whit, I wid've gied up everything for
her, and I did, but she dropped me in a second. In a fuckin second.
Dropped me for a total knob-end.

Geoffrey   You could still go tae college ain day.

Evelyn   Aye, spose. Dunno. Wonder if there's ony point.

Geoffrey   Wi college?

Evelyn   Wi onything really. Ken, when I think aboot the future
. . . I'm nae in it. I can see my mither and abiddy I ken, I can see
them a' . . . but I cannae see me.

Beat.

Och fuck it, gie me anither wine.

Geoffrey   Okay. Yiv got a 'something blank'.

Evelyn   Your French isnae good, is it?

Geoffrey   Nut. Mither pulled me ooto French classes at school.
She telt the heidmaster the language wid corrupt my innocence. I
wis allowed tae dae mair art instead.

Evelyn   Ah, your art. Och weel, cheers tae mithers. Fucking mental.

They clink bottles. **Evelyn** *drinks and* **Geoffrey** *stares at her face.*

Scene Thirteen

Geoffrey *and* **Clara** *dance. They are improving.*

Scene Fourteen

In **Geoffrey**'s *bedroom.* **Geoffrey** *and* **Clara** *stand by his single bed.*

Clara   This looks comfy.

Geoffrey   Aye.

Clara (*looks under pillow*)   No teddy?

Geoffrey   He's in the wash.

Clara *laughs.* **Geoffrey** *doesn't.*

Clara   Y'know, I had a security blanket till I was twenty-three. Can you believe it?

Geoffrey   Whit's a security blanket?

Clara   It's a blanket or a similar soft object that infants use for comfort during the transition from seeing themselves and their mother as one whole to the realisation that they're an individual and not physically linked to the mother.

Beat, **Geoffrey** *looks blank.*

Clara   It's a fairly common way of dealing with the trauma of separation. An object of comfort to replace the body of your mother.

Geoffrey   Security blanket. Nut, nivver heard o it.

Clara   Your eyes are so beautiful. So blue.

Geoffrey   Oh right.

Silence. **Geoffrey** *looks at* **Clara** *for a long time.*

Geoffrey   Your . . . um . . . your eyebrows look soft.

Clara   Thank you, Geoffrey. Shall we . . . sit down on the bed?

Geoffrey   K.

They sit down, a distance between them.

Clara   This is nice.

Geoffrey   Aye.

Clara   Shall we hold hands?

Geoffrey   K.

They hold hands.

Clara   Your hand is warm.

Geoffrey   Aye.

Clara   Shall we . . . Let's have a cuddle.

Geoffrey   K.

They lie back and try cuddling, but it's a bit awkward and arms and elbows are flying about.

Clara   Sorry . . . sorry . . . what about . . . I'll turn round.

She turns her back to **Geoffrey**. *He reluctantly cuddles her, keeping his distance.*

Clara   This is nice.

Geoffrey   Aye.

Clara   Could you . . . if you don't mind . . . move in closer.

Geoffrey   K.

He wriggles in closer.

Clara   I want to feel your breath on my neck. If you move in closer.

Geoffrey   Oh right.

He moves his head in closer to **Clara***'s neck. He starts to heavy mouth-breathe on her.*

Clara   Um . . . um . . . No, sorry. Not like that. Feathery nasal breath. From your nose.

Geoffrey   Oh right.

Clara   Feathery tickles on my neck.

Geoffrey   K.

He nasal-breathes on her neck.

Like this?

Clara   Yes.

Geoffrey   Like this?

Clara   Yes. It's nice. Really nice. And perhaps . . . could you stroke my back?

Geoffrey   K . . .

He starts stroking her back over her clothes.

I'm I daeing it right?

Clara   Yes. Great. But perhaps . . . if you don't mind, put your hand up my top. Put your hand on my skin. Feel my skin.

Geoffrey (*puts his hand under her top and strokes*)   K.

Clara   Oh . . . That's it . . . Ahh . . . Mmm, yeah, that's it. Keep breathing. Oh . . . yeah . . . Ahh . . . Ahh . . .

Scene Fifteen

Morning. **Edie** *is reading the paper to a certain extent. She looks up every second to see if* **Geoffrey** *and* **Clara** *have emerged.*

Clara *appears.*

Clara   Hi.

Silence.

It's a lovely deep bath you've got.

Edie   Aye, weel.

Clara   I had a lovely bath.

Edie   Hm.

Clara   Geoffrey's in the bath now. He's funny, he doesn't like sharing bathwater, does he? He emptied mine and now he's running a whole new bath.

Edie   And?

Clara   It just seems so wasteful. It's funny, you've got a whole cupboard full of lavender bubble bath.

Edie   Whit's funny aboot that?

Clara   I mean, I love a lavender bath, but a whole cupboard. Gosh.

Edie   Bessom.

Clara   Sorry?

Edie   Did you hiv a good night?

Clara   Great.

Edie   I didnae ken you wis staying ower. Else I wid've put the camp bed oot for you.

Clara   Oh no, I didn't mean to stay, but it got so late. We were having too much fun.

Edie   So I heard.

She goes back to her paper. **Clara** *doesn't really know what to do with herself.*

Edie   Ken whit I find funny.

Clara   What?

Edie   How my wee boy, as naive and pastey as he is, could get a grown woman tae go weak at the knees. When he's nae so much as accidentally brushed up against a wifie afore, and there's nae internet or dirty magazines in the hoose tae speak o. And I ken, I've checked under his mattress. Nut, nae contact wi anither female in the world. Oh. 'Cept his mammy o course. 'Cept his mammy.

Scene Sixteen

Clara *and* **Geoffrey** *dance. They are quite good – if not technically good, they're at least keeping up with the pace.*

Scene Seventeen

Edie *is playing cards with* **Thomas**. *She has bright red lipstick on. As soon as* **Geoffrey** *and* **Clara** *enter,* **Edie** *laughs hysterically as if* **Thomas** *has just told a joke.*

Edie (*laughs*)   Oh Thomas, you're hilarious.

Thomas   Ay?

Edie (*puts a hand on* **Thomas***'s forearm*)   Oh look, it's my son and his . . . Clara.

Thomas   Clara. Lovely tae meet you. Thomas.

Clara   Likewise.

Thomas   And whit hiv you kids bin up tae?

Geoffrey   Mum. Whit's that on your chaps?

Clara   What game are you playing?

Thomas   Poker.

Edie (*laughs*)   Oh Thomas, you randy old fool.

Thomas   Ay?

Edie   D'yous wint tae join us wi a game?

Geoffrey   Nut.

Edie   A board game? Boys against quines?

Geoffrey   Right, weel, we're off tae my room. I'll leave yous tae it.

Edie   Dinnae dae onything I widnae dae. That disnae leave much, does it, Thomas?

She laughs.

Thomas   Ay?

Geoffrey *and* **Clara** *exit to his room.* **Edie** *instantly goes in a mood.*

Thomas   Oh look, I've got a flush.

Lays his card hand down.

Edie (*trying to cool herself down*)   Tell me aboot it. That boy.

Some time later in **Geoffrey**'s *bedroom.* **Geoffrey** *and* **Clara** *lie on the bed,* **Geoffrey** *is stroking her back.*

Clara   What did you say happened to your dad again?

Geoffrey   I didnae.

Clara   Oh right, but he's not around, is he?

Geoffrey   He's deid.

Clara   I'm sorry. What happened?

Geoffrey   Lost at sea.

Clara   How awful, you must be –

Geoffrey   That's me bought the tickets for the Christmas dance on 7th December.

Clara   When did he –

Geoffrey   They're non-refundable, so it's legally binding.

Clara   Hey, could we stay at mine tonight?

Geoffrey   Nah.

Clara   Please, I've . . . got a double bed.

Geoffrey   Nah.

Clara   Please, Geoffrey. I'd quite like us to be together tonight.

Geoffrey   Are we nae taegither?

Clara   I mean . . . properly be together. Alone.

Geoffrey   Um.

Clara   It's what couples do when they . . . when they are falling in love.

Geoffrey   Falling in love. Whit's it like tae be falling in love?

Clara   You've never been in love? I'm not too experienced myself, but . . . It's the little things at first. Fizzy butterflies in your belly. Your eyes become wider, brighter. And you can't help but smile when you say their name, even think it. Your face aches from smiling. Always on the edge of laughter. You're full of energy but can't eat a bite. New colours burst into life. Then suddenly you're not afraid. Not afraid of the world. Not afraid of anything. And you could just lie like this forever.

Clara *is falling asleep.* **Geoffrey** *keeps stroking her back a while longer, then quietly leaves the bedroom to go to his shed.*

Edie *is sitting in the near dark kitchen,* **Geoffrey** *gets to the back door before* **Edie** *speaks.*

Edie   Geoffrey?

Geoffrey   Oh. You're up late.

Edie   You alright, son?

Geoffrey   Aye. Fine. Jist fine.

Edie   Good. Geoffrey, it has jist come tae my attention, whit wi all this girlfriend nonsense coming so suddenly and so . . . oot o the blue . . . that I've neglected some o my duties as a mither. Some o the facts o life. Somefar in my mind I kent this day wid come, that your curiosities aboot the female form wid be aroused. But you understand, I didnae wint my wee manny growing up too fast. I think you're ready for the birds and the bees.

Geoffrey   Oh right. If you think so. Are the birds the wifies and the bees the mannies? Oh wait. I ken, the birds eat the berries and they poop oot the seeds and then the seeds grow intae trees and then the bumble bees –

Edie   (*puts a finger over his mouth to hush him*)   How aboot I jist show you . . .

She lets her dressing gown slip down to expose a bare shoulder.

Scene Eighteen

Geoffrey *talks to the fisherman photo, washes red paint from his paint brushes.*

Geoffrey   Murray Mints.

He eats a Murray Mint.

Wid've bin good for the sea sickness I s'pose, ay?

Beat.

Mither tried tae gie me the birds and the bees. Wisnae quite whit I wis expecting.

Beat.

I have bin getting these feelings in my belly. Clara wis right. I feel a bit giddy in the stomach. Butterflies? Mair like puppies. Trying tae escape fae a scaffy bag thrown intae the River Lossie. Smiling when I think aboot her face. And the colours. The colours. Aye. I think I . . . might be falling in love.

Scene Nineteen

Sainsbury's.

Evelyn   You're in early.

Geoffrey   I didnae sleep. Bin painting all night, ken. Tomatoes on the vine. That's whit I've bin painting. It's the reds. I used so much reds. Rich reds that I didnae ken existed. Red jist started leaking. Blood dripping ooto the vines, swirling intae a pool o scarlet and crimson. I wisnae sure whit it wis meant tae be. Until I saw it, I think I saw it beating like a heart. Beating like my heart.

Beat.

Och weel.

Evelyn   Great. How's things wi Clara?

Geoffrey   Aye, it's aye, aye, aye, aye, it's . . . aye.

Evelyn   Glad tae hear it.

Geoffrey   Um, whit are those tiny wee French yogurts called again?

Evelyn   Petits Filous?

Geoffrey   That's them. That's the mannies. I've alwyes winted tae try them. Think I'll get some o them.

Evelyn   Wow Geoffrey, you're being quite reckless the day.

Geoffrey   I am. I am. Petits Filous the day, the morn – fa kens!

Scene Twenty

Edie *is in the kitchen, reading the papers, radio on. An opened jar of jam sits on the table.* **Clara** *enters, timidly.*

Clara   Morning, Edie.

Edie   Hm.

Clara   Lovely morning.

Edie   Ay?

Clara   It's a lovely morning.

Edie   Hm. Help yoursel' tae toast.

Clara   Oh, no thanks. I usually just have a piece of fruit and a functional yogurt.

She is intimidated by **Edie***'s stare. Silence.*

Clara   Right.

Edie   Ay?

Clara   Nothing.

Edie   I ken your type.

Clara   I beg your pardon?

Edie   Tree molesters. Judging me and my breakfast.

Clara   Oh gosh, no, sorry. I'm not judging, I just try to avoid bread products. I've got a sensitive stomach.

Edie   Is that right?

Long, uncomfortable silence.

Edie   Is Geoffrey nae up yet? It's nae like him tae stay in bed so late.

Clara   Oh, I don't know. He didn't . . . I thought he might've slept down here.

Edie   Nut, I've nae seen him.

Long, puzzled silence. **Geoffrey** *walks in the door, shopping bag in hand.*

Clara   Geoffrey.

Edie   And far've you bin?

Geoffrey   Jist at the Sainsbury's.

Clara   And last night?

Geoffrey   The shed.

Clara   You'd rather sleep in a cold shed than with me?

Geoffrey   I wis painting, nae sleeping.

Clara   Well, when were you planning to sleep? You know we've got a dancing lesson tonight.

Geoffrey   I dinnae like the dancing. It gies me shin splints.

Edie   Oh, your poor wee leggies.

Clara   But you love dancing.

Geoffrey   I love my painting. I realised last night. Butterflies. Puppies. Colour. Everything became clear.

Clara   What became clear?

Geoffrey *shrugs his shoulders.*

Clara   Is it just the dancing you don't like?

Pause.

Or is it me?

Silence. **Geoffrey** *takes Petits Filous yogurts out of his bag and puts them on the table. He avoids all eye contact with* **Clara**.

Edie   Whit the fuck is that?

Geoffrey   Whit?

Edie   Get that French muck ooto here.

Geoffrey   It's jist yoghurt. Nae need tae go feel.

Edie   Jist yoghurt? Jist yoghurt? Whit hiv I telt you aboot they European wyes? I've warned you. Get rid o them. Get rid o them. I'm nae hivvin debaucherous filth in my kitchen!

She picks up a jar of jam and throws it at the wall, leaving a big red stain. Silence. **Geoffrey** *is in shock,* **Clara** *is taken aback.*

Clara   Hm. Well I . . . No, well . . . you've made your feelings perfectly clear. I shall just have to . . . Right.

She cries.

Will you at least walk me to my car?

Silence. **Clara** *slowly exits by herself, slamming the door. The door quickly opens again, she pops her head round.*

Clara   Sorry. Didn't mean to slam –

She closes the door quietly.

Geoffrey (*looking at the mess*)   You sit doon . . . I'll tidy . . . Far d'we keep the brush?

He frantically looks about the kitchen, eventually finds the dustpan and brush, cleans up.

That's a silly jam. Jumpin off the table. Gied us a right fleg, ay?

Edie   Clara's gone –

Geoffrey   Aye.

Edie   Weel. Thank goodness for that. Nothing but trouble. You made the right choice.

Geoffrey   Aye. I ken.

Edie   I'm glad we can get back tae normal.

Geoffrey   Normal. Aye, let's get back tae normal. Toast? Think I'll put some toast on. Papers. There's your papers? And your cards? And I'll get a new jam. Wint some toast?

Edie   Nut. Oh, tell you whit, can you watch the toast till it's nearly done, then pop it manually and gently coz earlier when I put on toast I completely forgot aboot it, so when it popped I took a fleg and I fully pished mysel'.

Geoffrey   Hm. Dinnae think I'll bother.

They both start reading the papers in silence.

Edie (*thinking* **Geoffrey** *said something*)   Ay?

Geoffrey   Whit?

Edie   Whit d'you say?

Geoffrey   Nothing.

Edie   Oh.

They carry on reading.

Scene Twenty-One

Geoffrey *gets himself a Ribena carton. He speaks to the fisherman photo.*

Geoffrey   She smells o coconut. Did I tell you that? I wis painting fruit and foliage afore she came intae my life. Noo they're . . . different. Very different. I've painted a horse, slit fae its neck tae its groin, its womb is sliced open and there nestled inside, unharmed, is a sleeping human baby. And a skinny emaciated cat sitting on a living room windaesill, looking ootside tae a tree far his owner's grey and lifeless body hings fae a branch. And blood-spattered albino bats flying intae a cave which is actually the jaws o a tarry black monster wi hollow eyes that contain the emptiness o our existence. And then there's her. When a'hing goes dark I hiv her face pulling me tae the surface. I paint her a lot. Jist the wye she appears in my dreams.

He noisily finishes his Ribena.

Och min, it's a brave gravity that has drawn us taegither.

Scene Twenty-Two

Sainsbury's. **Geoffrey** *approaches* **Evelyn***'s desk, holding a packet.*

Evelyn   Hiya.

Geoffrey   Partially inverted refiner's syrup. Whit d'you suppose that is?

Evelyn   Must be some sort o processed sugar.

Geoffrey   When did the world get so complicated?

Evelyn   It's probably good for energy, but nae much else.

Geoffrey   Energy. That's good ay? I've bin painting you see. A lot. Nivver painted so much in my life. I got so immersed. My brain switched off. Didnae ken whit time it wis. Whit day it wis. Forgot tae eat. Forgot tae sleep. Forgot tae go tae the toilet. I even forgot tae go tae work on Monday.

Evelyn   On yoursel' Geoffrey. Here, could you dae me a favour? Can you buy some drink for me? Quite a lot o drink actually.

Geoffrey   Aye. D'you wint tae go tae the park again?

Evelyn   Nut. I'm hivvin a hoose-warming pairty the night.

Geoffrey   Oh right. Can I come?

Evelyn   Nut.

Geoffrey   How?

Evelyn   Dae I really need tae say it?

Geoffrey   Whit?

Evelyn   You're too old for my pairty.

Geoffrey   Oh.

Evelyn   And you're nae cool. And you cannae hold your drink.

Geoffrey   Is that all?

Evelyn   Nut, but it'll dae, ay?

Geoffrey   Can I tak you for a hot chocolate?

Evelyn   Nut.

Geoffrey   So I'll jist go and buy your drink then.

Evelyn   Aye. Twa twelve packs o mixed Breezers and a litre o vodka, cheers you're a life-saver.

Scene Twenty-Three

Strobe and disco lighting are on **Geoffrey**. *Remixed excerpts of the following songs, which refer to days of the week or the weekend, play loudly : Calvin Harris, 'Ready For The Weekend'; Rebecca Black, 'Friday'; Craig David, '7 Days (Sunship Remix); Whigfield, 'Saturday Night'; Basshunter, 'Saturday'; Katy Perry, 'Last Friday Night'; Black Eyed Peas, 'I Got a Feeling'.*

Occasionally his leg jerks or his hand twitches as if he is about to dance, but he doesn't. He is watching something. He wants to reach his hand out and touch it.

Geoffrey   I'm watching her dancing tae this . . . noise, which essentially sounds like a bunch o robots reciting the days o the week. She seems tae like it though. Singing along tae the days o the week wi her friend. Monday, Tuesday, Wednesday, Thursday . . . Very clever. Jumping up and doon taegither. Like a playgroup for adults. Some wee quinie's putting fags burns in her curtains. And this . . . group o young lads a'hind her. Wi plukes bigger than their brains. They've nae fully grown intae their faces yet. She's nae seeing them, but they're looking at her and her friend. Looking. At her in particular. They're pointing, and laughing, moving closer tae her. Ain lad wi an impractical haircut. He's moving closer. Tae her. He appears tae be harbouring a deep fascination wi her bottom. His friends gieing him nods and smiling. Pushing him. His hands reaching forth . . . he's touching . . . he's touching . . . Her eyes . . . look at her eyes. The anger and hate as she smashes a bottle across his face . . . I cannae look. At her look.

He looks at the fisherman photo.

Is this whit it feels like, Dad? How does it feel like this?

Scene Twenty-Four

Radio is on. **Edie** *seems distracted.* **Thomas** *knocks and enters.*

Thomas   Hallo, Edie.

Edie   How's it going, Thomas?

Thomas   Aye, nae bad, nae bad. I wis jist chatting tae Mrs Krimble. She wis at the Sainsbury's the other day, for her main weekly shop – she tends tae pop tae the Lidl for her daily odds 'n'sods, ken – and she telt me she seen your lad there.

Edie   Geoffrey?

Thomas   Aye. Course it's a free country and a' that. But, she says she seen him lingering – is that the word she used? – lingering, loitering aboot a young lassie that works there.

Edie   Why wid he be daeing that?

Thomas   I'll leave that wi you. I'm jist the messenger. I'll also leave you wi these. Sprouts.

He puts a small bag of brussel sprouts on the table.

Edie   Very kind thanks.

Thomas   There's mair sprouts far they came fae. Thought I'd tak you a wee droppy at first. Nae sure how much you'd get through.

Edie   Certainly nae as much as your wife.

Thomas   True, true. She could pack them awa like naebiddy's business. Onywye, cheerio. Edie.

He exits.

Edie *notices* **Geoffrey**'s *jacket and bag on his chair. She decides to go through his pockets, then his bag. She finds what seems to be a bottomless supply of Sainsbury's receipts. She becomes upset as she picks a few at random to look at in detail. Then, searching in his inside pocket she finds lots of Murray Mint wrappers, then a bottle of coconut bubbly bath. Shocked, she sits down to steady herself.* **Geoffrey** *comes in from being in the shed.*

Geoffrey   Whit happened?

Edie   This . . . this . . . whit's this, Geoffrey?

Geoffrey   Bubbly bath.

Edie   And whit flavour is it?

Geoffrey   Um. Coconut. I jist fancied a change.

Edie   A change? Yiv used lavender bubbly bath for forty-odd year, and noo you fancy a change? The divvil has got intae your heid. He's gied you an insatiable lust for the exotic. There's nae other explanation.

Geoffrey   Speak aboot getting your knickers in a twist.

Edie   I'm starting tae wonder if you tak after me at a'. I've gied you so much, Geoffrey, but I'm nae seeing it. I'm nae seeing my reflection in your eyes.

Beat.

Get oot. I need some time alone tae mourn.

Geoffrey   I'm going.

Geoffrey *grabs a bottle of bubble bath and exits.*

Scene Twenty-Five

Sainsbury's. **Evelyn** *is reading a magazine,* **Geoffrey** *approaches with a sandwich.*

Geoffrey   Hiya.

Evelyn   Ken this, I'll nivver understand fake tits.

Shows magazine.

Does this look desirable tae you?

Geoffrey *freezes.*

Evelyn   Ken. Got tae stop reading this shite. Daein my fuckin nut in.

Geoffrey   Sandwich.

Evelyn   Aye. It is.

Geoffrey   Did you ken sandwiches were invented by the Romans?

Evelyn   Is that right?

Geoffrey   Dunno. Did you hiv a good pairty?

Evelyn   Och, dinnae remind me. Fucking hell. I got . . . arrested –

Geoffrey   Arrested?

Evelyn   Shh. For assault. Then for swearing at police manny. These police folk, you'd think they'd be hard as hell but they're actually really sensitive. I mean, I've bin called a cunt plenty times but I've nivver went radge aboot it. And my flat's totally fucked. A'hing's got fag burns and drink spilt and my kitchen door's hinging off the hinges. Ohhh Jesus. Fuuuuck. I wis a prick tae think I actually had friends.

Geoffrey   I'm your friend.

Evelyn   Geoffrey. Dinnae be weird.

Geoffrey   How's his face?

Evelyn   If anything I've probably made it look better.

Beat.

How d'you ken that?

Geoffrey   You said.

Evelyn   Nut, I didnae.

Geoffrey   Dunno.

Evelyn   Ken whit, you widnae happen tae be responsible for the heap o Murray Mint wrappers outside my windaes?

Silence.

Hm. I think you should stop coming here. I think that's enough.

Scene Twenty-Six

A week later. The kitchen looks messy. Radio is on. **Geoffrey** *comes in with shopping bags.* **Edie** *jumps at the door going.*

Geoffrey   Tell you whit, that Lidl's okay actually. Wis surprised. It's got some good stuff. Jist popping the bags on the table.

He takes a pair of earmuffs out of his bag.

Look, Mither. I got you a pair o these. Ear muffins. Look. Will you look?

He puts them on **Edie**.

Geoffrey   Coz you dinnae like it when the door goes or the toaster pops, dae you? These keep the bad noises oot.

Takes items out of bag.

And I got you some tattie salad and a paper, Sudoku and a bratwurst, a sma' size panatone mixed fruit, and a jigsaw. Is that whit you wint? Coz you should be daein mair than listening tae the radio. Coz I dinnae ken if you're even listening.

Takes colouring books out of bag.

Look. Colouring books. They're jist pictures for you tae colour. The blue ain is pictures o the seaside. Green is pictures o fairms and the country. The red is o various forms o transport. Which ain d'you wint first?

Beat.

This ain? This ain? This ain? Ay? Jigsaw? The blue ain? Whit aboot the green ain? You like the countryside ay? Fae a distance.

Becoming flustered and overwhelmed, he keeps dropping the books.

Seven days and nae a peep.

Beat.

Och.

He gives up, walks out of the house. **Edie** *eventually walks out after*

Geoffrey.

Scene Twenty-Seven

Outside. **Geoffrey** *is waiting.* **Evelyn** *has just finished work.*

Geoffrey   Murray Mint?

Evelyn   Fuck's sake. You ken you're banned.

Geoffrey   I've nae bin in.

Evelyn   Still. I can get the security guard.

Geoffrey (*shrugs*)   Yiv changed your smell.

Evelyn   Aye.

Geoffrey   I liked the coconut.

Evelyn   I ken. Whit's in the scaffy bag?

Geoffrey   Oh aye, it's for you.

Evelyn   That's whit I wis dreading.

Geoffrey   I've painted you these. Three. It's a trilogy. In the first, you'll see it's a manny deid. Too distant tae mak oot fa it is or whit's happened, but there's a hint o red aroond the chest area. In the second instalment, you'll see the scene has bin magnified by 75 per cent. And you'll notice that the deid manny is beginning tae tak a likeness tae mysel'. Geoffrey Buncher. Lyin wi a hole far my heart used tae be. In the third instalment, which again is magnified by a further 75 per cent, you'll notice the scene centres around the heart. My bloody, still, but slightly warm, heart. My heart held in my hand. My bloody hand that cut oot my ain heart. Holding it up for all – i.e. you – tae see. My bloody heart. Wi a word carved on it. That word being your name. Evelyn.

Evelyn   You really need help, Geoffrey.

Geoffrey   That's how you make me feel. That's how . . . I feel.

He holds out the paintings for **Evelyn**, *she doesn't accept his offer. She starts to walk away, takes her mobile phone out.*

Geoffrey   Texting your boyfriend?

Evelyn   I dinnae hiv a boyfriend.

Geoffrey   I ken.

Evelyn   I ken you ken.

Geoffrey *follows her.*

Geoffrey   I jist wint tae watch you.

Evelyn   I've seen you watching me.

Geoffrey   Nothing wrong wi that.

Evelyn   I've heard your footsteps stop behind every lamppost.

Geoffrey   Nothing wrong wi that.

Evelyn   I've seen your shadow duck a'hind every parked car.

Geoffrey   Nothing wrong wi that.

Evelyn   You ken my shift patterns, ay?

Geoffrey   Nothing wrong wi that.

Evelyn   And how long it taks me tae get hame.

Geoffrey   Sixteen minutes. Unless yiv done some shopping then it's sixteen minutes plus howivver long it took you tae dae your shopping.

Beat.

Nothing wrong wi that.

Evelyn   Nothing wrong wi that. But tell me, whit if I wisnae hame sixteen minutes later? Whit if I took a different route? If I disappeared fae your sight? Whit wid happen? Wid you feel a bitty uncomfortable? Whit if I got hame an hour later? Wid your heart start beating faster? Wid blood rush tae your heid? Wid your palms sweat? Wid anger replace your harmless demeanour? Because one day I wilnae be hame sixteen minutes later. I wilnae be hame one hour, two hours or three hours later. And one day I wilnae be walking by mysel'. I'll be holding a boy's hand. A boyfriend. Holding his hand and fallin in love. Whit'll you dae when you see me in love?

Beat.

Evelyn   Nothin wrong wi that my airse.

She walks away. The sky rumbles with thunder. **Geoffrey** *is upset. He exits.* **Edie** *appears in the background.*

Scene Twenty-Eight

The next day. **Edie** *is doing a jigsaw slowly.*

Geoffrey   You ready for tea?

Silence.

Beans on . . . something.

Silence.

Mither, will you speak tae me?

Silence.

I'm nae sure whit I've done.

Thomas *knocks at the door and enters.*

Thomas   Jist Thomas.

Geoffrey   That's Thomas, Mither. That's Thomas closing the door.

Thomas *gently closes the door.*

Thomas   Hallo, Edie.

Geoffrey   That's Thomas saying hallo. Say hallo.

Thomas (*pause*)   Hallo, Geoffrey. And how's Edie?

Geoffrey   Jist . . . jist . . . jigsaw.

Thomas   Aye, a fine job your daein there, Edie. Ken you should start wi the corners?

Silence.

Righto. Geoffrey, I hate tae hiv tae say this, but, I come here as a neighbour and a friend. There's bin a major incident in the toon and I suspect the lads doon the station will eventually be lead tae you.

Geoffrey   Me?

Thomas   They'll be checking you hiv an alibi a'tween ten p.m last night and one a.m. this morn.

Silence.

D'you hiv an alibi a'tween ten p.m last night and one a.m. this morn?

Edie (*beat*)   Geoffrey wis helping me wi my jigsaw.

Thomas   Of course, Edie. I kent that wid be the case. As I say, jist tae prepare you. And Edie. Nae need tae panic. It'll jist be routine like.

Edie   Whit's happened?

Thomas   A lassie wis killed.

Beat.

Brutally murdered, in fact. Like an animal.

Beat.

A terrible mess.

Beat.

Poor lassie.

Beat.

Mind, this is all off the record, but . . . this lassie had bin seen wi you. In fact, I believe she got you chucked oot o Sainsbury's last week.

Geoffrey   Sai –

Thomas   But yiv got your alibi. Nae worries. (*To* **Edie**.) I'll see you later, Edie.

No response. He pats her shoulder.

Okey-dokey. Later, Geoffrey.

Thomas *exits. A long silence.* **Geoffrey** *quietly cries.*

Edie   That stupid dog's bin digging up our gairden again. The rose beds are ruined.

Geoffrey   I need a bath.

Edie   And she's bin poopin all ower our lawn.

Geoffrey   I need a bath.

Edie   Wis a dog hair in my tea cup.

Geoffrey   I need a bath.

Edie   Think she's bin in my kitchen.

Geoffrey   Mither.

Edie   Touchin my cups.

Geoffrey   I'm going for a bath.

Edie   Cups.

Geoffrey *heads for the door, pauses, but doesn't look back.*

Geoffrey   If you hear a scream, dinnae worry. I'm jist needing tae scream.

Scene Twenty-Nine

Edie *is wearing earmuffs.* **Geoffrey** *enters from outside with shopping and newspaper.*

Geoffrey   Think this'll be the last paper we read for a whiley. Folk are starting tae stare.

Edie   Paper.

Geoffrey   I'm sure it'll all blow ower soon.

Edie   Paper.

Geoffrey   Aye, paper. Luckily I've stocked up on essentials. Ribena. Bread. Tins o . . . stuff.

Edie   Paper.

Geoffrey   Aye.

Edie   Paper.

Geoffrey   D'you wint the paper? Is that it?

Edie   Paper-thin walls.

I've heard you speakin.

Used tae speak tae him aboot Mammy.

Asked him tae watch ower me.

Geoffrey   Ay?

Edie   But she pushed me oot.

Oot o your thoughts.

I heard you speakin tae him.

Couldnae hiv the dog messing up our gairden.

Ken how long the roses hiv bin growing?

A'wyes. A'wyes bin growing.

Dog wis in the gairden.

Diggin up the roses.

Making a mess o everything.

Yiv bin speaking tae a manny.

That nivver existed.

Geoffrey   Ay? But . . . that's my dad.

Points to picture.

Edie   I've nae idea fa that manny is.

Your daddy wisnae a manny.

Your daddy wis a monster.

He wisnae a manny. A monster.

She wis digging up the roses.

Hushed her up wi an axe.

Geoffrey   I see fa needed an alibi.

Phone rings. He lets it ring off.

No. No. No. NO. No. NO. NO. NO.

A long silence. He composes himself.

Tea, Mither ?

There is now a sense of angry people gathering outside, shouting, throwing missiles and bricks at various windows of the house. **Geoffrey** *spoons food from a bowl into* **Edie***'s mouth.*

Or maybes I should go ootside. Gie them whit they wint. Tear me tae bits. Spit in my face. Smash my heid wi a brick. Abiddy thinks I did it. S'pose I might've, in some wye. Yiv alwyes kent whit I winted afore I've kent mysel'. When I wis hungry. When I wis thirsty. When I wis tired and needed tae sleep. When I've bin grumpy and needed tae be by mysel'. When I've bin oot too long in the sun. When I've bin inside too long and needed some fresh air. And when I've needed tae change my pants. Yiv a'wyes kent when I've bin hurt. Yiv a'wyes stopped my hurt.

He goes to the window, shuts the curtains.

But onywye, I wilnae gie them whit they wint. Coz far wid that leave you. We're best sticking taegither.

Pause.

Geoffrey. Your son. Walking taewards you. Tiny, wee, final, steps, taewards you.

Reaching for your hand.

Edie *takes his hand,* **Geoffrey** *helps her to her feet. They hug.*

Geoffrey   Let's run you a bath shall we?

He smiles at **Edie***, she smiles back.*

Geoffrey   A nice wee bubbly bath.

They slowly walk arm in arm across the floor. They exit to go upstairs.

Narrative

Anthony Neilson

Narrative was first performed at The Royal Court Theatre, London on 5 April 2013, with the following cast (in order of appearance):

Olly	Olly Rix
Waitress/Imogen	Imogen Doel
Sophie	Sophie Ross
Brian/Hitman 1	Brian Doherty
Barney aka Noel/Lawrence of Arabia/Hitman 2	Barnaby Power
Zawe	Zawe Ashton
Chris/Chris as TV Exec/Chris as Therapist	Christine Entwisle
Director	Anthony Neilson
Assistant Director	Ned Bennett
Music and Sound Design	Nick Powell
Production Design	Garance Marneur
Lighting Design	Chahine Yavroyan

Credit

As ever, I must make a special point of thanking the brilliant cast. This play would simply not exist in this form if it weren't for their presence, their creative contributions and their personal support. Thanks also to my steadfast collaborator Nick Powell, who plays a much greater part in the creation of these plays than a mere text can ever communicate. Thanks to Dominic Cooke for his remarkable trust, and everyone at the Royal Court for their hard work and continually warm embrace. Finally, my thanks to the rest of the creative team, the stage management team – Jules and Brian – and everyone who drifted in and out of our rehearsal room, offering up their valued ideas and opinions. You were all a part of this story.

Notes for Production

There is a growing body of evidence that our use of the internet and related technologies is changing us on a neurological level. I believe it is also changing our perception of narrative. Structurally, *Narrative* is an attempt to find a modern, mainstream form that accommodates these changes and mimics the 'multi-tab' experience of internet surfing.

The text of *Narrative* is essentially a transcript of a live event, staged at a specific time, in a specific place and tailored to its participants. It was not written to be read, as such, and I have made no attempt to render it 'timeless' or 'universal'. As a result, it will either remain miraculously relevant or – more likely – date horribly. In either case, it may require some adaptation, depending on when and where you are staging it (especially if you live in a country without double-decker buses).

You will see that we used various clips culled from the internet as a kind of connective tissue. I have indicated the content of these clips and provided links, which may or may not remain active. It is up to you how closely you observe their content, or whether you use the clips at all.

You will also notice a couple of moments when we use the screen to flash up images. Unlike the clips, these images were not meant to support the narrative but to act as 'distractions' for the audience, in keeping with the formal conceit. In production, I ended up using this technique less than I had originally intended: partly for technical reasons but also because I was worried it would tip the piece into an 'experimental' area, which was not my intention.

As time goes on, and forms evolve, audiences may be more able to assimilate such distractions without getting unhelpfully stuck on their meaning. You should, if you wish, see this element as a 'free' area in which to distinguish your production and provide lateral/parallel comment or subtext.

The same could possibly be said of the video clips, with the caveat that you think carefully about their purpose in the text as it stands – particularly those that reinforce the symbol of the bison, and those that set up the events of the epilogue – and that you remain conceptually true to the spirit and themes of the play.

I am happy to enter into a dialogue about all of this and am contactable through my agent, unless I have died.

Anthony Neilson, 2014

Prologue

(**Note:** *This voice-over occurs over a slide show of the location described, only interrupted in the later stages by a subliminal frame – the content of which you may decide for yourself.*)

Narrator (V/O)   The earliest example of narrative art so far discovered dates back seventeen thousand years and can be found in the Lascaux caves of southwest France.

The central image of this painting – which may be the work of two to three artists – appears to depict a man with the face, or mask, of a bird in a violent struggle with a bison. The man has four fingers on each hand and an outsized penis. The bison is partly eviscerated, its entrails hanging in a loop from its body, and seems to have butted the man with its horns. The man appears to be falling backwards, either injured or dead.

Olly *is sitting in a café, texting.*

Narrator (V/O)   To the left of this central image, we see a rhinoceros. To its right, we find what may be a staff of some kind, with a bird atop it. The significance of these elements to the narrative is unclear.

Also unclear is the purpose of the narrative. Is it fiction or reportage? Is it a warning or a charm? Who is the protagonist? Is it the man or the bison?

Assuming, however, that the story told is what it appears to be – man wounds bison; bison kills man – this cave painting may be not only the first ever narrative but also the first recorded representation of mortality. Indeed, it is only if we assume the man to have been wounded or killed that the narrative has linear momentum. His death provides us with an ending and allows us to extrapolate his life.

Without this consequence, the painting in the Lascaux cave would be only a picture of a struggle.

A waitress approaches **Olly**.

Waitress   A guy said to give you this.

She hands him an envelope.

Olly   Who?

Waitress   He's . . . oh . . . I think he's gone now.

Olly *looks at the envelope.*

Olly   What did he look like?

Waitress   Just a guy. Can I get you anything else? Another coffee?

Olly   No . . . thanks.

The **Waitress** *lingers too long, as if attracted to him. She blushes, then leaves.*

With her gone, **Olly** *opens the envelope and takes out a photograph.*

(***Note:** The photograph, whenever looked at directly, is accompanied by a noise or noises.*)

He's shocked by what he sees and stuffs it back into the envelope.

He looks around the café, self-consciously, unsure if he's being watched.

He calls the **Waitress** *over.*

Olly   Excuse me . . . is this a joke?

Waitress   What do you mean?

In another area, **Brian** *and* **Sophie** *enter, having an argument.*

(***Note:** Two scenes now play. There can be overlap but allow the audience to get the gist of each.*)

Brian   You know what you are? You know what you fucking are?

Sophie   No, please tell me. Please tell me what I am?

Olly   This.

Brian   You're a quitter, that's what you are!

Waitress   I don't know. A guy just said to give it to you.

Brian   You're a fucking coward! People like you—

Sophie   People like me?

Olly   What guy, though? Where?

Brian   You never had to fight for anything your whole lives. You're born with a sense of entitlement, like happiness is a God-given right—

Olly   What did he look like?

Brian   And the minute you get a tiny sniff of anything less than perfect fucking bliss, that's it: you're off!

Waitress   I told you: just a guy—

Sophie   What are you talking about, people like me?

Olly   Tall, short, fat, thin—?

Brian   You . . . your whole fucking generation—!

Sophie   Oh right . . . so we should go back to the Good Old Days, should we? Stay with each other 'cause we're worried what the neighbours say?

Waitress   He was just . . . normal-looking.

Brian   I'm saying love is hard . . . !

Sophie   'Cos that really worked for our parents, didn't it?

Brian   Oh for fuck's sake . . . you're not your mother, OK? You're nothing like her.

Olly   Did he have a beard?

Brian   And I'm nothing like your fucking father, either!

Waitress   No, I don't think so.

Barney *enters, with a bison sock puppet on his hand and addresses the audience directly.*

(*Note: the other four actors improvise their scenes concurrently now – the lines that follow are only a guideline and can be used or not. They may take the scenes in whichever direction they wish. Do not attempt to delineate the scenes – the audience must choose which to follow, but allow Barney to be heard until established.*)

Barney   Gas bills, electricity bills . . . they seem to be just rising all the time!

Sophie   You really don't get a fucking thing I'm saying, do you?

Olly   He had no distinguishing features whatsoever?

Barney   I'm worried that I'm not getting the best deal from my service providers. It's all so complicated!

Waitress   I didn't really look at him—

Brian   Yes, I get what you're saying . . . What I'm saying is this is just the shit that goes on in your life and it never stops—

Barney (*Voicing puppet*)   No-um worry, Kemo Sabe! Leave it to um-Bison!

Karaoke-style music intro begins.

Olly   You didn't look at him?

Barney (*As puppet*)   Every month I'll check on line that you're getting the best deals possible from your providers! (*As self*) Will you, Bison?

Waitress   I did but I don't remember what he looked like.

Sophie   Fine, OK, but I can't just take your word for that—

Barney (*As puppet*)   And every time a better deal comes up, I'll change your accounts to the cheapest supplier!

Zawe *enters, microphone in hand, and sings a bad version of a song.*

(*Note: Although you may choose your own song, in the original production, **Zawe** sang David Bowie's 'Where Are We Now' which was appropriate thematically and because, having just been*

released, there was much talk of it on social media. Note also that
Zawe *got the lyrics wrong, singing 'Walking the Dog' instead of*
'Walking the Dead'. At one point, the screen displays an advert
for the album, emphasising that it's available 'In all formats'. The
music drowns out the other actors but they continue to improvise
their scenes. Again, these lines are only a guide. The chatter
should build to a cacophonous level.)

Sophie   I need to find it out for myself, don't you get that?

Olly   You don't remember?

Waitress   Look there's a lot of stuff going on . . .

Barney *responds to an unseen director.*

Barney   Oh what, you want it more—?

Waitress   The guy said to give this to you and I did—

Brian   Fine, ignore me, go ahead—

Barney   Oh right, OK . . . let me go back a bit . . .

Barney   retraces his steps.

Brian   Waste your fucking life like I wasted mine—

Waitress   I didn't know who he was, I didn't know if he was a
friend of yours or what—

Olly   All right, calm down—

Barney (*As puppet*)   Every month I'll check on line that you're
getting the best deals possible from your providers!

Sophie   You haven't wasted your life—

Barney (*As self*)   Will you, bison?

Brian   Forty-seven years old and fuck-all to show for it—

Waitress   I'm totally calm, I just don't get why you're taking a
tone with me—

Barney (*As puppet*)   And every time a better deal comes up, I'll
change your accounts to the cheapest supplier!

Olly   I'm not taking a tone with you—

Brian   Yes . . . I fucking have. And I just wasted *another* fucking year of it—

Waitress   Yes you are.

Sophie   Is that what you think?

Barney (*As self*)   And I don't have to do anything?

Olly   I'm not, but you have to admit it's pretty strange—

Brian   Except it's you that's wasted it . . . It's you that's wasted my fucking time!

Barney (*As puppet*)   Not a thing! Just leave it to the bison!

Now, suddenly, all the actors abandon their scenes simultaneously and join in with the chorus of **Zawe** *'s song. The singing is rowdy rather than tuneful the way a crowd sings.*

The song ends abruptly, perhaps even unresolved.

Darkness.

In the darkness, a digitised female voice, glitchy, stuttering, steadily degrading.

Voice   What did you expect of life?

(***Note:*** *On the screen, the first YouTube clip plays. The clip depicts a group of tourists in a National Park approaching a bison. The clip is called 'Bison Fury' and, at the time of writing, can be found here:* http://www.youtube.com/watch?v=F7VghMbLiMA *Over this:*)

Voice Why did you expect it? Who told you what to expect?

Still in darkness, the **Waitress** *drops a plate or cup, which smashes.*

Voice   What was expected of you? Who expected this of you? What did you expect of yourself? What do you expect of others? Of your friends, of your partners, of your children? Have they met those expectations? Was anything unexpected? Did you respond the way you expected? Why do we expect?

The voice breaks down, repeating this last phrase, disintegrating.

(**Note:** *The video clip stops just before the bison, inevitably, charges the too-close tourists. It freezes and fades with the* **voice**.)

Scene One

Olly *and* **Barney** *stare at the photograph, both amused and repelled.*

Barney   It's an arsehole! Jesus Christ, it's an arsehole! Isn't it?

Olly *shrugs.*

Barney   That's disgusting!

Olly   It's fucking gross, isn't it?

Barney   It really is. And you didn't see him?

Olly   No.

Barney   You don't have any idea who it was?

Olly   No.

Barney   That's unbelievable . . .

Pause.

Olly   So it wasn't you?

Barney   Me?

Olly   As a joke?

Barney   No . . . I mean, it's quite funny, but no. I wouldn't even think of it.

Olly   I'm not angry about it—

Barney   No—

Olly   I'd be relieved if it was you, to be honest.

Barney   I'm sure you would, but no . . . I mean, if I was going to play a joke like that, I'd have put it in your pocket or something

maybe, for you to find . . . but this . . . How would I even have
known where you were?

Olly   I don't know. Unless you followed me.

Barney   Followed you? Seriously?

Olly   I know.

Barney   You think I've got nothing better to do than follow you
around?

Olly   No . . . I know. I don't think it was you. I just don't know
who'd do that.

Barney   Did anybody know you'd be at that café at that time?

Olly   I didn't know myself. I only went in because I was early
for the audition.

Barney   And it wasn't some kind of set-up? There wasn't some
. . . camera crew hidden somewhere?

Olly   I thought that but no . . . I didn't see anything. And
wouldn't I have to sign a release form or something?

Barney   But why would anyone do that? Give a complete
stranger a photo of an—

Chris *walks onto the stage, interrupting them.*

Chris   Sorry. Excuse me. Sorry.

*They watch her take a central position on the stage and address
the audience directly. She is nervous.*

Chris   Hello um . . . this is a poem I wrote for my son, David.
It's called just . . . It's called 'For David'.

*She holds the note with trembling hands, gathers herself, then
starts. She is not a performer.*

David died a year ago
Such pain I hope you'll never know
My angel lived to seventeen
The most beautiful boy you've ever seen

Pause.

> They told us he had overdosed
> But we knew David was not morose
> Something else was to blame
> Finding out what became our aim.
> We knew he'd been on medicine
> To cure the acne on his skin
> But to our shock and dismay
> We found out it had been banned in the USA
> Vyoclozamine, the drug is named
> And we found out that it was famed
> For causing suicidal feelings
> Instead of its proper job of healing
> Since my baby passed away

Pause.

Chris

> I've dedicated every hour and day
> To making sure this drug is banned
> In every corner of the land
> I'll never rest until I'm done
> So please go to banvyoclozaminefordavid.com
> And take a moment to sign your name
> So no one else will feel this pain

Pause.

> I never wanted to have this task

Pause.

> Being a Mum was all I asked
> But with your help perhaps I could
> In David's name . . .
> Do something good.
> Thank you for listening.

She exits, but stops and turns back to the audience.

Chris   Oh and if you look on your seats, you'll find a leaflet which'll tell you some more about the campaign and the website and stuff. Thank you.

(*Note: the leaflets are there.*)

Olly *and* **Barney** *watch her go. Pause.*

Barney   And whose arsehole is it anyway? Is it his?

Olly   I don't know.

Barney   'Cos if it's his—

Olly   What?

Barney   Maybe it's an invitation.

Olly   An invitation?

Barney   Yeah, you know—

Olly   What . . . get a load of this?

Barney   Yeah, you know . . . have a bit of this.

Olly   Of this sweet candy?

Barney   Of this sweet, sweet candy.

Olly   Fuck, that's horrible. But then why would he leave?

Barney   Cold feet.

Pause.

Barney   It's not nice, though, is it? I mean – I'm no expert on anuses but that one looks particularly . . . sticky.

Olly   It's definitely a man's though, right?

Barney   It's close-up, true. It's hard to tell.

Olly   Maybe it's his wife's.

Barney   What—

Olly   I don't know. Maybe he gets some kind of thrill out of giving people pictures of his wife's arsehole.

Barney   No, come on: it's got to be a joke. Maybe he was watching you from across the street or something.

Olly   Yeah, but why me? There were lots of other people in there. Why did he single me out?

Olly   *begins to sing.*

(*Sings*) Am I an arsehole? I mean, I may be but I try my best to hide it. Is it obvious to everyone? Do people look at me and think: that guy's an arsehole?

Zawe *explodes into the room.*

Zawe   You're a fucking arsehole, you know that?! How dare you! How dare you fucking speak to me about my mother! What the fuck do you know about my mother or what she's been through?!

Olly   Nothing.

Zawe   My mother would do anything for me! My mother would fucking die for me! How dare you!

Olly   I didn't say anything about your mother—

Zawe   You should fucking wish anyone loved you as much as my mother loves me!

Olly   Fine. I'm sure that's true. I was just raising the possibility that maybe you're not quite as secure as you think you are—

Zawe   What the fuck do you know? You don't know a fucking thing about me!

Olly   No! That's exactly it! I don't. You don't know a person after just three months . . . you can't . . .

Zawe   Three and a half!

Olly   Fine . . . whatever . . . but you're right: I don't know you. That's my point.

Pause. **Zawe** *softens. She uses her hands to mimic cats' ears. She approaches him cutely, mewling.* **Olly** *sighs heavily. She butts her head against his leg.*

Zawe (*Baby voice*)   You do, dough. Doo do know me.

Olly   Jesus Christ!

Zawe   That's the thing about being soulmates. It's not about time. Something just connects. And I know . . . I understand: it's scary to think that this might be it; that we might never fall in love with anyone else again . . . but there's something much, much scarier—

Olly   Yes! Being trapped in a / relationship with you—

Zawe   There is no trap! / That's an illusion! You can walk away any time you want!

Olly   Which is what I'm trying to do!

Zawe   No, but don't you get it?! We're going to DIE, man! Do you get that? It's not miraculously not going to happen! You're not going to pass ninety, then a hundred, then two hundred, and someone says 'How come you're two hundred?' and you go, 'Oh I don't know, I just somehow didn't *die* for some reason'. NO! One day you'll wake up and that will be the LAST day you ever wake up! And that'll be it, you'll just be gone, nothing. You won't come back, not even as a zombie. Do you get that? Can you get your head around that?

Olly   So we're going to die: what does that have to do with anything?

Zawe   What does it NOT have to do with EVERYTHING?! If you abandon this – if you walk out . . . One day I'll die and you won't even be there. You might not even read about it, if I don't get famous. You might not even know I've died. You don't think that's tragic?

He doesn't really.

Zawe   Oh. OK. I see.

Olly   Oh come on . . . look . . . I like you and everything and I think it'll be very sad when you die. But you can't possibly feel this intensely about something after just three . . . three and a half months—

Zawe   No, you mean YOU can't. But you're not everybody, yeah? We're not all just people you've thought up in your head!

Olly   You don't love me, Zawe. You might feel like you do, but it's not real.

Zawe   Don't tell me what's real! I'll decide what's real, all right? Is that all right with you?

Olly   It's an infatuation—

Zawe   Fuck you. I'm not infatuated with you, you piece of shit.

Olly   OK. OK.

She looks panicky all of a sudden.

Zawe   Oh God, just . . . tell me what's good about me.

Olly   What?

Zawe   I just can't hear any more about what's wrong with me. Tell me five things that are good about me.

Pause.

Olly   There's lots of good things about you . . .

Zawe   Then just tell me five. Please.

Olly   Well . . . you're pretty . . .

Zawe   Am I?

Olly   Yes, of course.

She blushes.

Olly   And you're . . . kind. You're generous.

Pause.

Olly   Sociable.

Zawe   Sociable?

Olly   Yeah, I mean . . . I don't have to worry if I take you out that you won't . . . get along with people, or be shy. Aaaand . . .

Pause.

Olly   You're stylish. You dress well.

Zawe   I try to.

Pause.

Zawe   One more?

Olly   That's five.

Zawe   That's four. Pretty, kind, sociable, stylish . . .

Olly   Generous.

Zawe   That's the same as kind.

Olly   No it isn't.

Zawe   Pretty much.

Olly   Fuck . . . fine, you're . . . a good . . . singer.

Zawe   Do you think so?

Olly   Yes. You're a very good singer. OK?

Zawe   So I'm pretty, I'm kind, I'm stylish and sociable and generous and (*sings*) I can sing!

Olly *nods.*

Zawe   So why would you want to lose all that?! I mean, what do you *want* from a person?!

Olly   Oh God, look – it's just not going to work out, OK? There's nothing wrong with you—

Zawe   'It's not you, it's me'?

Olly   No . . . it's *not* me. Some things just don't work out. I'm sorry.

Zawe   OK, fine. Fuck you. You die alone. You just go and blip out of existence with nobody there to give a shit. Go on.

Pause.

Olly   OK, well . . .

He wanders towards the door.

Zawe   But not tonight. I'll be fine in the morning just . . . don't leave me here alone in this house, with all the memories—

Olly   What fucking memories?! Domino's Pizza? This is only the third time I've been here!

Pause.

Olly   You'll be OK.

Zawe   I won't. You don't understand: it'll be like a desert. Like a desert stretching out all around me, as far as I can see.

She looks bleak.

Zawe   Stay until the sun comes up.

Olly   I can't.

Zawe   Please.

Olly   You'll be all right.

Zawe   I won't.

Olly   You will. Really.

Zawe   Fuck you.

Pause. He opens the door.

Zawe   I want my jumper back!

Olly   What jumper?

Zawe   The jumper I bought you last week.

Pause.

Olly   Fine, I'll get the jumper.

Zawe   Tonight.

Olly   Not tonight—

Zawe   Tonight or I'll call the police.

Olly   And say what?

Zawe   That you stole it.

Olly   Well . . . good luck with that. I'll drop it off in the week.

Zawe   And the receipt.

She pronounces the 'p' in receipt. **Olly** *holds his temper.*

Olly   The what?

Zawe   The receipt.

She does it again. **Olly** *counts to five.*

Zawe   What?

Olly   It's *receipt.*

Zawe   What?

Olly   You don't pronounce the P!

Zawe   That's how it's spelt.

Olly   I know how it's spelt! Have you never heard the word before?

Zawe   What word?

Olly   *Receipt.* Have you never heard anyone say it?!

Pause.

Zawe   Are you done?

Olly   Done what?

Zawe   Assassinating my character?

He leaves.

Zawe *sits there. The sound of a desert wind, gathering force. The desert sun begins to blaze.*

Lawrence of Arabia *enters, in full Arab attire, sandy and* *exhausted. He kneels at the oasis and fills a canister with water, which he drinks needily.*

His thirst quenched, he sees **Zawe**. *She gives him a small wave and he half-waves back, as if he's seen her before somewhere.*

Lawrence *turns to address the audience.*

Lawrence   For his fortieth birthday, he decided to do something he had never done. He decided to jump from a plane. At precisely the right moment, he pulled on the ripcord, but his parachute failed to open. The emergency parachute also failed. As he fell towards the earth, he realised with certainty that he was about to die. 'Of course,' he thought, quite calmly. 'Why did I expect any different? I have jumped from a plane.'

Lawrence *exits.*

(*The next YouTube clip plays. It is called 'Is This What Grabriel's Horn Will Sound Like'* (*sic*) *and at the time of writing can be found here:* http://www.youtube.com/watch?v=KjZRygnibE0

The clip first shows text, read by a low American voice. This is the text:

> For the Lord himself will descend from Heaven with a shout, with the voice of an Archangel, and with the trumpet of God. And the dead in Christ will rise first.

> What will the trumpet of the Archangel sound like? Will it be a new sound? Or something all-too familiar, heard around the world?

The clip then cuts to home footage of suburban houses, the sky heavy with clouds, and the unearthly, thunderous sound of a horn blaring, seemingly coming from the sky.)

Scene Two

Brian *enters, talking on the phone*

Brian   Solomon? It's Brian. How's it going, my man? I know, we've been playing phone-pong a bit, haven't we? Message tennis. No, I'm grand, I'm grand. I was just calling to say I've just read Ep Three . . . Oh, it's terrific stuff. I tell you now, honestly, if the next three episodes are as good as the first three . . . I think we're talking about the best series yet. OK, so . . . There was just one thing I wanted to ask about: have you got the script to hand? Grand, well it's bottom of 25 . . . end of that scene in the wine cellar.

Pause.

Got it? OK, so I say 'Tell M'Lud I'll be up in a minute'. Exactly. Now then it says I cough, right? It says 'Finnegan coughs into his handkerchief'. Then it says 'He looks at the handkerchief' . . . Beat.

Brian   Yeah. And I was just wondering what the thinking was with that?

Sophie *enters, also on the phone but in a different space:*

Sophie   No, I haven't: I don't really watch movies much any more.

Brian   Why would they write that in, though? I mean . . . why end a scene on that?

Sophie   If I'm going to watch something, it's more likely a TV series, you know . . .

Brian   No, but it's the beat. It says 'He looks at the handkerchief . . . Beat'. What's that about? What happens in the beat?

Sophie   Or like a box-set or something . . .

Brian   But what do I see in the handkerchief?

Sophie   Yeah 'cos it's like reading a really good book, you know? It's the same feeling I used to get from that.

Brian   Phlegm? What, so he's just got a cold? Because that doesn't seem like a very dramatic storyline. You know . . . given that the manor's just been hit by a Doodlebug . . .

Sophie   I don't really have the time for books—

Brian   But if it was phlegm, I'd just shrug . . . who cares about phlegm?

Sophie   I don't know, my mind just starts to wander—

Brian   There must be something in it. Something in the phlegm.

Sophie   I think I've got ADHD or something . . . seriously—

Brian   Sol . . . you're the Producer: you don't know?

Chris *enters, also on the phone, also in a different space.*

Chris   Yes, I know he's very busy but he did say he'd meet with me before the next parliamentary session—

Brian   I'd like to know before the read-through, Sol: what does he see in the phlegm?

Sophie   Totally—

Brian   It's blood, Sol, isn't it? That's what he sees. Blood in the phlegm. Just tell me.

Pause.

Chris   But so did he definitely read the stuff I sent, because he said he'd read it?

Brian   Come on, Sol . . . I've been in this game a long time. I know what it means.

Sophie   It's just . . . to see something all wrapped up in, like, a couple of hours . . . it just doesn't feel realistic any more.

Brian   *Beat.* Beat is Final Face. He looks at the hankie – Final Face. Final Face isn't 'Oh, I've got a cold'. Final Face is terror. Final Face is fear.

Chris   Yes but when it was the by-election and you wanted the votes, it was all about how accessible he was going to be, wasn't it?

Sophie   Oh yeah, it's amazing. But you've got to stick with it—

Brian   Come on Sol . . . just say it: I'm dying, aren't I? That's what that means . . . hankie, beat. You're killing me off!

Sophie   The second season's better, the third season's fucking great.

Chris   I've been trying to get a meeting for over six months now!

Brian   Well who decides? Who decides that? Is it you, the execs, who?

Sophie   And what's brilliant is they don't mind killing people off.

Chris   There's people . . . children . . . being prescribed a drug that makes them suicidal . . . What's a higher priority than that?

Brian   And do the fans not get a say? Because you shouldn't underestimate how popular I am. He is. Finnegan is. I mean . . . you should see my mailbox—

Sophie   I'm not going to spoil anything—

Brian   No, look . . . I can play it, fine, I'd relish it . . . but this isn't about me—

Chris   I know it's not your fault . . . I'm just tired of getting messed around—

Sophie   Yeah, well . . . stick with it, it gets better—

Brian   Now an *illness* . . . a long-term illness . . . that could actually be good. I could play that. I could grow from that—

Chris   Well just tell him . . . I've got two hundred names on my petition already—

Sophie   Anyway . . . we shouldn't use up all our conversation—

Brian   That's all I ask, just . . . think it through, it's not too late.

Chris   Yeah, but that's two hundred votes he stands to lose right there—

Sophie   Cool. What time do you finish?

Brian   All right, buddy. I'll see you at the read-through and we can—

Chris   Oh listen, don't worry, I'm not going to let it drop—

Brian   Exactly. Sorry to be—

Sophie   OK . . . and I've got some interesting news—

Chris   You'll be sick of the sound of my voice, believe me.

Brian   All right, Sol, Cheers now. Bye.

We hear a medley of goodbyes over theirs.

Bye-bye, bye / All right then / Bye now / See ya / OK goodbye.

*And so on. **Brian** has hung up.*

Pause. Then he shouts angrily:

Brian   Fucking Oxbridge Twat!! Posh, stuck-up fucking
Oxbridge fucking Cunt!

Beat. Suddenly paranoid, he puts the phone back to his ear.

Brian   Hello?

Imogen *enters, whistling. She stands at the bus stop, and raises
her umbrella. She dips her shoe in a puddle and watches the water
shimmer.*

Chris *lights a candle.*

Chris   They finished building that Tesco's. It doesn't look so bad
as you thought. There's a few homeless people round the back but
they seem nice enough. I give money to the one with the dog. I
think most people do. I hope he buys dog food with it, not cider.

Pause.

Chris   Next time, I'll buy him an actual can of dog food those
ones with the ring-pull top.

Zawe *is having her palm read by* **Sophie**.

Imogen   It's funny what we care about and why.

(***Note:*** *on the screen, a photo of American singer Michael Bolton
appears, incorrectly titled Michael Burton.*)

Chris   Amanda . . . you remember Amanda . . . She gives money to Amnesty and I used to think that was really amazing, to care about people you'd never met who were so far away and nothing like you. But then she told me her dad used to lock her in the basement when she was little and it all made sense.

Chris   Maybe we don't care for anyone else.

Chris   Maybe when we cry it's only ever for ourselves.

Pause.

Chris   Anyway . . .

She exits, leaving the candle flickering.

(*The next YouTube clip plays. It is called 'Strange Sounds Heard Worldwide 2011/2012 – Corinthians 1552'. At the time of writing, it can be found here:* http://www.youtube.com/ watch?v=enyucbsd4kg

The clip begins with this text:

Since 2011, the sounds have been heard worldwide . . .

The clip is real footage taken in a snowy, presumably north American landscape. We can hear a strange and terrifying noise in the sky, to which the man's dog is reacting. We ended the clip after sixty-one seconds.)

Scene Three

Zawe *enters briskly, with* **Barney** *in tow.*

Zawe   OK, Noel, do you feel ready to do some improvising?

Barney   Sure, fine.

Zawe   You don't have a problem with that?

Barney   No, that's fine.

Zawe   OK, so what we want you to imagine is this: you're dissatisfied.

Barney   Right . . .

Zawe   Can we see that?

Barney   Dissatisfied?

Zawe   Yeah, can we see you being dissatisfied?

Barney   OK . . .

Pause.

Barney   What am I dissatisfied with?

Zawe   With life.

Barney   With life.

Zawe   With your whole life.

Barney   OK, got you.

He thinks for a moment. He sighs heavily, shakes his head.

Zawe   Whenever you're ready.

Barney   No, this is it, I'm doing it now.

Pause.

Zawe   OK, but don't internalise. Tell the story. Tell us how dissatisfied you are.

Barney starts to pace, fretfully.

Zawe   OK, good, but more. You're anxious, depressed, disappointed. You're not where you should be in life: your career's going nowhere; you don't like where you live; you haven't found your soulmate; you don't like your body; you hate your thighs—

By now, Barney's loping back and forth like some kind of gargoyle.

Zawe   That's good. That's great. And now SUDDENLY! . . . A tiny version of you jumps out of your body!

He continues pacing for a moment then stops.

Barney   Sorry, what? A tiny . . . ?

Zawe   A tiny version of you jumps out of your body.

Barney   A tiny version of me?

Zawe   Yes. A tiny version of you . . . exactly the same as you but, like, a metre high . . . jumps out of your body.

Barney   OK . . .

Zawe   Can we see that?

Barney   Yeah, I'll just have to . . . go back a bit.

Zawe   Whenever you're ready.

He starts to pace again, building momentum.

Zawe   OK, that's good . . . that's good . . . and . . . NOW!

He acts startled!

Zawe   Vocalise it.

Barney   Jesus Christ!

Zawe   Not that.

Barney   No, uh . . . Good grief!!

Zawe   What's wrong with you?!

He stops.

Barney   Is this . . . ?

Zawe   This is the voice of the Tiny You.

Barney   OK . . . sorry—

Zawe   What's wrong with you?!

Barney   I don't know, I'm just so . . . dissatisfied with my life.

Zawe   But you don't have to be!

Barney   Don't I?

Zawe   No, not if you use this . . . And Tiny You gives you a Footmouse.

Barney   A what?

Zawe   A Footmouse. That's the product.

He doesn't understand.

Zawe   It's a mouse for a computer but you operate it with your foot.

Barney   Oh . . . OK . . .

Zawe   You don't have to be dissatisfied!

Barney   Don't I?

Zawe   Not if you use this!

Barney *mimes getting the Footmouse.*

Barney   Wow . . . a Footmouse!

He mimes operating it with his foot.

Zawe   And now everything that was bothering you just goes away.

Barney   This is great!

Zawe   This is the best thing ever!

Barney   This is brilliant!

Zawe   You feel free—

Barney   Wow!

Zawe   You feel free and full of joy!

Barney   Yay!

Zawe   Show us joy.

Barney   Wowee . . . this is amazing . . . !

Zawe   Say the product.

Barney   Footmouse!

Zawe   Dance with joy!

He does.

Zawe   Say the product.

Barney   Footmouse!

Zawe   Again.

Barney   Footmouse! Footmouse! Brilliant! Footmouse!

For what seems like an age, he hops around grinning, shouting 'Footmouse'. Sad music bleeds in underneath. Then stops.

Zawe, *breathing heavily, gets up, unsteady.*

Zawe   OK, thank you.

Barney   OK.

She pushes past him.

Barney   Was that OK?

Zawe   Are you still with Marion . . . ?

Barney   No, actually I don't have—

She hurries out, as if to be sick. **Barney** *is left confused.*

Barney   What the fuck . . . ?

Glumly, he reaches up to grab a strap and now he's on an underground train.

On the screen, we see footage of his audition as if on YouTube: dancing like an idiot, grinning, shouting the name of the product, played out in agonising slow motion. The title of the clip is 'Footmouse Wanker' and it has been viewed nearly a million times.

In a different space, we see **Zawe** *enter, hyperventilating, having a panic attack. She slides out of view.*

Sophie *gets on the train. She takes out a mirror and applies* *lipstick.* **Barney** *watches her, longingly. She glances at him and he looks away.*

He puts earphones in and presses play on his audio device. We hear an audio drama, in American accents.

The next is all recorded:

Newsreader 1   Scenes of chaos today as the midtown branch of Unity City Bank was devastated by a huge explosion during the busy lunchtime period. We go now—

Static.

Barman   Hey, something's happening to the TV!

Magician   Attention, citizens of Unity! This is the Magician—

Barman   The Magician!

Magician   Today you have seen but a small demonstration of my power. I have the means to strike whenever and wherever I wish. If you wish to ever live in security again, my demands are simple: bring Elastic Man to me, in chains, by sunrise tomorrow. If you do not comply, I will engulf this entire city in the flames of Hell itself!

Sophie *finishes her makeup.*

Newsreader 1   Well . . . you all saw that: it looks like evil genius the Magician is behind this mayhem and he'll only stop if we bring him Elastic Man.

Sophie *stands.*

Newsreader 2   That's right, Jenny, except there's one problem: no one's seen Elastic Man for two weeks now! Elastic Man . . . if you're out there . . . if you can hear this . . . Unity City needs you now more than ever!

Newsreader 1   Save us, Elastic Man . . . save us!

Sophie *gets off the train.*

She meets **Imogen** *and they hug.*

(**Note:** *the actors can improvise around these lines for a more realistic feel.*)

Imogen   So come on . . . what's the story?

Sophie   The story?

Imogen   The big news you said you had—

Sophie   Oh—

Imogen   Is it something good?

Sophie   I don't know: I think you'll think it is.

Imogen   So tell me!

Sophie   Can we at least get a drink first?

Imogen   No, I can't wait that long!

Chris *approaches them, clutching a clipboard.*

Chris   I'm sorry to bother you . . . have you got a minute?

Imogen   Uh—

Sophie   I'm sorry we're in—

Chris   It's just this is my son, David. He passed on a year ago, from an overdose.

A mortified pause.

Sophie   Oh, I'm sorry . . .

Imogen   That's terrible . . .

Chris   It was recorded as a suicide but he was a very happy boy, as you can see, so we never believed he'd have done that. It turns out he was on a medication for acne called Vyoclozamine . . .

Sophie   I think I've heard of that . . .

Chris   You might have. It's actually banned in the USA because it's been linked to several suicides there but it's still being prescribed here—

Sophie   Really?

Chris   Well, it's cheap, you see. So I'm gathering names for this petition to have it banned over here as well—

Sophie   Yes, of course.

Sophie *takes the offered pen and signs.*

Chris   Thank you . . .

Imogen *signs next.*

Chris   You girls out for the night?

Sophie   Yeah, just catching up.

Chris   That's nice.

Imogen *hands back the pen.*

Chris   Thank you. And this is a leaflet: it gives you the address of the website and tells you a bit more about the drug and the progress we're making.

They take them.

Sophie   Good luck with it.

Chris   Bless you, thanks. Have a nice night.

She exits.

Sophie   That's fucking tragic . . .

Imogen   It's terrible. So anyhow—

They're in a bar – music playing.

Imogen   Give me the gossip, what's going on?

Sophie   Well, just that . . . I'm single again.

Imogen   No! Seriously?

Sophie   Yup. We split up, finally.

Imogen   How do you feel about that?

Sophie   Good in some ways. Bad in others.

Imogen   Oh, Sophe, I'm sorry, that's a shame.

Sophie   A shame? I thought you were dead against it?

Imogen   Me?

Sophie   I thought you thought he was a sleaze.

Imogen   Why would I think that?

Sophie   I don't know: because of the age difference.

Imogen   Did I say that?

Sophie   Yes! You said he was old enough to be my father.

Imogen   Well yeah, like . . . age-wise. But he wasn't your father. That's the important bit.

Sophie   I can't believe you're saying this . . .

Imogen   You didn't listen to me, did you?

Sophie   You know . . . it was a factor, when I was weighing it up . . . I could hear your voice—

Imogen   God, I was just winding you up. Christ, my first boyfriend was twenty-five when I was fifteen.

Sophie   Seriously?

Imogen   Totally. Underage sex and everything. And I mean *everything*.

Sophie   You've never told me that. That's actually quite dodgy, isn't it? Being twenty-five and shagging a fifteen-year-old?

Imogen   Didn't seem that bad at the time. It's not like I was forced or anything.

Sophie   He could have gone to jail for that.

Imogen   Still could, I guess. Just as well we stayed friends!

They leave this venue and move to another one, with different music. On the way, they take out their phones and refer to them constantly from now on.

Imogen   But, like, that wasn't my problem with your man. It just looked like it could have got pretty serious.

Sophie   It was, for a while.

Imogen   I was just thinking ahead. I mean, like . . . twenty years' difference: if he croaked at seventy, you'd be on your own at fifty. And you don't want to be on the shelf at fifty.

Sophie   Fifty's not that old.

Imogen   It is if you're a woman. Can't have kids; tits have dropped, arse has dropped; neck does that vagina thing . . .

Sophie   What century are you living in? People are starting new lives at fifty . . .

Imogen   Still got the barren womb. Men want fertile women: always have, always will.

Sophie   You're actually quite old-fashioned, aren't you? You sound like my grandmother.

They leave the venue and walk through the streets.

Imogen   So what went wrong? In your relationship?

Sophie   Nothing went wrong, exactly . . .

Imogen   Were you arguing?

Sophie   Not really. But we weren't having much fun either.

Imogen   You think you could do better.

They sit down by a water feature.

Sophie   I think I could do different.

Imogen   But you have to commit to someone eventually.

Sophie   No, you don't . . .

Imogen   No, but then it's just fucking . . . musical chairs. Wherever you are when the music stops.

Sophie *opens her bag.*

Sophie   D'you want an apple?

Imogen   An apple?

Sophie   Yeah, you know . . . fruit? Do they have fruit where you come from?

Imogen   Fine, yeah, let's get crazy. An apple.

Sophie *produces a knife from her bag.*

Sophie   D'you want it peeled?

Imogen   What the fuck is that?!

Sophie   It's a Swiss Army knife.

Imogen   You can't carry a knife around!

Sophie   Why not?

Imogen   I don't know . . . can't you get arrested for it?

Imogen *takes the knife from her.*

Sophie   Why? My dad gave me that when I was about twelve. It's more a tool than a knife.

Imogen   You're the tool.

Imogen *opens the knife, unfolds the various implements, fascinated.*

Sophie   See, now you've confused me again. D'you think I made a mistake?

Imogen *lets them snap back into place.*

Imogen   About what?

Sophie   Ending it.

Imogen   I guess you just weren't happy. If you were, you would've stayed.

Sophie   Maybe I would've got happy again. That's what he said.

Imogen   There's someone out there that's right for you. You'll know when you know.

Sophie   That's bullshit, that's just rhetoric.

Imogen   Yeah, probably.

Imogen *sticks the knife in* **Sophie**'*s neck.* **Sophie** *stares at her in surprise.*

Imogen   Oh my God . . . !

Sophie *staggers away, clutching her neck.*

Imogen   Oh my God, Sophie, I'm sorry, I don't know why I did that!

Blood jets from **Sophie**'*s neck in long arcs, spattering into the water. She drops to her knees, falls forward.*

She twitches violently then expires.

Pause.

Imogen   Sophie . . . ?

The world shifts on its axis, visibly darkening. The other actors appear on the stage, watching **Imogen** *reproachfully.* **Olly** *and/ or* **Barney** *drag* **Sophie**'*s body away.* **Chris** *stares at her before following them out.*

Brian *reads, and his voice is dislocated, unearthly.*

Brian   The little boy lifts the air rifle, takes aim and squeezes the trigger. The rifle pops! and the bird falls from the tree. The little boy walks through the leaves to where it lies and watches it stop, like a watch stops.

Imogen, *beside herself with panic, runs away.*

Brian   There was nothing in his nine years to explain why he would shoot a bird. But here it lay, this thing that once flew.

Slowly, **Brian**'*s voice returns to normal.*

Brian   And suddenly, for the first time, the boy understands the direction of time; that it moves only forward; that he cannot turn it back. For some reason, this surprises him. In killing, he knows he cannot kill. In taking a life, he realises he is powerless.

He sways slightly, drunk and stoned. They both are.

Brian   What do you think?

Zawe   Wow.

Brian   Wow?

Zawe   It's just like . . . Mind? Blown.

Brian   OK . . .

Zawe   You're a poet. Simples.

Brian   Except it's prose.

Zawe   Prose can be poetry, man. A song is poetry. A good meal is poetry.

Pause.

Zawe   A duck is poetry. A brick—

Brian   Yeah, I get what you're saying.

Zawe   It just speaks to me, you know? I just completely get where you're coming from.

Brian   I'm just sick of relying on other people's words, you know? I want to write my own words.

Zawe   Totally. I so get that. I want to write my own words. My Mum would've loved that. She would've loved you.

Brian   Why?

Zawe   Just . . . she would have: she was a poet too.

Brian   An actual poet?

Zawe   A fishmonger. But she used to sing. She used to make up songs and sing them to me.

Brian   Like what?

Zawe (S*ings*)   You are a Princess, you are the best . . . everything you do is amazing . . .

You will have the moon and stars and everything your heart desires—

Pause.

Brian   Nice.

Pause.

Zawe   But then she stopped.

Brian   Singing?

Zawe   Yeah. When her brother died.

Brian   Shit.

Zawe   She was brought up in an orphanage but then in her twenties, she went and found her real parents and she found out she had a brother and they got very close. But then I was maybe eleven, twelve? He got killed in a car crash.

Brian   Shit . . .

Zawe   Never sang again. Never even listened to music. Said it made her head go funny.

Pause.

Brian   Must have been difficult.

Zawe   For me? No . . . that was why she was so brilliant. She was just so determined I'd have the childhood she never had. Never hit me, never judged me, never stopped me doing anything . . . just gave me love and belief and confidence . . . yeah. And that's a precious gift, man. No matter what happens in life . . . I know . . . that I was loved. A lot of people don't ever know that.

Brian   No.

Zawe   Lot of people, they just jump from one relationship to the next. Because they're insecure. They're worried they'll lose themselves.

Brian   Tell me about it.

Zawe   You know what I mean?

Brian   I do. But it's the times as well: everyone's told they're entitled to nothing less than perfect happiness. Soon as that initial state of bliss wears off, they move on.

Zawe   Totally: that's so right.

Brian   Nobody wants depth anymore. The shallow, the insecure; that's what's prized.

Zawe   That's so true: nobody wants anything real.

Brian   They want to be lied to. Lies sell the truth doesn't. I guess you know that, in your business. No offence.

Zawe   No, hey . . . totally: it's bullshit. I just work with the creative people: the actors, the directors. I don't come up with the campaigns or anything.

Brian   Look, we're just as bad. So-called artists: we all help sell the lie. It's worse in some ways. We know that adverts are lies but art . . . it's supposed to tell the truth. It's supposed to tell people the truth about themselves, so they won't feel so fucking . . . alone. But we sold out. And for what? For money, for fame. For fucking awards. The fucking BAFTAS, the Oliviers: they should give out white feathers at these things not fucking statues.

Zawe   Cool, totally. So would you turn one down if you got one?

Brian   Ah, well . . . now that depends on a couple of things . . .

Cross-fade to: **Barney** *sits in a bar, waiting.*

He hears a strange, throbbing noise. **Imogen** *enters, in a state of extreme distress, shaking, snotty, her makeup running.*

Also, she seems to have sprouted horns. Bison horns.

Barney *stares at her, unsure what is happening.*

Imogen   Is it Noel?

Her voice echoes, strangely. She jumps at the sound of it.

Barney   I'm waiting for Sophie.

Imogen   Yes. Yes. I'm . . . Sophie. That's me . . . Sophie.

Barney *speaks loudly, as if to backstage crew:*

Barney   You don't LOOK like Sophie.

Imogen   I . . . Don't I?

Barney   You don't look like the PICTURE of Sophie on the WEBSITE.

Imogen   No. I've changed my hair.

Her voice echoes forcefully. She tests it:

Imogen   I've changed my hair. (*Panicked*) I've changed my hair!

Pause. **Barney** *gets up and retreats towards the exit.*

Imogen   So . . . then . . . can we have a drink then? Can we just have a drink and get on with it?!

Barney   Get on with WHAT?

Imogen   With the school. No! With the science. Shit! With the . . . *scenery.*

Barney   You're not **Sophie** though! This is meant to be with Sophie!

With a frustrated scream, she exits the stage. Lights go down on **Barney**, *still confused.*

Cross-fade back to **Brian** *and* **Zawe:**

Brian   The exact same sound?

Zawe   The exact same sound, man . . . all over the world. 2011. There's loads of clips online. It's freaky as shit.

Brian   Yeah, well . . . it wasn't the fucking Rapture.

Zawe (*Shrugs*)   Who knows?

Brian   Well, we all know. Because it wasn't. There weren't chariots in the sky and fucking Christians vanishing.

Zawe   Not this time . . .

Brian   Oh what . . . so it was like a drill? Like a fire drill?

Zawe   I'm just saying—

Brian   Are you religious?

Zawe   What?!

Brian   Fair enough if you are—

Zawe   No . . . fuck . . . religious? I'm like . . . the least religious person I know!

Brian   Until now.

Zawe   Fuck religion, man! All of that stuff. The Rapture . . . it's fucking . . . American bullshit!

She passes him the joint, exhales.

Zawe   I just sometimes think . . . what if we were wrong? What if we were wrong and they were all right?

Brian   Then we'd be fucked.

Zawe   We'd be totally fucked.

Brian   But they're not. They're insane.

Zawe   No, I know, totally. Just sometimes you should ask.

Pause.

Brian   You know what I like about you? You surprise me.

Zawe   Is that good?

Brian   It's good for me. Usually I can figure people out pretty quickly.

Zawe   Figure them out?

Brian   Yeah, you know: make sense of them. But you . . . you're a challenge.

Zawe   I'm a very simple person.

Brian   It's fine . . . a bit of mystery's good. It's attractive.

Zawe   I don't want to be a mystery, though. That's not what I want.

Brian   What do you want?

Imogen *appears between them, breaking the mood. That strange, throbbing noise again. They look awkward, as if she shouldn't be on stage. She's trying to control her panic.*

Imogen   Hey.

Pause.

Zawe   Hi.

Imogen   What's happy? No. What's happened? Happening.

Zawe *raises her hand to point at* **Imogen**'*s horns.*

Imogen   What?

She reaches up, only now discovering her horns.

Imogen   Oh no, what the FUCK?! What the fucking fuck is THIS?!

Brian (*To* **Zawe**)   I should probably call you a cab.

Imogen *runs to a mirror.*

Zawe   Oh. Right. Yeah. I guess it's . . . pretty late.

Imogen   I've got horned! D'you see that?

Zawe   Don't want to keep you up.

Imogen   I've got funky horns!!

Brian   No, you're not keeping me up. I thought I was keeping you up.

Zawe No . . . wow . . . I'm such a night owl.

Brian Maybe we should move to the living room.

Zawe Have you got music?

Brian I have. I even have some gospel music.

They start to leave.

Imogen When are you going?! You're supposed to stain on!!

They are gone.

Imogen What if I don't?! What have I donut?! What have I *done*?

Olly *and* **Barney** *enter. They hesitate for a moment, seeing* **Imogen**, *but continue with the scene.*

Barney So come on . . . what's the big news?

Imogen *points at* **Olly**, *excited.*

Imogen Youth! I know you!

Olly OK, well . . . you know that audition I went to the other day?

Imogen I was the waitress! In the cape! In the café. Remainder? Remorse. Remember? It was meat!

They ignore her. Pause. She runs off stage, taking the strange noise with her.

Barney Oh yeah: the advert?

Olly Yeah, well . . . thing is . . . it wasn't an advert. It was a film.

Barney Oh, right. Why didn't you say?

Olly I wanted to but I couldn't. They made me sign something saying I wouldn't talk about it. I'm not even supposed to tell you now but I just . . .

Barney What, is it . . . a big film?

Olly   Yeah, well . . . big-budget, yeah.

Barney   What, like Hollywood?

He shrugs.

Barney   Hollywood?!

He can't help but smile.

Barney   So come on . . . what is it?

Olly   It's stupid. It's a kids' film really. It'll probably be absolute shit and I'll never work again.

Barney   What is it?

Pause.

Olly   Elastic Man.

Pause. **Barney** *nods.*

Olly   I'm Elastic Man.

Pause.

Barney   Is it a decent part?

Pause.

Olly   Well . . . it's the lead, I suppose.

Barney   It's a film of Elastic Man?

Olly   It's a film of Elastic Man and I'm playing Elastic Man.

Barney   What's it called?

Pause.

Olly   Elastic Man.

Barney   Brilliant.

Olly   Yeah?

Barney   Oh . . . yeah. I used to love Elastic Man. They're making a film of it?

Olly   Yeah . . .

Barney   Big-budget?

Olly   Massive. Fucking massive. Guess who's playing the villain?

Barney   Who?

Olly   Clooney.

Barney   Clooney? Is he playing the Magician?

Olly   I think so . . . I haven't seen the script yet—

Barney   It must be the Magician. That's his arch-enemy.

Olly   You'd know better than me. I never really read comics.

Barney   Wow. So who's playing Elastic Man?

Pause.

Olly   Me.

Barney   Uh-huh.

Olly   That's what I'm saying: I'm playing Elastic Man!

Pause.

Barney   Yay! Elastic Man! That's great! You're playing Elastic Man! This is brilliant! Yay!

Barney *begins to dance around, like he did in the Footmouse audition. It gets a little disturbing.*

Barney   Wow! Wowee! Elastic Man! Elastic Man! Brilliant! Amazing! Elastic Man!

Eventually he tires and slumps into a seat, obviously devastated.

Olly   Are you all right?

Barney   I'm brilliant. That's great news . . .

Olly   'Cos that was a bit . . .

Barney   No, no . . . that's terrific news. I'm happy for you, mate, I really am. Couldn't have happened to a nicer guy.

Olly   Thanks.

Pause.

Barney   So wow . . . that means . . . I know Elastic Man!
Elastic Man is my mate. My best friend . . . Elastic Man! That's
something isn't it?

Olly   It could be a disaster.

Barney   No, no way. It'll be huge.

Olly   People will go to see it, yeah. But I'm still going to be
prancing about in a fucking skin-tight suit playing a guy whose
body can stretch like elastic. I could end up looking like a total tit.

Barney   But a rich tit. A famous tit.

Olly   A famous tit . . .

He ponders this, while **Barney** *pours himself a stiff drink.*

Olly   But listen . . . Noel . . . I told you because . . . well, because
you're my mate. But also because . . . I'm going to be away for a
few months filming and . . .

Pause.

Olly   Well, you know we've been talking about moving on . . .

Pause.

Barney   Oh. The flat.

Olly   Kind of makes sense to do it now, don't you think?

Pause.

Barney   I mean, it films in July so I'll stay on until it's all done.
So there's plenty time to find someone.

Barney   Nah. Another flatmate? Too old for that. I'll find a
one-person place.

Olly   You'd be better staying here. You won't get anything
decent on your budget.

Barney *drinks.*

Barney   On my budget.

Olly   I didn't mean it like that.

Barney   No, sure . . . but I'll just have to move, won't I? Out of London.

Olly   That won't do you any good . . .

Barney   Maybe it will. Maybe that's the best thing. Get this stupid acting idea out of my head. Maybe it'll save my life. 'Thanks, Elastic Man! How can I ever repay you?!'

Sophie *appears, on the screen, as if on a Skype call.*

Olly   Come on . . . don't be like that.

Imogen *hurries onto the stage – the sound again – and looks up at the screen.*

Imogen   Soapy?

Sophie *starts to talk but there's no sound.*

Imogen   Soapy, I can't heart you! Turn on your michael! Sophie, turn on your mic!

Barney (*To* **Olly**)   Has something changed?

Chris *enters, slowly, shedding her leaflets as she does, leaving a trail.*

Imogen   Sophie, can you hear me?!

Sophie *leans in and turns off the screen.*

Imogen   Sophie?

Imogen *turns to see* **Chris**. *They stare at each other, desolate.*

Chris   He wasn't taking it.

Her voice echoes too, like **Imogen***'s.*

Imogen   Taking what?

Chris   The drug. The acne drug. Vypo . . . vyspo . . . clora . . .

Pause.

David wasn't taking it. His flatmate found the boxes.

Pause.

He told me he'd been taking it.

Pause.

Imogen   Can you see me?

Chris   Yes.

Imogen   Does my voice sound weird to you?

Chris   A bit. What's wrong with you?

Imogen   I did something.

Chris   What?

Imogen   Something terrible. The worst thing you could ever do, ever.

Chris   Why?

Imogen   I don't know. I don't think there was any reason. Can you do something for no reason? Something bad?

Pause.

Chris   I hope so.

Pause.

Chris   That's me done then.

Chris *puts on a pair of the bison horns.*

Chris   What now?

Pause.

I suppose I go.

Pause. S*he starts to go, but then hesitates. She turns to* **Imogen**.

Chris   Which way should I—?

Lights out.

Scene Four

In the darkness, we hear the voice of the **Narrator**.

Narrator (*V/O*)   The Democratic People's Republic of Korea, commonly known as North Korea, is a country in East Asia, in the southern half of the Korean peninsula.

On the screen, footage of Korean military propaganda plays: missiles paraded through the streets, huge armies marching, crude animations of attacks on America.

Narrator (*V/O*)   Its capital is Pyingyong but only a thousand people live there, with the majority of its four billion citizens living in rural areas devoted to noodle farming, its second biggest industry after arms production.

Zawe *bursts in, as if chased. She slams the door shut and presses against it, her breathing fast and shallow.*

Narrator (*V/O*)   North Korea is a single-party state under a united front led by the Korean Workers Party, or KPP. It is a totalitarian state with an elaborate cult of personality built around its leader, currently Kim Yung Guy, and the flow of information is so tightly controlled that most North Koreans remain unaware of their own mortality.

Zawe *drops to the floor and crawls to a place of safety.*

Narrator (*V/O*)   Women in North Korea must wear school uniforms until the age of fifty, despite the fact that they are not allowed to attend school. Punishments for contacting the outside world range from execution to the barbaric practice of turtling, which involves turtles.

Brian *enters, looking for her.*

Brian   Zawe? Zawe?

Narrator (*V/O*)   Genetically, North Koreans are closer to squid than human beings. One in five of its citizens serve in the armed forces. The national dish is boiled terrier. North Korea has declared itself a nuclear state, although some experts claim that their missiles are only drawings and therefore incapable of causing widespread destruction.

Brian *finds her cowering.*

Brian   Zawe, what the fuck are you doing?! What's wrong?!

Narrator (*V/O*)   Despite this, in 2012, UN Secretary-General Button Moon sanctioned sanctions against the country and relations with the West continue to deteriorate.

Brian   What's wrong, darling? What's happened?

He helps her to sitting. She's hyperventilating.

Brian   All right, just breathe. You're all right. Where's your bag? Have you got your bag?

She nods, taking a paper bag from her pocket. **Brian** *helps her to put it to her mouth.*

Brian   That's it, just breathe, nice and slowly—

The bag deflates and inflates as she does.

A television executive appears. It is quite obviously **Chris** *in disguise. She's placed paper bags over her horns to hide them.*

Exec   We think it's brilliant.

Brian *is still trying to manage* **Zawe**.

Brian   Oh . . . Great—

Exec   Everyone's *very* excited.

Brian   Excellent.

Exec   Um . . . notes . . . we do have some notes—

Brian   Of course—

Exec   Now the . . . hitman character—

Brian Yep . . .

Exec We love him! He's a great character.

Brian Oh . . . great, thank you—

Exec In fact, we like him so much, we'd like two of him!

Brian Two of him?

Exec Yes. A pair of hitmen. People like two hitmen. They like the banter between them.

Brian The banter?

Exec Yeah. They like them quirky. Almost comedic.

Brian Comedic?

Exec Not that they're funny but you know . . . if they talk about . . . just normal stuff.

Brian Normal stuff.

Exec Yes, they talk about normal stuff but . . . they kill people in an unusual way.

Brian Unusual?

Exec Yes: not with a gun . . . with . . . something quirky.

Brian Quirky.

Exec Yes, like . . . a glue gun or . . . a blanket!

Brian A blanket?

Exec What do you think?

Brian Honestly?

Exec Oh yes, of course . . . be completely honest. That's all we want, is for you to be honest.

Brian The 'hitman' in my script is an ex-member of the Ulster Volunteer Force. They go to people's doors and shoot them in the head. With a gun. Most of them aren't very bright and they're very fucking far from funny, let me tell you. So if you're asking me what I think, honestly: I think you're talking shit.

Pause.

Exec   You're right. I don't know what I'm talking about. I'm not qualified to be a Television executive. I'm going to be a therapist instead. Rain.

Now we are in a therapist's. **Chris** *has put glasses on.*

Zawe   Wedding.

Therapist   Water.

Zawe   Reflection.

Therapist   Mirror.

Zawe   Smudge.

Therapist   Smudge?

Zawe   Mirror.

Therapist   No.

Zawe   Yes.

Therapist   No, stop—

Zawe   Bus.

Therapist   No, Zawe—

Zawe   No, Zawe.

Therapist   Why did you say smudge?

Pause.

Zawe   Did I say smudge?

Therapist   I said mirror, you said smudge. Do you know why?

Zawe   Oh. My mum didn't like mirrors. She used to spray over them with furniture polish so they were all smudged and smeary.

Therapist   Why did she do that?

Zawe   She didn't like to look at herself. She said she didn't recognise the person looking back.

Therapist   So you grew up in a house without mirrors?

Zawe   I had my own mirror. Just a little one.

Therapist   You don't have a problem with them?

Zawe   Now? No.

Pause.

Zawe   I don't like the full-length ones.

Therapist   Why not?

Zawe   I don't like how tall I am. I look like a tree. I feel like I walk like a tree would walk, if a tree walked.

Therapist   You feel like you take up too much space?

Zawe   I feel like if someone was going to start shooting, I'd be the first one they picked.

Sophie *appears on the screen.* **Imogen** *runs on again, addresses the screen.*

Imogen   Soaky wait! When are you? Sophie turkey mink on, plead!

Now **Sophie** *looks directly at her.*

Imogen   Sophie please . . . I'm soppy! You had to forget me, please! I'm scarce!

Sophie   They're coming for you. You *bitch*.

She turns the camera off.

Imogen   Wait, who? Who's coming?

Thriller-style music. **Barney** *and* **Brian** *enter, dressed as ultra-cool hitmen. Wearing the obligatory shades.* **Brian** *carries a glue gun.* **Barney** *drags a blanket.*

Imogen *hides. The music stops.*

Brian *sniffs the air. They've affected appropriate accents.*

Brian   She's close. Not long now.

Barney   What'll we do when we find her? Kill her?

Brian *holds up the glue gun.*

Brian   Let's just say she'll come to a sticky end.

Barney   Sex.

They move on, then **Brian** *stops suddenly, turns on* **Barney**.

Brian   Wait a minute . . . what?

Barney   What?

Brian   What did you just say?

Barney   Sex.

Brian   Sex?

Barney   Yeah, sex. As in genius. It's what people say if something's good. You know: I just got a new Ferrari. 'Sex'. As in 'brilliant!'

Brian   Do people say that?

Barney   Yeah. Totally.

Brian *scrutinises him.* **Barney** *shifts uncomfortably.*

Brian   Did you make it up?

Barney   What?

Brian   Are you trying to start a word?

Pause.

Barney   No . . .

Brian   Are you trying to re-contextualise a word?

Barney   What do you mean?

Brian   You know what I mean: like 'wicked' or 'sick'.

Pause.

Barney   I've heard people say it.

Brian   Have you? Look at me.

Pause.

Brian   Take off your glasses.

Barney   Why?

Brian   Take them *off.*

Barney *takes his glasses off and holds* **Brian***'s gaze.*

Brian   Have you heard anyone say that?

Long pause.

Barney   No.

Brian   No.

Pause. **Brian** *shakes his head.*

Brian   No one would know. Even if it caught on . . . who would know?

Barney   *I* would! *I'd* know.

Brian *puts his shades back on.*

Brian   Let's get this done.

They exit, to the thriller-style music.

Olly *enters, also wearing shades, and a puffy coat. He carries a rolled up screenplay, which he places down.*

He looks around furtively, then takes a battered envelope from his pocket. From the envelope, he takes out the picture of the anus. He stares at it, chewing his lip nervously.

Zawe *enters. She looks glamorous but too thin, and despite wearing ludicrously high heels that accentuate her height, she bends down to compensate.*

Zawe   Well, well!

He jumps, stuffs the photograph into his pocket.

Olly   Zawe?

Zawe   Look at you, the big movie star!

Pause.

Olly   What are you—?

Zawe   I'm here now.

Olly   You're directing?

Zawe   No . . . God, no: I'm doing the interview. They'll edit me out, don't worry. Replace me with the various presenters. But it's a step in the right direction.

Olly   To . . . ?

Zawe   To being seen.

Olly   OK.

Zawe   Is that OK?

Olly   Bit of a surprise but OK. So how are you? You look good.

Zawe   I am good. I'm brilliant, actually. New career, new flat . . . new relationship.

Olly   Great.

Zawe   Oh, listen . . . for what it's worth? You were SO right about us not being soulmates.

Olly   Well . . .

Zawe   I don't know what I was thinking! Just a crazy time, you know?

Olly   It happens.

Zawe   Bullet? Dodged.

Pause.

Zawe So how about you? You've done well.

Olly Not yet.

Zawe Hey . . . we're doing the PR, so . . .

Olly It's bound to do well.

Zawe I'll know when *you* die, that's for sure. OK . . . so just take a seat . . .

Reluctantly, he takes off his coat to reveal his ridiculous, skin-tight Elastic-Man suit.

Zawe *Hey . . .*

Olly Don't.

Zawe *Very* stylish.

He sits on the stool. **Zawe** *touches her ear.*

Zawe OK, are we good?

Pause. Bizarrely, she adopts an American accent:

Zawe OK . . . first question: were you a fan of Elastic Man as a child?

Pause.

Olly Are you going to do it like that?

Zawe (*Normal accent*)   Like what?

Pause.

(*American accent*) Were you a fan of Elastic Man as a child?

Pause.

Olly Well . . . I was certainly aware of the comics and I saw a few of the cartoons, mostly because of my younger brother who was a big fan. I was probably more into Batman when I was a kid. But yeah, I certainly knew of the character, I mean—

Zawe Wait a sec . . .

She touches her ear again, nods. In her normal accent:

Zawe   OK . . . so your producer says you shouldn't say that stuff about Batman. Just focus on Elastic Man. And be more positive generally. You're a big fan, you always were, yada, yada—

Olly   OK.

Zawe (*American accent*)   Were you a fan of Elastic Man as a child?

Olly   Yes, I mean . . . who wasn't? I read the comics and I saw the cartoons.

Faintly, we hear the sounds we associate with the anus.

Olly   I wouldn't say I was an obsessive fan but I certainly enjoyed what I read of them and, you know . . . he's such an iconic character so . . .

Zawe *giggles.*

Zawe   Exactly . . . and how will you approach the character?

Olly   Well, in the same way—

Zawe   (*Normal accent*) Could you put the question in the answer?

Olly   Well . . . you approach a character like Elastic Man in the same way you approach a character like . . . Hamlet or Macbeth.

The anus sounds.

Olly   In some ways, it's actually harder than those parts because it's more outside your experience. I mean . . . we all know what it's like to be a stroppy teenager or a bit ambitious; but here's a man who suddenly has the power to stretch like elastic . . . He can stretch himself to the size of a football field; he can stretch his neck and look in a window ten storeys up, you know . . . What does that do to your body? What does that do to your mind? How does that kind of power change you? Those are really interesting questions, you know? It's meaty stuff.

Again, **Zawe** *giggles.*

Zawe   Exactly . . . So is it intimidating to work with George Clooney?

Olly   George . . . Gorgeous George . . .

Anus sounds.

Olly   You do have to pinch yourself, you know . . . I'm wearing the costume and we're on this huge set and there's George Clooney playing the Magician . . . it's quite surreal. But George is such a professional . . . He knows you're going to be nervous and he knows how to put you at your ease . . . It helps that he's very funny and very generous with his time. There's no starry-stuff. Pretty soon you're just relating to him as you would to any other actor. And he's doing something very interesting with the Magician so I think people are going to be surprised and very pleased.

Giggle.

Zawe   Exactly. So finally . . . can you say the famous catchphrase for us?

Olly   I knew you'd ask me that . . .

She nods. He squirms.

Olly   I actually said it for the first time the other day.

She nods.

Olly   Seriously, you want me to say it?

She does. Pause.

Olly   STRETCH IT!

He reddens.

Zawe (*Normal accent*)   Really?

Olly   What?

Zawe (*Normal accent*)   I don't know . . . do you want to do that again?

Olly   Not really, no.

Zawe   Your producer says to do it again but with more conviction.

Olly *looks beyond her, to the unseen producer.*

Olly   Shouldn't we save it for the film?

Zawe *touches her ear.*

Zawe   He's asking if you should save it for the film?

Pause. She nods.

Zawe   No, it'll sell tickets. So . . . (*American accent*) can you say the famous catchphrase for us?

Pause.

Zawe (*Normal acccent*)   You can get up. Use the space.

Olly *climbs down off the stool, paces.*

On the screen now – for the first time – we see the anus, clear and close.

Olly *sees it and turns away. The anus fades. With energy,* **Olly** *strikes a heroic pose and shouts:*

Olly   STRETCH IIIIIIIIIIIT!!

Zawe   Brilliant!

He can't speak for shame.

Zawe   OK, we're done.

He nods. She extends her hand, the accent dropped now.

Zawe   It was *so* lovely to see you again. I hope it goes really well for you: lots of sequels . . . ELASTIC MAN Two, Three; Four, Five . . .

He nods, aware his producer is watching.

Olly   Hopefully . . .

Zawe   See you on the big screen!

She exits.

(*On the screen, the next YouTube clip. It's called '101-year-old woman grows horns on her head' and at the time of writing can be found here:* http://www.youtube.com/watch?v=mcmwru_fl44

It depicts a very old peasant woman from China with a long, horn-like growth protruding from her forehead. The clip was re-edited for time.)

Scene Five

Brian *enters, raging, followed by* **Zawe**.

Brian   Jesus fucking Christ!! With the actor? With this fucking . . . guy who's playing fucking . . . *Plastic Man* or whatever?!

Zawe   He's an ex-boyfriend—

Brian   Oh right . . . so that makes it OK does it?

Zawe   It doesn't make it OK but it's not as bad.

Brian   Oh right . . . so I can just fuck any of my ex-girlfriends can I? And you'd be OK with that?

Zawe   I wouldn't be OK with it—

Brian   No, you're fucking right you wouldn't!

Zawe   But it would be better than someone new.

Brian   How? How is that better? Cheating is fucking cheating!

Zawe   No, it's just like . . . going back in time a bit.

Brian   Going back in time?

Zawe   We'd already had sex. So we just had it one more time than we'd had it before.

Brian   Are you seriously trying to use science-fiction to justify this?

Pause.

Zawe   Look, I'm sorry, yeah? I know it was wrong. We were just . . . talking about old times . . . and I got too drunk. It didn't mean anything.

Brian   Oh well that's a comfort. It's great to know that you betrayed me for something meaningless. That makes it so much better!

Pause.

Brian   I mean, why even tell me about it? If it didn't mean anything—

Zawe   You wouldn't want to know?

Brian   No! Why would I want to know?

Zawe   I thought you'd want to know.

Brian   Don't fucking pretend it's about me! The time for thinking about me was just before your knickers came off! That was the time for consideration! No . . . You had a squalid little secret troubling your conscience but instead of just living with it, you decided to dump it into my fucking brain!

Zawe   You wouldn't tell me?

Brian   Oh no. No: you do *not* get to turn this round on me! I haven't done that. You've done it and now you've told me. And now it does mean something. Now it *has to* mean something.

Pause.

Brian   Do you want to be with this . . . fucking . . . Olly guy?

Zawe   No!

Brian   No?

Zawe   I told you—

Brian   Right. It was meaningless. So do you want to be with me?

Pause.

Brian Zawe: do you want to be with me?

Pause. A long pause. **Brian** *crumbles.*

Brian Oh Jesus. Oh Jesus Christ, I'm an idiot.

Zawe You're not.

Brian I am. I am. Hollywood. Fucking Hollywood.

Zawe Hollywood?

Brian I thought this was it. You and me: I really thought this was that great fucking Love thing they fill our heads with. But it's not, is it?

Pause.

Brian Oh Christ, don't you ever learn? Don't you ever fucking learn?

Pause.

Zawe I do love you.

He nods.

Brian Prove it.

Zawe Prove it?

Brian Marry me.

Pause.

Zawe Marry you?

Brian Why not?

Pause.

Zawe I can't.

Brian Why not? If you love me?

Pause.

Zawe It wouldn't be right.

Brian   Why not?

Zawe   I just told you I slept with someone . . .

Brian   Exactly. And by doing that, you've fucking smashed the trust we had. Do you understand that? You fucking . . . *girl*! You stupid fucking *girl*. Do you have any idea how hard it'll be to rebuild that?

Zawe   No, Brian, why don't you tell me? Why don't you tell me like you've told me everything else, from all your years of wisdom?

Brian   Hard. Long and tiresome and fucking *hard*.

Pause.

Brian   But I'll make you a deal, a one-time offer: marry me. Say it now and I'll just trust you. I'll use my emotional fucking etch-a-sketch and make like it never happened. Just commit, absolutely, here and now. Free pass.

Pause.

Brian   What do you say?

Pause.

Zawe   I do love you . . . I just . . .

Brian   Fuck you. Fuck you.

Pause.

Brian   What the FUCK do you know about love? Hmm? Oh no, wait a minute, I know: your mother loved you. That's why you're so secure, right? That's why you have panic attacks and hide under the bed all day: that's why you're in therapy: that's why you fucked fucking Plastic Man! Because you're so secure! Because your mother fucking loved you so fucking much!

Pause.

Brian   But what if she didn't, Zawe? What if she didn't love you?

Zawe *shakes her head.*

Brian   Come on . . . like you said: You've got to ask the question sometimes. What if you're *wrong*?

Pause.

Brian   Because tell me this . . . who did *she* learn it from? Your mother was brought up in an orphanage. You told me she was treated like shit. So where did she learn how to love? I'll tell you: from books. From the TV. From fucking Hollywood. She gave you stuff, she showered you with unqualified praise, she told you you'd inherit the fucking Earth and it was all fucking bullshit! A simulation: a cheap, superficial imitation of love by someone who didn't know the meaning of the word. And thirty years later, what's the result? You. You. A fucking . . . Easter Egg of a person.

Pause.

Brian   You don't know who you are, you don't know what you want, you don't know what you think . . . Life throws shit at you and you collapse and you know why? Because there's no core to you, no foundation, none of the things that real love . . . genuine, complex, awkward love . . . builds. Your mother loved you like a child loves a doll. She didn't know any other way. And you know what? Neither do you.

Pause. **Zawe** *nods. He's crossed a line and he knows it.*

Zawe   And what about you? Were you loved?

Pause.

Brian   I don't know, Zawe.

Pause.

Brian   But I can sleep, you know? I can spend more than ten minutes in silence. I can look in a fucking mirror.

Pause. Lights down, in conventional style.

Sophie *appears on the screen.* **Imogen** *enters – that same unearthly sound.*

Imogen   Soppy . . . wait! Please . . . call you head me?

Sophie *looks at her.*

Imogen   Sophie please . . . judge tall to me! Please!

Pause. The image of **Sophie** *speaks – her tone is fairytale dark.*

Sophie   Why should I?

Imogen   Because I'm sordid! I'm so funky sordid for who I did. I can't go off like this. I'm a total wren, look at me!

Pause.

Sophie   Why did you do it?

Imogen   I don't know! The night was in my head and then I just did it. It was like my arm did it.

Sophie   Your arm?

Imogen   Like a mustard spasm.

Sophie   Oh come on . . . . Obviously you hated me on some level.

Imogen   No, I loathed you! You're my best friend!

Sophie   Am I supposed to feel sorry for you? At least you're still in there. At least you're still a part of it.

Imogen   I know but look at me . . . I've got horns! I've got fucking horns now! And my voice sounds weird and my weirds are word and I don't fit anywhere . . .

Pause.

Imogen   I know I don't dessert your hell but I'm scarred, Sophie! I'm so fucking scared . . .

Pause.

Sophie   They're going to need a reason. A reason why you did it.

Imogen   But what if there isn't one?

Sophie   Then they'll write you off. Is that what you want?

Imogen   No . . .

Sophie   Then give them a reason. One that makes sense to them.

Imogen   Like what though?

Pause.

Sophie   What about that boyfriend? The one who was twenty-five when you were fifteen.

Imogen   What about him?

Sophie   Well . . . technically . . . you were abused.

Pause.

Imogen   Yeah but that didn't—

Sophie   But maybe it *did*. Maybe you've been lying to yourself.

Imogen   What so . . . I stabbed you?

Sophie   You had a lot of anger. Years of suppressed anger and something triggered it. Something like . . .

Pause.

Sophie   The apple.

Imogen   The apple?

Sophie   Did that mean something to you, the apple?

Imogen *tries to think.*

Sophie   Did he *eat* apples?

Imogen   Yeah, probably . . .

Sophie   Did he *like* apples?

Imogen   I think so.

Sophie   Do you remember him eating an apple?

Imogen   I guess so . . .

Pause.

Imogen   But did he abuse me though?

Sophie   Did you ever do anything you didn't want to?

Pause.

Imogen   Sometimes I wasn't in the mood . . .

Sophie   But he did it anyway.

Imogen   Yeah. But I just went along with it.

Sophie   Of course you did. You were only fifteen. You didn't know any better.

Imogen   I guess . . .

Pause.

Imogen   He did tell me to keep it a secret. He didn't want anyone to know he was my boy-band.

Sophie   So he knew. How it would look. That's good. What else?

Pause.

Imogen   He licked me in my school uniform. Liked me. To wear it.

Sophie   Good. You're remembering.

Pause.

Imogen   And sometimes he . . .

Sophie   Sometimes . . .

Imogen   Sometimes he'd make me choke on his cod, which made me crikey, not properly, but 'cos I was neatly sick! And then . . . and then he'd cumberbatch on my façade!

She's crying now.

Sophie   Good. The first step is acknowledgement. You need to acknowledge that you were abused.

She nods.

Sophie   Say it.

Pause.

Imogen   But won't he get into trousers?!

Sophie   Fuck him! He should have thought about that at the time.

Pause.

Sophie   Do you want back in or not?!

Imogen   Yes.

Sophie   Then *say* it! Say it and it'll be true!

Pause. **Imogen** *turns to face the audience.*

Imogen   I was abused.

Pause.

Imogen   I was abused as a child.

Suddenly – brightness! A mirrorball! Jaunty music! A party atmosphere.

(*On the screen, a YouTube clip plays. It was called 'Kittens on Decks' and showed kittens trying to climb aboard a record player turntable. At the time of writing it can be found here:*

http://www.youtube.com/watch?v=onvi3aewfe4 *but any extremely cute animal video would suffice.*)

The cast all enter, smiling and happy, and gather round **Imogen***, patting her, hugging her, and offering platitudes:*

You've been so brave.
If there's anything I can do.
We need more people like you.
You mustn't blame yourself.
People like you are the real heroes.

Imogen *accepts their embraces, happy but bewildered.*

Imogen   I'm fine, really . . . I'll be fine.

And now they leave.

> Just hang on in there.
> If there's anything you need-
> If you ever want to talk-
> Just be kind to yourself, OK?

Imogen   I will. Thank you. Thanks for all your support.

The party's over and she's left on the stage with **Chris**, *who still has her horns covered, and is still pretending to be someone else.*

Imogen *is ashamed.*

Imogen   Will you tell?

Chris   Tell what, dear?

Imogen   You know what.

Chris   I don't think I do . . .

Imogen   Yes you do.

Pause.

Imogen   I know it's you. I saw you before.

Chris   I don't think so.

Imogen   I did! You were collecting names, for your son. But he didn't die like you thought he did. You had horns, like me.

Chris   I think I'd remember having horns, don't you?

Imogen   Did you ever find out why? Why he killed himself?

Chris *looks uncomfortable.* **Imogen** *is crying.*

Imogen   Do you think I'm evil?

Chris   I don't think anything.

Imogen   But you know what I've done—

Chris   I don't *know* . . . anything.

Imogen   Yes. You do.

Pause. Letting the façade drop, **Chris** *reveals her horns.*

Chris   I'll tell you what I know: I used to think DEAL OR
NO DEAL was a load of superstitious shite! But now I watch it
twice a day! And Every . . . Single . . . Fucking . . . Number has a
meaning!!

Pause. She regains her composure.

Chris   You're back in. That's all that matters.

Chris *pushes a few pages of script into* **Imogen**'s *hand.*

A microphone is placed on stage.

Zawe *storms in, raging.*

Zawe   You're a fucking arsehole, you know that?! How dare
you! How dare you fucking speak to me about my mother! What
the fuck do you know about my mother?!

Taken by surprise, **Imogen** *hurriedly searches for her lines on the
page.*

Imogen   Oh fuck—

Zawe *joins her at the microphone.* **Imogen** *reads:*

Imogen   Nothing! I just said—

Zawe   You're not the Queen of suffering you know? We're all
survivors.

Imogen   Um . . . You keep saying that! But what the fuck have
you survived exactly?

Zawe   OK, fine . . . You win: you win the Suffering award. Here:
here's your crown of thorns, Great Queen of Suffering! We're
sorry that we burden you with our problems once in a while!
We're sorry that this relationship can't always be about you!

*Over time, the scene becomes more real, the scripts less used, the
stage more taken.*

Imogen   I don't want it to be about me! I don't want to talk
about my shit . . . Jesus Christ: I'd give my left tit to never have

to talk or think about it ever again! You're the one that keeps dragging it up and then the minute I start talking about it, you start fucking nodding and telling me how you feel my fucking pain!

Zawe   I do though.

Imogen   Why? Because your mother didn't love you?

Zawe   Yeah well we can't all have been abused and killed our best friend and been to prison, yeah? That doesn't make my pain less valid than yours, though, does it?

Imogen   No, but that's not what I'm saying—

Zawe   No, you're saying I don't have any pain.

Imogen   Christ, no . . . you obviously have pain; you've obviously got a fucking ton of pain. I just don't think it comes from where you think it comes from.

Zawe   Right. Because you know better than trained therapists.

Imogen   I just don't know where you get the idea that your mother didn't love you. Jesus . . . I wish my Mum had made up songs about how amazing and fucking wonderful I was! All I got was how I should marry the first man who showed any fucking interest in me!

Zawe   But it was a lie, don't you get that? They were just stupid songs and then they stopped! They just fucking stopped and I had nothing!

Imogen   But you didn't have nothing though! OK, she stopped singing . . . She was obviously majorly depressed . . . but she fed you, she looked after you, she supported you . . . What the fuck else did you want from her? What do you think love is?

Zawe   I think that love . . . is what I feel for you.

Imogen   Is it, though? See, this is what I don't get . . . You say your mother didn't love you because she wasn't loved, right? So if you weren't loved . . . how can you say you love me?

Zawe   I don't know. I think maybe it's a miracle.

Imogen   A miracle?

Zawe   Like I was meant to meet you. So I could understand what love is.

Imogen   Woah . . . wait a second, where are we going with this miracle shit? Meant to meet me?

Zawe   That's what I feel.

Imogen   Meant by who, though?

Zawe   I don't know. By whatever means us to be together.

Imogen   OK, listen . . . reality check . . . because we need to fucking address this, here and now: YOU are NOT a lesbian.

Zawe   What?! How can you say that? How the FUCK can you say that!

Imogen   Come on—

Zawe   What the fuck have we been doing this last month?! What was all that if I'm not a lesbian?!

Imogen   Letting me eat you out doesn't make you a lesbian, Zawe.

Zawe   I'm going to . . . do that to you, I told you! I'm just waiting till after I get my molars out!

Imogen   Come on—

Zawe   It's nothing personal, I just don't want to get an infection.

Imogen   Zawe . . . come on . . . I love you—

Zawe   And I love you—

Imogen   But seriously: there's no future in this.

Zawe   No . . . don't say that. There is a future. This is the future.

Imogen   This is?

Zawe   Not now, this is the past; but this bit coming up . . . is the future: see? There. That's the future. Just not any more. Now it's this bit . . . see? The future. And we're still together.

Pause.

Imogen   Zawe . . . I'm so grateful to you for everything you've done for me. You've supported me and cared for me and that's how I know: that's how I know that you were loved. But you're looking for something, and this isn't it.

Pause.

Zawe   Fine. Just go then.

Imogen   Zawe.

Zawe   That's what you want isn't it? To leave. You leave, you're left: over and over and over until it all stops.

Pause.

Zawe   And maybe that's OK. Maybe *that's* what's meant to be.

Pause.

Imogen   Look, we're both tired. Let's just . . . get some sleep and then—

Zawe   No. Just go.

Imogen   Go where?

Zawe   Go home.

Imogen   What, now? It's the middle of the night . . .

Zawe   So?

Imogen   So I know you're not good with nights.

Pause.

Imogen   This doesn't have to be a big scene. Let's just wait until the morning—

Zawe   No.

Unusually forceful.

Zawe   Just go. I'll be fine.

Imogen   Will you?

Pause.

Imogen   Will you call me tomorrow then?

Zawe *shrugs.* **Imogen** opens the door.

Imogen   Zawe—

Zawe   I want those shoes back.

Imogen   The shoes you bought me? They won't even fit you . . .

Zawe   I'll take them back to the shop.

Imogen   Fine. But I don't have the receipt.

She pronounces the p.

Zawe   It's all right: I kept it.

Imogen *leaves. The sound of the desert wind.*

Zawe *walks to the oasis and looks at herself, reflected there.*

Zawe (*Sings*)   You are a princess. You are the best. Everything you do is amazing . . .

Then she falls silent.

(*The next YouTube clip plays. It's called 'strange sounds all over the world, Jerusalem, Houston, New York, Belgium etc.' and at the time of writing can be found here:*

http://www.youtube.com/watch?v=IfvLn8MBjws

The section used runs from 0.10 to 1.00. The clip is real footage shot in New York by a young man hearing a loud, strange noise in the sky. He offers a profane commentary.

'I'm hearing uh . . . I'm lookin' out my window right now . . . hearin' some strange fuckin' sounds out there. I've no idea what the hell they are . . . it's . . . rattling the earth around here, we're in Long Island, January 18th (2012) . . . and it's fuckin' loud. You hear that? You hear that shit?! 'Fuck is that shit? I've no idea, like . . . it's comin' straight

out of the sky. What is that? This is for all you YouTube
people . . . you hear that?'

(***Note***: *there are many such clips on YouTube covering the spate
of noises heard in 2011/2012 and you may find more appropriate
clips for your production, if you choose to include them at all.*)

Lights up.

Barney *brings a cup of coffee to* **Olly**.

Olly   Aw, thanks . . . .

Barney   It's good to have you back, man.

Olly   It's good to be back. Bit of normality.

Barney   Just for the weekend is it?

Olly   Back on Tuesday.

Barney   So . . . tell me all about it: how's it going? How's
George?

Pause.

Olly   He's fine.

Barney   Is he a nice guy?

Olly   Yeah, he's a nice guy. But he's not a *normal* guy, you know
what I mean?

Barney   Yeah, well . . . he doesn't have a normal life.

Olly   No, he doesn't. He's got Barack Obama's personal
number. Like . . . that's one of his mates: the President of the
United States.

Barney   Wow.

Olly   Yeah but it's just so different from what I'm used to. I
mean, you might as well be mates with fucking . . . Hansel and
Gretel, you know what I mean? It's just completely unreal.

Barney   Yeah but you're in there, mate. You've been selected by
the big grabber-thing of life. The golden doors have opened.

Olly   I've got the feeling they might shut in my face.

Pause.

Olly   I've been invited round to Russell Crowe's house next weekend.

Barney   Wow. Why?

Olly   It's just what they do. They just invite you round because . . . you're new.

Barney   That's nice, I suppose. They're trying to make you welcome.

Olly   I guess. But it's not like kicking back with a few mates, you know? You're always on edge.

Barney *nods.* **Olly** *gets up.*

Olly   Just going for a piss.

He leaves. **Barney** *looks at* **Olly**'s *cup of coffee. A villainous look comes over him: checking the coast is clear first, he picks up the cup and lets a sliver of spit falls into the coffee. He puts the cup back.*

Olly *comes back.*

Barney   So tell me . . . give me all the gossip.

Olly   You know what? Could we just not talk about it for a while?

Barney   OK . . .

Olly   I'll tell you all about it tomorrow. I'll take you out for a Chinese. I'll pay.

He sips from the coffee. **Barney** *watches.*

Barney   Brilliant.

Olly   I just want to be normal for a while.

Barney   Well . . . this is the place to do it.

Pause.

Olly   Honestly? I've been feeling quite weird recently.

Barney   Weird?

Olly   Yeah. Bit paranoid.

Barney   About what?

Pause.

Olly   It's stupid.

Barney   What?

Pause.

Olly   You remember that picture?

Barney   What picture?

Olly   Remember: that picture of the arsehole?

Barney   Oh yeah. Did you find out who it was?

Olly   No. I still don't know. No, it's not that.

Pause.

Olly   It's just it's been . . . preying on my mind.

Barney   Why?

Pause.

Olly   You know how we were wondering whose arsehole it was?

Barney   Yeah—

Olly   Well I know this is stupid . . . but I was thinking . . . what if it's not his, or his wife's . . .

Pause.

Olly   What if it's mine?

Barney   Yours?

Olly   What if it's a picture of my arsehole? What if there's a picture of my arsehole out there? What if when this movie comes out, someone puts it online and says, look everybody: Olly Rix's arsehole!

Pause.

Barney   But . . . how would they have got a picture of your arsehole?

Olly   I don't know. I know it doesn't make sense. I just had the thought. And now I can't seem to get it out of my head.

Barney   Yeah, but it's completely ridiculous.

Olly   I know.

Barney   It's probably just anxiety. It's like when you think you've left the oven on.

Olly   Yeah. Except sometimes you have left the oven on.

Barney   Yeah, well, that's where the analogy breaks down.

Pause.

Barney   Look . . . you're under a lot of pressure. The mind does funny things.

Olly *nods, looking stressed.*

Olly   You're my friend, right?

Barney   Of course I am.

Olly   You're my best friend.

Barney   Yeah . . .

Pause.

Olly   Would you . . . look?

Pause.

Barney   At?

Pause.

Barney   At the picture?

Olly   Yeah.

Pause.

Olly   And then . . .

Pause.

Barney   Oh no . . .

Olly   It'd just ease my mind. If I knew, for sure.

Barney   No! Jesus . . . I'm not looking at your . . . !

Olly   Noel, please: I've got no one else to ask.

Barney   Ask Clooney! Ask Russell-fucking-Crowe!

Olly   I can't ask them to look at my arsehole!

Barney   So why are you asking me?! Why don't you do it?!

Olly   I've tried!

Barney   What and you couldn't see it?

Olly   Not properly. I couldn't be in the position I had to be in and hold the picture up for comparison.

Barney   Take a photo of it then!

Olly   Do you know how difficult it is to take a photo, one-handed, of your own arsehole?

Barney   No, I have to say I don't . . . !

Olly   I'm not asking you to rim it! Just take a look!

Barney   Absolutely and utterly not.

Olly   It's just an arsehole—

Barney   No. No . . . it's not just an arsehole, it's a man's arsehole and it's your arsehole and those are pretty much the two things that . . . you know: it's the line I won't cross.

Pause.

Barney   Anyway . . . how would I know?

Olly   You might.

Barney   How?

Olly   There might be some distinguishing marks.

Barney   Like what? Have you got a mole or something? A birthmark?

Olly   No, I don't think so.

Pause.

Olly   But what about the spokes?

Barney   The *spokes*?! What the fuck are the *spokes*?!

Olly   The lines that come out from round it—

Barney   Jesus . . . what: count them?! Like the rings on a tree?!

Olly   No, but they must be quite unique to each person. Like fingerprints.

Barney   Oh, right . . . the spokes of your anus are like fingerprints?

Olly   They must be, mustn't they?

Imogen *enters with an envelope.*

Barney   I really don't know; I'm pretty sure they don't dust for them at crime scenes!

Imogen *gives* **Barney** *the envelope.*

Barney   What's this?

Imogen   I don't know. I was just told to give it to you.

Olly   We're not in a café, are we?

She exits. **Barney** *opens the envelope.*

Olly   That's strange: I'm sure that was the waitress from the café . . .

Barney *is staring at the letter.*

Olly   What is it? It's not another arsehole, is it?! 'Cos that'd be—

Barney   It says I've died.

Pause.

Olly   What?

Barney   It says I've died.

Olly   You've died?

Barney   Supposedly.

Olly   Of what?

Barney   It doesn't even say.

Pause.

Barney   This can't be right. Is this right?

Pause.

Barney   So what? That's it? We don't get to finish this story?

Pause.

Barney   Unbelievable! That's it! Done!

Olly   Shit. I can't believe that.

Barney   Can you believe that?!

Olly   No.

Pause.

Barney   Fine, I mean, if that's what's been decided! I just don't think it's fair on other people. They're not going to see how it turns out!

Olly   It's shitty.

Barney   It is, isn't it?

He's getting tearful. **Olly** *gets up and goes to him.*

Barney   We were going for a Chinese.

He dissolves into tears. **Olly** *holds him in his arms until he's calmed.*

They separate and **Olly** *offers his hand.*

Olly   Well . . . it's been a pleasure.

Barney *takes it.*

Barney   It has. It really has.

Olly   We nearly got there.

Barney   Yeah. Nearly. That's me though isn't it? Nearly. Nearly got married. Nearly had kids. Nearly got that part in Call the Midwife. Nearly, nearly, nearly.

He goes to leave but stops.

Barney   Hey, Olly?

Olly   Yeah?

Barney   I wish I could have been happier for you, mate. I just wasn't written that way.

As he exits, **Brian** *enters. They shake hands in passing.*

Brian *sits down and addresses the audience.*

Brian   I've used the bus all my life: double-decker buses, now . . . not your single deck, bendy things, which you'll notice they're phasing out. They're phasing them out because there's no order to them. There's an order to a double-decker bus.

You start your life downstairs, at the front of the bus, with your ma. You're either in a pram or in her arms: either way she wants you close to the doors. When you outgrow the pram, she moves you to the middle, but still downstairs. Eventually, you start making trips without her, and as you get bolder and more confident, you start moving to the back: but you're still downstairs.

Round about ten, twelve, you've got friends and you want to be

part of the adult world; so you make the big move . . . Upstairs.
But you sit right at the front, so you can pretend you're driving.
The more friends you make, the further back you move; you pretty
much colonise the middle top deck until you hit puberty and then
it's back of the bus, baby . . . all the fucking way! Drink, drugs,
sex, music . . . it all happens at the back of the bus. And you stay
there well into your twenties.

Then you turn thirty. You're properly an adult now. You don't
want to sit with the assholes at the back but you're still young at
heart, so you move back to the middle of the top deck. Now and
then, you get together with your mates and you sit at the back just
to show you've still got it; but left to your own devices, you start
the incremental move forward.

Past forty, something strange happens; just now and then, you sit
in the very front seats, only now you're fucking glad you're not a
bus driver.

Past sixty, the knees are starting to go, the stairs are unappealing
and the people on the top deck are starting to scare, annoy,
confuse you. Who needs it? So you move downstairs again, but
at the back, where you can nurture that last scrap of defiance. But
sure as shit stinks, you'll start that slow move forward, just to get
a little closer to those rearwards doors.

And then . . . then you're properly old. Christ, you're doing
well to be getting the bus at all; why make life more difficult for
yourself? What's the point?

And there you come to rest: downstairs, at the front, shortest
possible distance from the exit; in the seats your long-dead ma
made you give up for the old folks, all those years ago.

(*The last YouTube clip plays, against music. It's called 'Man
Attacked by Angry Bison' and at the time of writing it can be
found here:* http://www.youtube.com/watch?v=I9jROXrd9sE

*The clip shows a man at a rodeo being caught on the horns of a
bison and flung through the air. It plays out once in real time, then
again in slow motion.*)

Epilogue

In the darkness, a vast, frightening sound from the sky.

Then silence.

Then again – the noise. A horn? So loud the building shakes.

*One by one, the cast – even **Sophie** – drift back onto the stage, wondering what the noise is. They murmur among themselves.*

Again the noise – terrifyingly loud.

The cast look up towards the sky . . .

Once more, we hear the digitised voice:

Voice   What did you expect of life?

Why did you expect it? Who told you what to expect?

What was expected of you? Who expected this of you? What did you expect of yourself? What do you expect of others? Of your friends, of your partners, of your children? Have they met those expectations? Was anything unexpected? Did you respond the way you expected?

Why do we expect?

Why do we expect?

Why do we expect?

Whatever it is they see up there, they each take in their own way.

Fade to black.

Rantin

Kieran Hurley

**Created with Liam Hurley, Gav Prentice,
Julia Taudevin and Drew Wright**

Rantin was originally presented at Cottiers Theatre, Glasgow on 17 April 2013 as part of the Auteurs Project, a collaboration between the National Theatre of Scotland and the Arches, and Behaviour 2013 with support from the Esmée Fairbairn Foundation.

Performers (in alphabetical order)

Kieran Hurley
Gav Prentice
Julia Taudevin
Drew Wright

Director	Kieran Hurley
Set and Costume Designer	Lisa Sangster
Sound Designer	Matt Padden
Lighting Designer	Paul Claydon
Dramaturgy and additional text	Liam Hurley

A Note on the Original Production

This is a show made up of songs and stories. It is, to use a phrase that I think was coined by John McGrath, a ceilidh-play. As such music is very important to the show, and various musical themes and textures are used repeatedly, in a way which we think is very important to how the stories hang together. This document contains words and lyrics and only the very occasional stage direction where music might start. The rest is up to you to re-imagine.

When staging this play, it is important to think of the audience as a vital part of the event. In the spirit of a ceilidh you should all feel very much like you are sharing the same space. There are occasional references to the Arches in Glasgow, where our original tour opened. These should change to reflect whatever space the show is being performed in. Similarly, if the play is being performed in Scotland, Emma's scene should be adapted to be set in the same town that it is playing in. The local detail should describe Emma passing immediately outside the venue where we are gathered. When touring in Scotland, this should be adapted and updated constantly.

Kieran Hurley

Intro

As the audience enter we are playing some tunes from the hi-fi. Chatting, getting a drink. We're setting up the space. Towards the end of this we'll encourage the audience to fill up their drinks and go for a pee and stuff. When it is time to start we open with a song.

Song: MacPherson's Rant

Trad. Arr.

Additional words by Drew Wright and Gav Prentice.

Drew   Farewell yon pitheid dark and dank
Farewell farewell to thee
Macpherson's time will no be long
In yonder colliery

Chorus:

All   Sae rantingly, sae wantonly
Sae dauntingly gaed he
He played a tune an' he danced aroon
Below the gallows tree

Drew   Forgive the man whose rage betrayed
A wound that cannot heal
Fae the Iron Burgh's great canal
Oot to the toons o' steel

Chorus

Drew   In the smirr and smelt o' the Central Belt
We worked wi strength and pride
But then the fall, we lost it all
Oor wives and mithers cried

Chorus

Drew   Farewell to steel, and ships and coal
The pride o' industry
What price the cost? Oor greatest loss
Was solidarity

Chorus

The song ends.

Gav *says thanks for coming, and introduces himself. He probably cracks a joke about the show being credited as 'by Kieran Hurley' but since it's by all of us that's kind of as if we're a band called Kieran Hurley who just happen to have a member of the band whose name is also Kieran Hurley. Like Van Halen. Or Manfred Mann.* **Gav** *introduces everyone else.*

Julia *explains that this show was nearly called Till Apples Grow On An Orange Tree. Then at one point it was going to be called Pie Suppers In The Sky, and then we nearly called it Ah'm No Hairy Mary Ah'm Yer Maw, but we thought better of that, so now it is called Rantin.*

Kieran *explains that we're going to tell some stories, and sing some songs. Each little song, story, or moment is like a turn, or a track in a set list at a gig. As we tell these stories we'd like you to imagine that they are happening in Scotland, right now outside this theatre, as we speak.*

Drew *explains that what we're offering is a collection of fragments really. We're not trying to show the whole story, that would be impossible. There's no central character here, just some imagined ideas of different people, with different stories, perspectives, next to each other trying to co-exist. Which in some way is what the process of making the show has been like.*

Once this has clearly run its course, **Gav** *suggests we start.* **Kieran** *asks to dim the lights.*

Kieran   If this was the start of a film, we imagine that at this point you'd see a map of Scotland as if viewed from above. The map is green and blue and grey.

Underneath the speaking, **Julia** *begins to sing.*

<u>Song: Soraidh Leis An Ait</u>

Trad. Arr.

Julia   Soraidh leis an àit
An d'fhuair mi m'àrach òg
Eilean nam beann àrda
Far an tàmh an ceò
Air a moch a dh'èireas
Grian nan speur fo ròs
A'fuadach neul na h-oidhche
Soillseachadh an Stòrr

Kieran   Imagine that now. The map, as the camera slowly moves in on it. Closer. Bigger. And the place names become clearer in a kind of old-looking calligraphy like on pirates' maps. Or maybe it's more like chalk on a chalkboard. Or maybe your map is more of a sans serif font like on Google. And then Drew's voice, in voiceover says:

Drew   This is a story that has multiple beginnings, an abundance of middles, and no clear end. It starts, for our purposes, right here under this old railway arch in Glasgow, with each of you here. But it also starts, among other places, above our heads, here:

Howard (1)

Julia *becomes* **Howard**.

Julia   This man is called Howard. He is sixty-seven years old. He clutches his crumpled boarding pass in his hand. Origin: New York JFK. Destination: Prestwick International Airport. A one-way ticket. The print has been smudged slightly from the sweat from his thumbs over the course of his six-hour journey across the Atlantic.

He has never left America before now.

He has been saving, preparing, for this moment. For this. He thinks about the military pipe music his granddaddy used to play, back home in Lincoln, Nebraska.

He thinks about the hours he's spent up late, by himself, Googling the real meaning of those mysterious and ancient sounding words.

He hadn't considered until recently that he might actually move there. But here he is.

He has brought a phrasebook of Scots words with him for the journey.

Drew   Stravaig: verb; to wander. Noun; a journey without purpose.

Gav   Dwam: noun; a stupor or a daydream.

Kieran   Fankle: verb; to tangle, to twist. Noun; an entanglement, a state of disorder or confusion.

Julia   Fankle. Wow.

It took Howard a long time to really think of Scotland as an actual place where people are born and live and die. For longer than that it had been an ambiguous reference point, somewhere utterly relevant to who he is but in an invisible and underacknowledged kind of way. It later became a semi mythical place, a point of explanation – a Babylon and a Zion. The fire of the clearances that packed his ancestors off to Canada, their subsequent journey south. Howard thinks about this journey often. He feels it, in his bones.

He was fifty years old when he first watched *Braveheart* and it changed his life. Even if some of it was made up, sure, I mean Howard's nobody's fool. But that very week he bought himself a kilt. Jeez Louise he felt powerful. His varicose roots swelled out of his Celtic warrior legs, and he knew at that moment that one day those warrior muscles were going to take him Home.

Since then he has been real sad about Mel Gibson drink-driving and beating up his wife. And the anti-semitism. That had really got under Howard's skin, particularly due to his deep affection for the work of Rabbi Burns. Just kidding. Come on, Howard is not an idiot. He knows that Scotland's bard is not really a rabbi. That's just his name.

He wrote Mel's agent a letter telling him how badly he felt that Mel was letting the side down. Before this he had watched

Trainspotting on late night pay-per-view and was so intrigued. This is so fucking exotic, Howard thought. My people are the most complex sons of bitches on this godforsaken earth.

This explains a lot.

Macpherson (1)

Drew   While Howard flies above our heads, in Thurso, Helen, a police officer, gets in, kicks off her shoes and puts on the telly.

Julia   In Perth, Robert and Stephen, two finance co-workers are having awkward sex in Robert's flat, right now, at this minute.

Drew   And over in Methil, East Fife, Albert Macpherson, fifty-nine years old but looking at least fifteen years older, wearing his big coat and wooly hat, sits in a small bar, doing his usual routine of getting absolutely blootered.

Kieran*, now in Macpherson gear, picks up a pint.*

Kieran   Ready Gav?

Gav *nods.*

Drew   One, two, three!

Gav *plays a loud part on the electric guitar while* **Kieran** *necks his pint. The music stops.* **Kieran** *is Macpherson. He sits.*

Kieran   Basically it's aw fucked, right? All ay it. The whole thing. Fucking fucked.

Julia   This is Macpherson.

Kieran   Fucked I'm tellin ye. Beyond repair. Kaput. Done for. Broken watch. Doon the pan.

Julia   Look at him. He is totally steaming.

Kieran   Oot the game.

Julia   Banjoed.

Kieran   Absolutely fuckin totalled.

Julia   And testing the patience of the other punters.

Kieran   Fifty-three pound a week. Eh? RATBAG. Look efter number one, eh? Listen listen listen listen – here. Listen! Tae me. Here. You.

Macpherson singles out an audience member.

Kieran   Aye you, fuckin, mere! Whit do you dae? Whit, whit do you dae?

This requires some improvisation. **Macpherson** *asks the audience member what they do for a living. The audience member replies.*

Kieran   That's shite! Naw, no offence, just cosay it's aw shite. Nowhitamean? Nowhitamean but? The whole fuckin… SHITER.

Julia   Macpherson will probably get moved on in a minute. But he's used to that. Getting moved on is a bit of a theme in his story.

Kieran   Listen tae me right. Ah'll tell you what to dae about it. The whole system right is a broken watch. Right. It is. Listen. Naebody can hink ay the other possibilities, eh?

Macpherson *necks another drink.*

Julia   He's moved from town to town. Coatbridge, Motherwell. Now Methil. Looking for work and finding it. But like a spurned and jaded lover, the work just kept packing up and leaving.

Kieran   A broken watch. Cause a watch right it's an invention right. That people just made up. Aboot how to organise the world, how tae go about it! And noo we cannae imagine a world wiout it. Right. And that's the system. But it's fucked noo, and we're aw starin at the scrapheap ay broken clocks hinking fuck dae we dae no – we cannae see past these hings! But here's the real truth – IT WAS ALWAYS FUCKED IN THE FIRST PLACE! EH? EH? NOWHITAMEAN BUT?

Macpherson *points to the same audience member he singled out before.*

Kieran   HE DOES. HE FUCKIN KNOWS. ASK HIM if you dinnae believe me. Fuckin pile ay broken watches built on one idea ONLY: look eftir number one. Look eftir number one eh? NUMERO UNENTO. Look eftir number one! Which is the same as tae say: it's dog eat dog. DOGS EATIN DOGS OOT THER **Macpherson**. The hing is. Hing is but: is your dog gonnae eat ma dog? Aye. Nowhitamean? You fucking laugh then. You nowhitameanbut don't you? And who's the top dogs eh? Eh? RATBAGS. You know what a mean. Aye ye dae. Aye ye fuckin dae.

Julia   And now he sits. Building walls around his shrinking, sozzled, fading world.

Kieran   Dog eat dog eh? An foreigners an aw. Whit? Coming here for the rat race and setting their dogs on us aw. Whit? Aye!

Julia   Time to move on Macpherson.

Kieran   Every man for himself, eh? Every man for himself. Staring straight ahead, ignoring every other cunt, elbowing them oot the way to the front ay the queue to dig our own mass grave. BROTHERS AN SISTERS. We shall overcome EH? Aw they roses will turn to bloom eh? RATSHITE. Yous can aw believe in your fairytales but I believe in what I see in front of me. And ah've got a truth for you. AYE. I'll show yous aw. Aye, ah no whit youse aw see when you look at me, WASTER – intit? WASTER. Aye.

Julia   Time to move on son.

Kieran   Fuckin sponging off, fucking sponging, drone, drone, drone, Macpherson, a fuckin waste ay space get rid ay um! AYE!

Macpherson *points to the audience member again.*

Kieran   HE KNOWS. Fuckin dinnae believe me ask this cunt. Eh? Eh? You want tay know what a learnt eh?

Macpherson *points to the audience member again.*

Kieran   He does! He fucking does so FUCKING SHUT IT THE

LOT AY YOUS! Here it is: rat race is for rats. And here's the hing: WE'RE AW FUCKING RATS!

Julia   RIGHT YOU, THAT'S IT, GET OUT!

Kieran   AYE FUCK YOUS AW I WAS LEAVING ANYWAY! RATS!

Short stories (1)

Julia   In Inverness, Harry packs his bags and scribbles down the collection code for his ticket on the Caledonian sleeper to visit his dad down in Brighton.

Drew   In the corner of Da Wheel bar in Lerwick, Seamus, reading a book on folklore, has just learned about selkies; seal people who would appear to unsuspecting strangers in human form. He thinks to himself; that'd be a beezer fancy dress.

Kieran   Right now, Asjad, eight years old, runs through Govanhill in Glasgow, singing a song that they learned at school today. He already knew the song, but this was the real version, like from the olden days. Magic! So now he runs, skipping and hopping past the fruit stalls, the halal butchers, the Irish pubs, away from his mum shouting after him in Urdu, past the bookies, past the old blue rinse ladies, past the Romani kids playing football, past the block lettered sign on the evangelical church telling all below that Christ Died For Our Sins, past all this, schoolbag swinging, at the top of his voice singing.

Song: Ah'm No Hairy Mary Ah'm Yer Maw

Taken from You Cannae Shove Your Grannie Off The Bus/ It Was Murder Michty Murder In The Hoose.

Trad. Arr.

Kieran   Ah'm no Hairy Mary, Ah'm yer maw

All   Singing Ah'm no Hairy Mary, Ah'm yer maw
Singing Ah'm no Hairy Mary
Ah'm yer maw's canary
Ah'm no Hairy Mary, Ah'm yer maw

Gav   In Dundee, Shuggy is making a huge pot of stew for about ten people. He liked to have a big batch ready for when everyone piled in after a night oot.

Julia   In Coatbridge, Angie is thinking about football. She's just sat at home, calculating the likely points total required for Albion Rovers to achieve a play-off spot at the end of the season.

Kieran   And at her kitchen sink, in Balmedie, Aberdeenshire, in a house she's lived in for sixty-seven years, Ruth, seventy-eight years old, is doing the dishes, by a window that looks on to the site of the Trump International Golf links. She think to herself, fit like is that Trump? I'd throttle him. She has a song that she sings to herself, in moments like this, to stop her smashing her plates in anger. At this moment, as she stacks another mug up on the rack, she is singing that song in her kitchen. It goes like this. I'm sure she'd love it if you wanted to join in.

Song: Donald You're A Loser

Words by Drew Wright.

Based on Donald Where's Your Troosers
by Andy Stewart and Neil Grant.

Drew   I've just flown in from the USA
I'm rich and I always get my way
But all I ever hear you say is

All others   Donald you're a loser!

Drew   I promise jobs and wealth creation
For your obliging servile nation
Wages well below inflation

All others   Donald you're a loser!

Chorus:

Drew   Let my hair blow high my hair blow low
Greed is the only life I know
Wheesht you cheeky so-and-so

All others   Donald you're a loser!

Drew   With my entourage of spooks and goons
We're here to help you save the dunes
But fit like are they local loons?

All others   Donald you're a loser!

Drew   They live in slums they live like pigs
Why aren't they working on the rigs?
How they tormernt me with their jigs

All others   Donald you're a loser!

Chorus

Drew   I'll seize the Menie for the few
A playground for my playboy crew
It isn't for the likes of you

All others   Donald you're a loser!

Drew   Did I tell you about my Hielan' grannie?
Came fae the Isles she was thrawn and canny

Kieran   Even she'd think you're a fanny!

All others   Donald you're a loser!

Chorus

Miriam (1)

Julia becomes **Miriam**.

Kieran   In Clydebank, right now, on the number 61 bus, there is drizzle on the window-panes, there is a crumpled trod-on *Metro*, there is a stale smell of pee, and, there is a woman.

Julia   Too much rain here.

Kieran   This woman is called Miriam.

Julia   Too much.

Kieran   She is forty-two years old. Born two and a half thousand miles away in Ramallah, occupied territories of the Palestinian West Bank. But now, she is here, in Clydebank. On her way to her first shift in a new job. A cleaning job.

Julia   Here.

Kieran   She has been driven here, buffeted and blown here on the roch wind of forces beyond her control. But she pushes on anyway. Well she has to, right? She feels the disapproving gaze of the woman in the seat opposite hers. She looks up. The woman instantly looks away, staring out the window, at nothing. She thinks to herself:

Julia   I'm here you know. I'm here too.

Kieran   She thinks:

Julia   You don't have to pretend you can't see me. And you can't just wish me away. Grumpy cow.

Kieran   She thinks:

Julia   So grumpy and sad, all these faces!

Kieran   She thinks the faces on the bus have seemed to be slowly getting more tired, more sad these last couple of years.

Julia   It is not for me this wet place. It doesn't look like anyone on the number 61 bus wants to be here. Who knows who it is really for, this place? But it is not for me.

Kieran Someone once said to her, Scotland, it is a mongrel nation. And she laughed thinking of the small scabby yappy dog that always leaves a shit on the street where she lives and wakes her up in the morning. A nation like this she thought.

Julia Why would anyone want to live in a yappy shit dog nation like that? So strange.

Kieran She feels the woman opposite look back at her, and this time Miriam shamefully avoids her gaze. A man gets on the bus.

Gav Awrite Jim!

Kieran Picks up a *Metro*. Glances at it. Shakes his head.

Gav Heavy times man. Wooft! Heavy duty.

Julia Maybe this is the problem for these people. Too much wind, too much rain. Too much heavy duty times. Half the world want to be here, in this place, away from their own stories. And these people think they have heavy duty times.

Kieran She thinks about the job that waits for her at the other end. Earlier, on the phone, her son had said, this is good. He said, this shows you belong here now. She sighs, and puts in her earphones.

Julia A wee present from my son.

Kieran Presses play on her iPhone.

Julia A wee present from my son. What is this music? This, my son's music. London music.

Kieran Before she arrived here she was in London. Her son is still in London. A young man now.

Julia Always loving the music from this place, always in the shops in Brixton.

Kieran She thinks of him. Her son. And sunlight. She thinks of sunlight.

Julia   My son, he would say, why not apply for citizenship?

Learn for the test. Then you can go back and visit Ramallah if you miss it so much. No. There is nothing for me there either. No one. Not now.

Kieran   Avoiding the scornful eyes of the woman sat opposite her, and staring out the window of the bus, Miriam looks through the open flat grey grass, the council hedge rows, and tries to imagine, home. The garden path, with the broken paving stones, the sweet smell of the flowers, dry earth, moist cool shade. The distant rumble of construction in the air. She can feel it fading. These days, she feels that memory slowly fading, washed away in the cold drizzle of this strange place.

Gregor

Drew   Let's leave Miriam there for now, and move out along the Firth of Clyde, up the coast, and out to sea, where, in the lounge bar of a passenger ferry, sits this young man, right now.

Song: Griogal Cridhe

Trad. Arr.

Additional lyrics and music by Gav Prentice.

Julia   Ba hu, ba hu, ba mo leanabh
Ba mo leanabh, ba
Ba hu, ba hu, ba mo leanab
Chan eil thu ach tlàth
Dhìrich mi dhan t-seòmar mhullaich
S thèirinn mi'n taigh-làir
S cha d'fhuair mise Griogal Cridhe
Na shuidhe mu'n chlàr

Kieran   Gregor crosses the Minch, towards the mainland, away from Stornoway for the last time, never to return. Well, until the summer at least. I mean he'd maybe have to come back for a summer job and that. But still.

The wee old woman behind the ferry bar polishes the glasses and rearranges the crisps.

Look, it's not like he was off to join the army, or train in finance, or become a total sell out or that. Not like most of his pals from school. He was off to do sociology. And history of art, if you must know. In Glasgow. It was a good thing, he was doing. This was his chance. There's only so long you can stay on the island after all. I mean if you really want to find out about the world, about yourself, if you really want to contribute, you have to get out. And let's face it, it's not like you can afford to move back with an arts degree. Even if you wanted to.

The whisky of the moment is Glenmorangie. 3.35 for a double measure. That's not a bad deal, if you like that stuff. The flickering lights of the puggy catch his eye. He'd get up and play it later. He'd laid his coins out on the table. Not now though.

This isn't one of those sad stories alright? This isn't about the island mourning another lost son.

The houses would keep being sold off. Holiday homes for folk from Shropshire. And Edinburgh. And Kent. Folk who could afford them. And fair fucks to them at the end of the day. That's just the way it is. So you move on don't you? Why should he be any different?

Gav   I thought one day we'd all agreed
We'd never take the gold
We'd never take the king's and queen's
Now I'm the only one unsold

Julia   Ba hu, ba hu, ba mo leanabh
Ba mo leanabh, ba
Ba hu, ba hu, ba mo leanab
Chan eil thu ach tlàth

Kieran   At his seanair's place in Bragar, his seanair had told him you better not come back, a failure. His grannie hadn't liked that at all and said he absolutely must come back or else what will we do? But this wasn't like all those Gaelic laments she used to sing to him when he was wee. Ok? His childhood lullabies. Aye, that stuff matters but this was not fucking like that. Don't let this become another lament. Ok? Please.

Gav   So all I've had I've gave away
And all you've had you've kept
Which do we judge the better life,
That which laughed or that which wept?

Julia   Òbhan òbhan òbhan ìri
Òbhan ìri ò
Òbhan òbhan òbhan ìri
'S mòr mo mhulad 's mòr

Kieran   At the other end of the mainland Glasgow awaits.

With its university tower, its old dusty books, its promise of knowledge of worlds beyond his stacked high on its shelves. With its river, its shipyards, its art galleries, its Style Mile, and the ghost of displaced Gaels before him haunting its tenement closes. He'd get up and play the puggy in a bit. Not now. He wasn't in the mood. Not now.

Gav   It's past my bed
And I'm past my best
And I'm not gonnie like this
One little bit

Howard (2)

Gav *chats to the audience about Gaelic, asks if anyone speaks it. He explains the brutal lyrics of Griogal Cridhe, the Glen Lyon Lament. But, he says, if you imagine it's all about hills it sounds lovely.*

Gav Anyway, who remembers this guy?

Drew *becomes* **Howard**.

Drew The time is now *(**Drew** checks watch and says the actual time.)* Prestwick local time, and Howard is still above us in the clouds. He flicks through the in-flight entertainment options, but his mind is somewhere else.

Somewhere between the twin poles of *Braveheart* and *Trainspotting*, Howard had felt the universe offering him an explanation of himself.

So why now? Exactly this month in, 2014? Howard doesn't think this is a life crisis or anything like that. Even with everything that's happened with Angie. And the dog.

Well, Howard doesn't know exactly why. Retirement offered him some options he supposed. But he'd like to think it went deeper than that. A fever in the blood, an ancestral reaction. Some kind of calling, surely. It had to be. Right?

He settles on the screen that shows the progress of the flightpath. The little graphic of his aircraft edges ever closer towards place names that sound both familiar, and alien, all at once. He whispers them to himself. The shape they make on his tongue brings a tremble of anticipation, a tiny clenching of his teeth.

Lanark.
Methil.
Bridge of Allan.

His pupils dilate. There was a word for this. He reaches for his phrasebook.

Gav   Yivvery: adjective; anxious for, waiting, hungry.

Drew   The jigsaw to Howard's soul has been missing a piece, and by gosh he might just be about to find it.

He returns his phrasebook to the net sleeve on the back of the seat in front of him, next to the in-flight emergency procedure information and the Visit Scotland brochure which stares back at him, with the words: Discover The Land that inspired Disney-Pixar's *Brave*.

My people, thinks Howard. My people, here I come.

Macpherson (2)

Kieran *becomes* **Macpherson**.

Julia   Zoom in on that map in front of Howard right now, to one of the place names that caught his eye. Methil. Where that old boy Macpherson has just been booted out the pub.

Look at Macpherson. Staggering up the pier. We don't know everything about his story after he was moved on, but we do know that the winds are whipping up a storm, and at this precise moment Macpherson has just realised he has lost his house key.

Kieran   AW FUCK YOU. Why!

Julia   There is a roch wind blowing through the harbour. Macpherson's been feeling these winds all his life. We don't quite know everything that goes through his mind, as he gives up his search. We know he feels the winds bite right deep into the marrow of his bones.

Kieran   IT'S AW FUCKED ANYWAY!

Julia   Going nowhere, Macpherson abandons himself to this moment.

Kieran   AW AY IT!

Julia   The waves crash their welcome of him. And he welcomes them. Staggering up the pier, he feels mighty, like the waves. Invincible.

Kieran   The whole fuckin . . . shiter!

Julia   As tall as the cranes on the docks, silhouetted against the twilight of the sky, like a giant gallows of Macpherson's life.

Kieran   Beneath the gallows tree ay the sea . . . FUCKED!

Julia   Time to move on Macpherson.

Kieran   I'M STILL HERE YOU BASTARDS!

Julia   Time to move on son.

Kieran   I'M STILL HERE!

Julia   Salt, metal, concrete, the cold bite of the rushing air, dancing with him to the tune of his whole story.

Kieran   When the boats come in the RATS WILL COME ASHORE, eh! RATS the lot ay thum.

Julia   Waves rising then breaking. Collapsing like all of it collapsed. The shipping. The coalfields. The oil. The power plant.

Kieran   AW FUCKED!

Julia   And right now, it's Macpherson's turn to collapse.

Kieran   Fuck the lot ay thum. Every one ay yous. Fuck yous aw.

Julia   Watch him. As he, with no house keys and no place to go, rantingly, wantonly, throws his tired body to the open wind. He is kaput. Done for.

Kieran   Doon the fuckin . . . pan!

Julia   There at the end of the pier. Macpherson the ranter collapsing, awash in his own mind as he falls to the concrete. And the waves collapse around him.

Song: MacPherson's Rant (reprise)

Julia, **Drew**   Sae rantingly, sae wantonly
Sae dauntingly gaed he
He played a tune an' he danced aroon
Below the gallows tree

Kenny

Kieran *becomes* **Kenny**.

Gav   And in Edinburgh, right now, alone in a high-class private dining room in the centre of town, there is this man.

Kieran   The ink is practically still wet on the contract that lies on the marble-topped table. Oh, man, thinks Kenny. That was good. Fuck. That was big. A big deal.

He knew they'd sign, the Chinese delegates, and they did, goddammit. They left like a shot after it was done, maybe some kind of shock, who knows, who cares. They signed that bitch. Yes.

Right now, he's not thinking about the flight he has to take tomorrow, private jet, 7am to London. He's not thinking about his need for sleep. He's not thinking about wee Jamie back home and how he says he doesn't like his new nanny and how Kate says they need to 'spend more quality time together'. He's not thinking about the niggling feeling he gets, in bed, that she might after all, be right. No. Not right now. In this moment, as we speak, all that matters to Kenny is the thrill of the chase and the kill: they fucking signed.

Oh man, that feels great! It's not for no reason they call us venture capitalists, he thinks. A venture, right? A risky or daring undertaking. A journey in which one jeopardises one's own safety and security. We are the frontiersmen. The front line of economic growth.

He looks out. Out from the wide and high glass window in this top floor private room, out over Princes Street. Rooftops, the skyline. All silent behind the thick glass, like a hologram. Suited men and women, once rushed off their feet now quietly lining up for the bus, a late day in the office. A group of drunk lads spilling up towards the strip bars on Lothian Road. Some kids, horsing about on the corner, a woman with her screaming children, an old guy waiting, dumb, at the traffic lights: it's green you fucking moron you can cross. The Walter Scott monument, the gardens, the castle itself. Inspiring Capital. You see, there's money to be made here, always, if you've got the nerve, the balls to go out and get it.

Yes. The system works. It worked for him didn't it? Deals, big deals like the one just signed lying on the table, that's what's going to keep this thing going. Sacred documents those, the holy scriptures that keep the whole dream alive. You see, he himself is living proof that the thing ain't broke. Nothing needs to change round here as long as there are people like him around with that hunter's instinct, with the will to win the race. And it's only a rat race if you're losing.

The waitress scurries along the floor picking up abandoned bottle caps. He pours himself a long glass of imported premium Czech lager. Here's to us, he thinks. In these hard times, we are the wealth *creators*. And if all you have to *wait* for it to trickle down then I'm sorry. Maybe you could dig yourself out of your own hole, like I did. And if you don't like that idea, well, there's nothing more any of us can do to help you.

But at least we're here, right? The ad*venture*rs. The last of a mythic breed, facing danger at all costs, winning prosperity against the odds and bringing it home. We've got it covered, he thinks, as he watches the people of Edinburgh pass by below. Really, we are your saviours. No need to thank us though. You wouldn't anyway. Don't worry about it. You're fucking welcome.

Shona

Julia *becomes* **Shona**. *She holds a golf club in her hand.*

Kieran   While this is happening, Brian is kicking mud off his heels before stepping in the front door of his castle home, after an evening stroll on his family's private acreage. Such history, he thinks. Such proud heritage.

Gav   In St Andrews, Collette sits in a café, patiently explaining to a friend how the town was built on the sugar, coffee, slaves, and blood of her people.

Kieran   And in Stirling, Sanjit, a first year economics student from Devon, prepares for a presentation on Adam Smith's theory of The Invisible Hand. Seems the idea is that the free market and profit motive will make us all treat each other alright, and that an invisible hand will carry the less fortunate along, and keep the bullies all in check. Sanjit is really hoping he hasn't misunderstood this. That would be embarrassing.

And in Port Glasgow…

Julia   Twenty oors a week ah used tay dae but noo they've goat me doon fur nine.

Kieran   This is Shona. She is fifteen years old. Part-time supermarket checkout worker. And high school student. Part-time also. Right now she is sitting underneath an electricity pylon, on a hill, looking down over Port Glasgow where she lives. She is fucked off.

Julia   Mr Grant says naebody ever takes a stand anymair. Mr Grant that's my history teacher right. He says we're a pathetic. Oor generation. That's whit he says, he says we're a pathetic.

Kieran   She is dealing with some Big Shit.

Julia   Have any of yous ever heard ay the Luddites? Mr Grant telt us aboot them, they were like these weavers. Huv you ever heard ay Ned Ludd? He was no really a real guy right. He was like a fairy story guy right, who was famous for smashing fuck ootay stuff. That wiz his hing right. And he lived in Sherwood Forest. He was sortay like a jakey Robin Hood.

Kieran   She is addressing the people of the town below.

Julia   So Ned Ludd was like the king of the Luddites. Except they were real. They were like these weavers right, fae the north ay England. You getting aw this aye?

Kieran   The people of the Port can't hear her, of course. They're not listening. But she doesn't care. She's used to that.

Julia   Anyway, Mr Grant is lit that: English workers, he says, English workers, are just the same as us. Well ah could telt you that masel. Fucksake.

Kieran   Shona's mum and dad had moved them up from Liverpool when she was four.

Julia   20 oors, doon tay 9. Magrit at work says it's cause ay aw they Polish. Ah'm lit that Magrit, ah need they oors. It's cause ay ma maw's hingmy . . . my Maw, she cannae . . . Ah need thum. Magrit. And she's goin: it's only gonnae get worse cause it started wi the Irish and it's gonnae be the Bulgarians noo and aw. I'm lit that: ye cannae say that Magrit and she's lit that: ah know ye cannae but it's fucken true.

Kieran   She takes a big swig of Mad Dog Twenty Twenty.

Julia   But Magrit's full ay pish but. It's no the Polish. It's they fucken machines. Ye cannae go anywhere and no hear: unexpected item in bagging area. Lit that: quantity needed. Pure lit that: quantity needed. Fucken voice man.

And you git the folk jus daein their shoppin getting ragin at aw us staff cos they cannae understaun the hing when it doesnae work right. It's jus lit that: unexpected item in bagging area. And they're lit that: whidyemean! And it's jus lit that: unexpected item in bagging area. Unexpected item in bagging area. You figure it oot. Deal wi it. Prick.

But you dinnae get a machine calling in fur sick days but dae ye. Naw.

And you git daft Magrit gettin humpty wi the Polish. And you git the Polish gettin Magrit and mair like her oan thur case. And you git aw the staff gettin humpty wi each other, checkin the rota aw suspicious an that. And you git my maw, pure chuckin pelters at me – how are you no workin? Nine oors have you any idea – gien it aw that.

Turnin oan each other. Everywhere. And it's no right, cause I'll tell you what it is, it's lit this: back in the day we used tay huv jobs makin stuff. And growin stuff. But then we wurnay needed. Noo it's just buyin stuff. And sellin stuff. But you need a job sellin the stuff tae be able tae buy the stuff. And noo they're sayin we're no even needed fur that.

Aye. Surprised ye there eh? Didn't see that coming did you Port Glasgow? Am smart enough tae huv this figured oot. So here's a hing:

Kieran   The town below begins to light up as darkness settles.

Julia   Why were the Luddites named efter Ned Ludd? A wee rocket. A wee fucken fairy bampot. A pure hooligan, smashing stuff up. A ned. Ned Ludd.

Any ideas? Naw. Didnae think so. Well I'll tell ye:

He was famous for smashing fuck ootay stuff and so were they.

Cos when they brought in machines tae dae the weavers' job fur them the Luddites said naw. And they smashed the machines. And then they kept daein it. And then it spread.

And everyone started daein it, till they hud tae send in the fucken army cos they didnae stop until they were trampled intay the ground and they paid fur it wi their lives.

What do you say to that?

Mr Grant says there is dignity in stauning up. Daein whit's right.

And my maw's at hame, wi her hingmy, cannae work, gien me aw that. Nine oors.

Mr Grant says naebody ever takes a staun anymair. Well let's just fucken see aboot that.

Are you wi me? Are ye?

Unexpected item in bagging area? Aye. Too fucken right there is ya stupit fucken cow!

Short stories (2)

Kieran   While Shona descends the hill, golf club in hand, and thinking of everyone, turning on each other, everywhere, in a bus shelter in Aberdeen, Liam, fourteen years old, takes a permanent marker from his pocket and writes 'ALL POLES GO HOME' underneath a drawing of a swastika. He's drawn that the right way round, aye? He's sure that was the way his brother taught him.

Julia   In Stranraer, Kelly writes a letter to her daughter's father in prison. She didn't like the fucker but it was best to keep in touch.

Kieran   Near Rosneath, by the mouth of Loch Long, Cheryl, 38, clears a bookshelf in her estranged deceased mother's house. Over the other side of the bay, nuclear submarines haunt the waters below the surface. It's so quiet here, she thinks.

Julia   And in Elgin, Ingrid Agnieszka Willis forces her way out of her mother's body, takes her first breath in this world and lets out an almighty scream of life.

Song: The Invisible Hand

Words and music by Gav Prentice.

Gav   There is a story that if only you try
The future for us all is mapped out in the sky
That as sure as the sun and the stars and the moon
The money will flow and the people will bloom
An invisible hand will guide us all along
Hold us up if we're weak and knock us back if we're wrong
And if it's in this hand that you place your faith
Then we will grow
And we will grow
And you will see his good grace
But nobody knows where we can go
With the invisible hand around our throat

Kieran   Right now, Amanda, Holyrood MSP, lies soaking in

Dead Sea bath salts, sipping cold white wine in a candle-lit
bathroom in the high-ceilinged Georgian flat in Stockbridge in
Edinburgh, where she lives, by herself. How had it come to this,
she thinks. What would her dad think? But you have to look out
for number one, don't you? She'd earned this.

Charlie, a drug dealer in Dumfries, walks down Buccleuch Street
packing two hundred pills, casting a nervous eye over his shoulder
for stop and search units.

While in Dundee, Kim puts pen to paper on the block purchase
of a whole estate of new build flats for private let. She thinks to
herself, this land is my land.

Gav   There's plenty of time to make it back to work
And collect the gold watch for the time that you've served
Play by the rules and let the hand do the rest
And if you work
And if you work
Then you will see his good grace
And upon you will shine his face
But nobody knows where we can go
With the invisible hand around our throat

Emma

Julia *becomes* **Emma**.

Drew   While Macpherson lies face down, unmoving, on the Methil pier, giving up on the world and on everyone in it; while Miriam travels through Clydebank on the number 61 bus shirking the disdainful looks of her co-passenger; and while Howard moves, hopefully, expectantly through the clouds above us, meanwhile, right now, here in Glasgow . . .

Song: Come All Ye Tramps and Hawkers

Trad. Arr.

New lyrics by Gav Prentice, Julia Taudevin, and Drew Wright.

Gav   Come all ye fellow citizens
Whoever you may be
Across the country up and down
Come listen now to me
I'll tell to you a rovin tale of places I have been
From up into the snowy north
And south to Gretna Green

Julia   Emma walks the streets of Glasgow. She's here for a purpose. She's here on work.

She's here to find out what the people of Glasgow think about communication and connectivity. In their area. And whether or not their experience would be positively enhanced by greater access to community building features and the integration of accessible social elements.

You know, apps, and that.

Emma works for a market research company. For an internet provider company. For a market research company that's now working for an internet provider company. It's not a shit job. It was just a bit . . . you know.

Town to town, gathering vital consumer data. Standing on

shopping high streets, clipboard in hand, seeking co-operation from passing shoppers.

Kieran   Please indicate overall how well connected you feel by your service provider in your area
a. very well connected
b. well connected
c. neither well nor poorly connected
d. poorly connected
e. very poorly connected
f. other

Drew   You've maybe seen me in your toon
A clipboard in my hands
Seeking your opinion
On certain high street brands
And while the vast majority
Ignore or pass me by
I've spotted one, she looks like fun
A twinkle in her eye

Julia   They'd put her up in the Jury's Inn. Not a dream job this. But it had come at a good time. She'd started on the phones, but you got better pay with this. I mean, she does miss you know, working next to other people. Fag breaks, lunch breaks, people to chat with. But at least this way she got to see the country, right? Campbeltown, Alloa, Peterhead . . .

Kieran   All ye barmen and ye barristas
If ye be single men
I'm in town for one single night
And could do with a friend
Nae ties, nae guilt, nae questions
Will I expect of thee
If only you will open your arms and hold tight on to me

Julia   She never stays in any place for long. But long enough to never quite be back home either. Home. What even is that? Home is wherever she lays her hat. I mean, she never wore a hat, but you get the picture. Her trusty satnav helps her out on her long hours driving from one town to the next, pulling over at the services. KFC. Maccy Ds. M&S Simply Food.

Kieran   Would the offer of improved connectivity and communication in the place where you live entice you to consider switching to a new Broadband service provider?

a. I would be very enticed by this
b. I would be somewhat enticed by this
c. I would be neither enticed nor put off by this
d. I would be somewhat put off by this
e. I would be very put off by this
f. other

Julia   Tomorrow, she'd get up, go into town and get to work. But now, with the whole night ahead of her, she walks these streets she's never been on before, and might never be again, looking, for something. Something to do, someone to talk to. She'd popped her head in to the Grant Arms but it was just old formica tables and an old guy playing darts. Not her scene.

Gav   I could try to sell my camera
And drink the money down
Both to kill the memories
Of another empty town
It's not to keep me warm at night
Or to keep black dogs at bay
And it's no to find ma destiny
But something else tae dae

Julia   Right now, alone, and looking for company, Emma stands on Argyle Street. Hardly a dream job this. But she was only here for one night, and she bloody well intended to make the most of it. Soon she'd be on the road again. KFC, Maccy Ds, M&S Simply Food. But every now and then, turning a corner and suddenly finding herself along a wide open coast, a flock of gulls flying overhead. Or looking out and witnessing a rugged mountainside, and her, tiny moving through it . . .

This was the way. Match.com had yielded an interesting looking fella she could go and meet. He'd suggested a bar called Box. Was that creepy? Who knows? Maybe it'd be fun.

And at this precise moment, not knowing where the road takes her, and looking for, something, Emma passes the Blue Lagoon chippy, the twenty-four hour shop, she glances up to her left and sees a shiny black sign with the words 'The Arches' written on it.

She didn't need to go home. She didn't need a home. Each day a new town. Who knows who she might meet? The company needs her to fill her forms with answers. But right now, Emma just wants to fill her life with stories. Come on Glasgow, she thinks. I am in you. And I won't be for long. What stories do you have for me to take with me? Every day is a new chapter.

Come all ye fellow citizens
Whoever you may be
Across the country up and down
Come listen now to me
I'll tell to you a rovin' tale of places I have been
From up into the snowy north
And south to Gretna Green

Gav   Come aw ye scruffs and scroungers
That never work a day
Come aw ye tired strivers
That could never work again
You know that they divide us
But you know we're all the same
It's not how they reward us
It's how they play the game

Drew   Always thinking positive
And practising my smile
Eating soggy sandwiches
While eating up the miles
I never thought I'd be like this
Footloose and fancy free
But if you think I chose this life
I didn't, it chose me

Miriam (2)

Julia *becomes* **Miriam**.

Kieran   Back in Clydebank, and here's Miriam, on her way to her new job, still sitting on the number 61 bus, this minute, as we speak. The woman opposite her still scowls. As Miriam glances up, the woman stares out the window, away from her again, insistently.

Julia   I'm here. I can see you. I'm here.

Kieran   She still listens to the same track on her son's iPhone.

The rest of the songs are awful, she thinks. But she actually likes this one.

Julia   Good music, this.

Kieran   The bus is fuller now, with more people.

Julia   All these heavy duty faces. Heads down, staring away, no talking. And her. She still wants to pretend I'm not here. Like that will make her problems go away. Strange place this.

Kieran   She thinks of the sunlight, dry earth, moist shade. Fading.

Julia   All these people, desperate to be somewhere else. None of them look like belonging here, being here. Not really. Chasing, reaching for something, reaching for not here.

Kieran   With her son's music still playing.

Julia   It's good music this. Sunlight music.

Kieran   She imagines.

Julia   What if they all heard this music, with their heavy duty faces? Maybe all the bus would sing along? Maybe even this woman here.

Kieran   And she laughs slightly, to herself.

Julia   A mongrel nation. All of us, riding on the back of this funny yappy dog. All looking somewhere else. How strange. All wishing the other wasn't here. None of us with more belonging than the next one. Each of us just here. What if we all just decided to be here? To look at each other, just here. This big funny mongrel.

Kieran   And at this exact moment, right now, Miriam is looking around the number 61 bus, at all the different faces of its passengers, and in her mind's eye she sees; each passenger on the bus, nodding to her son's music, looking each other in the eye, and singing. Recognising each other. Here. Right now. And so she takes her son's headphones out of her ears, and turns the volume right up loud. The woman opposite shoots her a sharp, angry look, affronted. But this time Miriam catches her eye, and holds it. Here. As the noise blares from her open headphones, bemused, surprised, disgruntled faces turn to her, and with a glint in her eyes, she meets them. And as the bus trundles along through this cold strange place a warm smile grows across her cheeks.

Macpherson (3)

Kieran *becomes* **Macpherson**.

Gav   Who remembers Macpherson, collapsed on the Methil pier? While all this other business has been going on, he's still been here.

Julia   On the pier in Methil, Macpherson the ranter lies face down.

Macpherson *coughs and splutters.*

Julia   But he's still here. The storm has died down. And Macpherson's still breathing.

Drew   To me? It's a positive sign.

Julia   And he's not alone.

Drew   You wouldn't have struck me as a man of faith, but good on you.

Kieran   What, the, you fuckin . . .?

Drew   Yes you. Lying face down. Deep in prayer, I'm sure. But you're about forty degrees off. Mecca's that way, sunshine.

Kieran   Fuck's the Bingo got tae dae wi it?

Drew   Ah, good question. Well, it's a lottery. And nearly a full house for you tonight, Macpherson.

Kieran   You an angel? Am I deid! Where's ma fuckin keys?

Drew   Do I look like an angel, Macpherson?

Kieran   Then fuckin . . .

Drew   A body meetin a body coming through the Rye. That's you and I.

Kieran   Where d'you come fae? You come fae ower there?

Drew   The sea? Aye. I did. I stepped out of the water, peeled off my skin, and left it hanging on the coat hooks in the Empire Bar. Beside the brollies.

Kieran   Wan ay they fuckin fairytale seal cunts?

Drew   That's right, son. I'm a selkie. I'll be slipping away in a moment or two. But before then, I'm curious to know: what exactly is it that you feel the world owes you Macpherson? Besides a painless exit. Dignity. Recognition. Some respect. A decent pension. Some brotherhood. Some tenderness, am I right?

Kieran   Ma life! Has been one fuckin . . .! Drone!

Drew   Of course it has! But there is a different drone Macpherson, and I don't mean military surveillance. You must understand, in the art of the great music, the drone represents the eternal. The commonality with all that is.

Kieran   Havers.

Drew   Aye, no doubt. But you, my pished pal, you have your part to play in this muckle sang. But you won't find your voice on your knees, or in apologies. The drone doesn't waver. Or haver. It doesn't care if you've lost your house keys. It's a tone deeper than grievance or anger.

Kieran   Rat race is for rats. That's the end of it.

Drew   Except it's not, is it Macpherson? There's a second part to that phrase and you know it. We're not rats. We're human beings.

Kieran   You're a seal.

Drew   So you say. But then according to you I'm also a mythical character from ancient folklore so you can indulge me a bit of life-changing wisdom.

Kieran   Talking pish fairytale cunt. I don't believe you exist! Heh! What do you say to that SELKIE PRICK? None ay this pish you cannae see, don't believe it. Lived experience. Lived fucking experience. Eh?

Drew   Ah, very good. Rational evidence, the true spirit of the Scottish Enlightenment. But you can see me can't you? Thought so. You don't believe in the things you don't see? Well, believe in me.

Kieran   Fuck you. Aw pish!

Drew   Indeed so, indeed. It is, as you say, all pish. But it's all we've got. And it's a story that you're in whether you like it or not. So what way is it gonna go Macpherson? Eh? What happens when we turn the page? This is more complex than you know. This is more complex than I know. This is about you, me, and we, the heart that beats, the shore and the sea.

Kieran   And how would you know, eh? I don't know who you fuckin are but who the fuck do you think you are, eh? Trying to tell me. How would you fuckin know how it is?

Drew   These questions, Macpherson; you, me, us – all of us – how we fit together in something better than a broken watch these won't be answered once and for all tomorrow. Or this September. Or lying face down on the Methil pier. But we are where we find ourselves. And we have to start somewhere. I'd say that storm will be back. So what'll it be? Oh baws, there's my lift. Left half a pint sittin in there and all.

Kieran   Aye well fuck off then. Go on. I don't need your fucking advice.

Drew   Fair enough, Macpherson. But you're back on your feet aren't you?

Pause. **Gav's** *mandolin starts up.*

Drew   I'll see you around.

Time to move on Macpherson. May the road, as they say, rise up to meet you. Just maybe not quite so suddenly as tonight. Sair yin.

The selkie goes to leave.

Drew   Oh, and, eh . . . top pocket mate. Always the last place you look.

The selkie exits

Macpherson *taps his top pocket. He goes into the pocket and takes out his keys. He stares at them.*

Macpherson *looks up to where the selkie left. Looks at the audience. Back to his keys. And then he stumbles off.*

Song: Coatbridge 1967 (Rantin version)

Words and music by Gav Prentice.

Gav   There was no summer of love
In the towns that caught no sun
But the homes were warm enough

When the kids were on the run
From the Pope and Bible John
And filling out the same old form

Prove your conscience, prove your age
Prove you make an honest wage
And you're more than them today

Then by the time you've ran away
You've a debt you must repay
And nothing left of worth to say

Chorus:

All   So if you don't believe
In the things that you don't see
Then come believe in me
I can take up all your pain
Hold it out beneath the rain
'Til it all gets washed away

Just stay

They make a desert, call it peace
And then between their gritted teeth
Tell you all the words you need

They give you not a penny more
You read your paper by their glow
And still at night you hear the drone

Of all the workers coming home
Kids at the football bang the gong
And still at night you hear the drone

They'll give you not a penny more
So you can lie here all you want
But still at night you'll hear the drone

Chorus

Howard (3)

Kieran *becomes* **Howard**.

Julia   Still up in the sky, but closer, much closer now, sits this man.

Kieran   Howard is still staring at the digital avatar of his aeroplane on the tiny screen in front of him. The numbers tick off the altitude counter. Descending. He reaches for his phrasebook.

Gav   Rant: verb; to frolic, romp, revel. Noun; a merrymaking, rough frolic, a lively song of joy.

Kieran   Soon, the runway will rise up to meet him. He feels the sacred soil of his ancestors call to him, an ancient pull, so much stronger than gravity. He imagines leaving the airport, the last of the sunlight swelling in the sky above, his heart opening to this moment. Light drizzle flecking his face. The bright runway lights. His heart opening to this moment. He does not yet know that when this moment passes, he'll be surrounded by the words Pure Dead Brilliant in big letters.

As he imagines venturing out from the airport, in pursuit of history, heritage, communities of the ancient tongue, he doesn't know that days from now a man in a service station on the road to Fort William will tell him that nobody speaks that Gaelic stuff anymore, and to be honest he's not really sure why they bother doing the road signs in two languages.

Drew   Ranter: verb; to sew a seam across roughly, to darn coarsely, to join, to attempt to reconcile statements which do not tally.

Kieran   There are many things he doesn't know about the story playing out below him. He doesn't know about a young man crossing the water on a boat leaving an island with no plan of going back. Or a small boy, who runs through the streets of Govanhill, singing.

352   Contemporary Scottish Plays

Drew   Or about a schoolgirl who, at this moment, walks towards a supermarket with a golf club in her hand.

Julia   Or a travelling market researcher walking the streets of Glasgow, looking for company.

Gav   He doesn't know about a woman on the number 61 bus on her way to her first shift at work imagining all the people singing.

Drew   Or a venture capitalist in Edinburgh surveying the people below.

Julia   Or a drunk man on the coast, having a moment of clarity, or was it delusion, as a stranger teaches him that all things are connected, all our futures are shared, and each of us has our part to play.

Kieran   And he doesn't know that when he steps off the vessel, standing on the tarmac between the plane and the shuttle bus he will immediately experience a shattering disappointment and inevitable defeat. He will feel instantly homesick for Lincoln, Nebraska. But in a strange way, in that moment, he will look at himself, his body, his own hands, as if for the very first time. As he steps onto the shuttle bus, a young Paisley-born woman will observe in passing that it looks like rain. Yes, Howard will say, exchanging a smile. It's looking very dreich.

During the next song, the following happens. **Drew** *becomes* **Howard** *in place of* **Kieran**. **Kieran** *briefly becomes* **Gregor**, *still sitting on the boat looking at the puggy.* **Julia** *becomes* **Emma**, *arriving to meet her date.* **Kieran** *becomes* **Kenny**, *looking out the window at Princes Street.* **Julia** *becomes* **Shona**, *arriving at the supermarket with a golf club in her hand.* **Kieran** *becomes* **Macpherson**, *sitting at home, shell-shocked and clutching his house keys.* **Julia** *becomes* **Miriam**, *sitting on the bus, looking around and smiling. Throughout all of this,* **Drew** *remains as* **Howard**.

<u>Song: Ae Fond Kiss</u>

Words by Robert Burns. Arrangement by Gav Prentice.

Gav   Ae fond kiss, and then we sever;
Ae fareweel, alas, for ever!
Deep in heart-wrung tears I'll pledge thee,
Warring sighs and groans I'll wage thee.

Who shall say that Fortune grieves him,
While the star of hope she leaves him?
Me, nae cheerful twinkle lights me;
Dark despair around benights me.

I'll ne'er blame my partial fancy,
Naething could resist my Nancy:
But to see her was to love her;
Love but her, and love for ever.

Had we never lov'd sae kindly,
Had we never lov'd sae blindly,
Never met – or never parted,
We had ne'er been broken-hearted.

Julia   Right now, as Howard circles up ahead, he doesn't know any of this. All he knows is that he's trying to see himself as part of a story. That is what he wants. To be part of something bigger than himself.

Drew   And he doesn't know, that he's part of it already. A story with no single through-line, and no fixed centre. And that at this exact moment, down below him, under an old railway arch in Glasgow, a man in a tartan baseball cap is talking to a room full of people about him right now. And that each of those people in the room are part of the story too. A story that has multiple beginnings, an abundance of middles, and no clear end.

Julia   Rantin: noun; a noisy mirth, a celebration.

Kieran   As Howard returns his Scots language phrasebook to its place in the seat in front of him, musing on the variants of the word 'rant' and feeling perplexed as to how a rant can be both an expression of anger and a song of joy all at once, he doesn't know that that same man is about to take off his cap. Walk across the stage. Pick up a guitar with two strings on it, and sing a song. A song which is both an expression of anger, and a song of joy and hope, all at once.

Drew *becomes* **Drew** *again, and goes and gets the two string guitar.*

Gav   And that when that song ends the performance will end. And the people in the room will get up out of their seats, and so will Howard. And the last note on the keyboard will play, and the lights will dim. And the people will leave and go out into the world. And the story will continue.

The cast sing Freedom Come All Ye *by Hamish Henderson. Additional lyric by Drew Wright:*

And an Arab lad fae yont Gaza
Dings the fell gallows o the burghers doon.